In thy name, At thy lotus feet...

| | akhaṇḍa-maṇḍalākāraṁ vyāptaṁ yena carācaram | |

(Which) pervades the entire unbroken form of the circle (of creation), moving and unmoving

| | tat-padaṁ darśitaṁ yena tasmai śrī-gurave namaḥ | |

To That beautiful and benevolent Guru through whom that state was revealed (to me), Salutations!

COPYRIGHT

YogSadhna Inc., Minneapolis, MN

Editor: Sunita Pant Bansal

Proofreader: Rina Tripathi

Cover Design: János Gräfl

Page layout design: Mandeep Singh | Mady'sin Design

Pictures by: Gaurav Arora, Mitchell Manz, and Tóth Milán

ISBN # 978-0-692-37554-9

29 28 27 26 25 24 23 3 4 5

Published 2015.

Printed in India

It is my calling to share with you the practices that could empower you as a practitioner (Sādhaka), be established in health (Swastha), share with you the tools of well being of mind. May whatever I share be of benefit to you, may my senses be of help, may my mind be worth of guidance and being guided, may my whole being be of service...

may each fragment of my being, be for UNIVERSE.

DEDICATION

Dedicated to my father, "Late Shri Radhey Shyam Arora," whose subtle teachings and love permeate each cell of my being, and who made me the person I am today and the person I shall be.

Dedicated to *Mahāmaṇḍaleśvara* Swami Veda Bharati, in whose Ashram I wrote this book.

In Thy Name, At Thy Lotus Feet

CONTENTS

Acknowledgement I
Author's Note III
Editor's Note V
Foreword VII
Reviews VIII
Transliteration Key XV

Mudrā Basics

Introduction 02
I Origin and History of *Mudrā* 13
II Textual References of *Mudrā* 16
III Psychology of *Mudrā* by Ágota Seszták 25
IV Philosophy of *Mudrā* by Siddhartha Krishna 28
V Science behind *Mudrā* 36
VI Benefits of Hand *Mudrā* 82
VII Guidelines for the Practice of *Mudrā* 85
VIII Types of *Mudrā* 97

Hand *Mudrā*

I *Vyāvahārika Hasta Mudrā: General Mudrās*

1 *Abhiśeka Mudrā: Mudrā* of Anointing an Idol with Water via Conch 106
2 *Acalāgni Mudrā: Mudrā* of Eternal Fire/Flame 107
3 *Agrā Mudrā: Mudrā* of Salutation to the Teacher Outside and Within 107
4 *Añjali Mudrā: Mudrā* of Salutation to the *Guru* and Six Higher *Cakras* 108
5 *Arcita Mudrā: Mudrā* of Greeting and Salutation 108
6 *Aśoka Mudrā: Mudrā* depicting a moving *Aśoka* Tree 109
7 *Ātmāñjali Mudrā: Mudrā* of Offering from the Soul 109
8 *Āvāhana Mudrā: Mudrā* of Invocation 109

9 *Bhramara Mudrā: Mudrā* depicting Silence, Bee, Crane, or Sexual Union 110
10 *Buddha-pātra Mudrā:* Upholder of Law 110
11 *Haṁsa Mudrā: Mudrā* of Inner Rhythm 111
12 *Hansī Mudrā: Mudrā* of Peace and Restoration 111
13 *Hṛdayāñjali Mudrā: Mudrā* of offering from the Heart 112
14 *Kailāsa Mudrā: Mudrā* of Contemplation and Salutation to the *Sahsrāra Cakra* 112
15 *Kacchapa Mudrā* (Turtle *Mudrā*): *Mudrā* of *Liṅga* with *Yoni* 113
16 *Latā Mudrā: Mudrā* of Union and Entwinement 113
17 *Mukula Mudrā:* A gesture of Virginity/Unbloomed Flower Bud 113
18 *Namaskāra Mudrā: Mudrā* of Salutation and Acknowledgment of Divinity in Everyone 114
19 *Nidrā-Hasta Mudrā: Mudrā* of Cajoling One to Sleep 114
20 *Nidrā Mudrā: Mudrā* for Deep Sleep 114
21 *Paṅkaja/Padma Mudrā: Mudrā* of offering Flowers to Deity/ *Mudrā* of Full-bloomed Lotus 115
22 *Padma-kośa Mudrā: Mudrā* of Blossom, Lotus Bud, Brilliance 115
23 *Puśpāñjali Mudrā: Mudrā* for holding Flowers 115
24 *Puṣpa-pūṭa Mudrā: Mudrā* for offering Flowers, Rice, Water, Alms 116
25 *Śakti Mudrā: Mudrā* for Calming the Energy Flow 116
26 *Śikhara Mudrā:* A gesture of Strength and Steadiness 117
27 *Sūcī (needle) Mudrā* I: Elephant Tusk, Universe, or Transgression 117
28 *Sūcī (needle) Mudrā* II: Astonishment, Anger, Threat, and Turning the Potter's Wheel... 118
29 *Sūcī (needle) Mudrā* III: Concentrated Energy: Healing *Mudrā* 118
30 *Sūrya Prāṇa Mudrā: Mudrā* for Soaking in Solar Energy 119
31 *Tattva Mudrā*: A gesture of Truth 119
32 *Vajrapradama Mudrā: Mudrā* of Unshakable Trust 120
33 *Vajra Mudrā: Mudrā* of Thunderbolt or Unshakable Knowledge from Emptiness 120
34 *Vitarka Mudrā:* A gesture of discussion/preaching of Buddhist Teachings 121

35 *Yoga Mudrā*: A gesture of Union ... 121

II *Cikitsaka Hasta Mudrā*: Therapeutic *Mudrās*

1 *Apāna Vāyu Mudrā: Mṛta Sañjīvanī Mudrā*: Life Saving Gesture ... 126
2 *Daṇḍa Svāsthya Mudrā: Mudrā* for Healthy Back ... 128
3 *Gaṇeśa Mudrā: Mudrā* for Aiding Digestion ... 130
4 *Garuḍa Mudrā: Mudrā* for Immunity ... 132
5 *Girivara Mudrā: Mudrā* to Release Water Retention ... 134
6 *Kāyākalpa Mudrā: Mudrā* for Detoxification ... 136
7 *Kṣepaṇa Mudrā: Mudrā* for Letting go/ Detachment ... 138
8 *Liṅga Mudrā: Mudrā* for increasing Heat/ Solar Energy ... 140
9 *Mahā-jñāna Mudrā: Mudrā* for Detachment/ of Supreme Wisdom ... 142
10 *Mahāśīrṣa Mudrā: Mudrā* for Relieving Headache ... 144
11 *Mṛga Mudrā/Bidāla Mudrā: Mudrā* for Blood Pressure ... 146
12 *Muṣṭi Mudrā: Mudrā* for Digestive Fire ... 148
13 *Pūṣan Mudrā: Mudrā* for Nausea ... 150
14 *Sandhi Mudrā: Mudrā* for Healthy Joints ... 152
15 *Śaṅkha Mudrā: Mudrā* for Speech Disorders ... 154
16 *Śūnya Mudrā: Mudrā* for Balancing Air Pressure in Ears ... 156
17 *Śvāsa-Nālikā Mudrā: Mudrā* for Healthy Bronchioles ... 158
18 *Śvāsi-Cikitsā Mudrā: Mudrā* for Asthma ... 160
19 *Surabhī Mudrā:* Wish-fulfilling *Mudrā* ... 162
20 *Tse Mudrā: Mudrā* for Depression ... 166
21 *Ūru Mudrā: Mudrā* for Easy Breath ... 168
22 *Varuṇa Mudrā: Mudrā* to Relieve Congestion ... 170
23 *Viparīta Namaskāra/ Madhumeha Mudrā: Mudrā* for Diabetes ... 172

► ***Yoga Tattva Mudrā:* Five Element *Mudrās***

24 *Pṛthivī Mudrā:* Earth Gesture ... 178
25 *Jala Mudrā*: Water Gesture ... 180
26 *Agni Mudrā:* Fire Gesture ... 182
27 *Vāyu Mudrā*: Air Gesture ... 184

28 *Ākāśa Mudrā*: Ether Gesture 186

▶ ***Pañca Prāṇa Upāsanā Mudrās*: Worship of Five *Prāṇa Mudrās***

29 *Prāṇa Mudrā:* Forward and Incoming Energy Gesture 192
30 *Samāna Mudrā:* Balancing and Mixing Energy Gesture 194
31 *Vyāna Mudrā*: Dispersing Energy Gesture 196
32 *Udāna Mudrā*: Uprising Energy Gesture 198
33 *Apāna Mudrā*: Downward and Outward Energy Gesture 200

▶ ***Cikitsaka Sparśa Mudrā:* Therapeutic *Mudrās* of Touch**

34 *Adhama Sparśa Mudrā: Cin-hasta Mudrā* 206
35 *Madhyama Sparśa Mudrā: Cinmaya Hasta Mudrā* 210
36 *Ādya Sparśa Mudrā: Ādi Hasta Mudrā* 214
37 *Mahad Sparśa Mudrā*: *Yoga Hasta Mudrā* 218

▶ ***Prāṇāyāma Sparśa Mudrā – Mudrā* to direct the *prāṇa***

38 *Nāḍī Śodhana: Viṣṇu Mudrā* 226

III *Ādhyātmika Hasta Mudrā:* Spiritual *Mudrās*

1 *Abhaya Mudrā: Mudrā* of Fearlessness 232
2 *Agni-Śalā Mudrā: Mudrā* of *Vedic* Fire Ceremony 234
3 *Agni-Cakra Mudrā: Mudrā* of the Fire Vortex 236
4 *Agni-Cakra Samāna Mudrā*: *Mudrā* of Fire Pacification 238
5 *Bhūmi-sparśa Mudrā: Mudrā* of Earth as Witness 240
6 *Cin Mudrā: Mudrā* of Supreme Consciousness 242
7 *Dharma-cakra Mudrā: Mudrā* of Right Action 246
8 *Dhyānī Mudrā: Mudrā* of Contemplation 248
9 *Jñāna Mudrā: Mudrā* of Supreme Knowledge 252
10 *Hākinī Mudrā: Mudrā* of Concentration 254
11 *Kubera Mudrā: Mudrā* of Eternal Abundance 256
12 *Mātaṅgī Mudrā: Mudrā* of Divine Expression 258
13 *Sāñjali Mudrā: Mudrā* of Loving Offering 260
14 *Saṅkalpa Mudrā: Mudrā* of Resolve 264

15 *Śiva Mudrā/ Īśvara Mudrā: Mudrā* of Supreme God 266
16 *Śiva Liṅga Mudrā: Mudrā* of Cosmic Oval 268
17 *Uttarabodhi Mudrā: Mudrā* of Supreme Enlightenment 270
18 *Varada Mudrā: Mudrā* of Divine Boon 272
19 *Yoni Mudrā: Mudrā* of Cosmic Womb 274
20 *Vajra-padma Mudrā: Mudrā* of Unshakeable Trust 276

► ***Sapta Cakra Mudrā: Mudrās* of Cakra**

21 *Vairāgya Mudrā: Mudrā* of Detachment *(Mūlādhāra Cakra)* 282
22 *Bhairava/ Bhairavī Mudrā: Mudrā* of Eternal Energy *(Svādhiṣṭhāna Cakra)* 284
23 *Agni Namaskāra Mudrā: Mudrā* of Salutation to Fire *(Maṇipūra Cakra)* 286
24 *Pūrṇa Jñāna Mudrā: Mudrā* of Complete Wisdom *(Anāhata Cakra)* 288
25 *Viśuddhi Mudrā: Mudrā* of Eternal Purity *(Viśuddhi Cakra)* 290
26 *Kāleśvara Mudrā: Mudrā* to Transcend Time *(Ājñā Cakra)* 292
27 *Śakti-jāgaraṇa Mudrā: Mudrā* of Awakening *(Sahasrāra Cakra)* 296

► ***Gāyatri Mantra Mudrā – Mudrās* in the practice of *Gāyatri***

28 *Sumukha Mudrā* 303
29 *Sampuṭa Mudrā* 304
30 *Vitata Mudrā* 305
31 *Vistṛta Mudrā* 306
32 *Dvimukha Mudrā* 307
33 *Tṛmukha Mudrā* 308
34 *Caturmukha Mudrā* 309
35 *Pañcamukha Mudrā* 310
36 *Ṣaṇmukha Mudrā* 311
37 *Adhomukha Mudrā* 312
38 *Vyāpakāñjalika Mudrā* 313
39 *Śakaṭa Mudrā* 314
40 *Yama Pāṣa Mudrā* 315
41 *Granthi Mudrā* 316
42 *Unmukhonmukha Mudrā* 317

43 *Pralamba Mudrā* 318
44 *Muṣṭika Mudrā* 319
45 *Matsya Mudrā* 320
46 *Kūrma Mudrā* 321
47 *Varāhaka Mudrā* 322
48 *Siṁha-krānta Mudrā* 323
49 *Mahā Krānta Mudrā* 324
50 *Mudgara Mudrā* 325
51 *Pallava Mudrā* 326
52 *Surabhī Mudrā* 327
53 *Jñāna Mudrā* 327
54 *Vairāgya Mudrā* 328
55 *Yoni Mudrā* 328
56 *Śaṅkha Mudrā* 329
57 *Paṅkaja / Padma Mudrā* 329
58 *Liṅga Mudrā* 330
59 *Nirvāṇa Mudrā* 330

▶ ***Ṣaḍaṅga-Nyāsa Mudrā: Mudrās* of Touch, to Protect & Awaken**

60 *Hṛdayāya Mudrā*: *Mudrā* to Awaken the Heart 336
61 *Kavacāya Mudrā*: *Mudrā* to Shield the Body 337
62 *Netra-trayāya Mudrā*: *Mudrā* to Awaken Insight 338
63 *Phaṭ Mudrā: Mudrā* to Release Negativity 339
64 *Śikhāyai Mudrā: Mudrā* to Awaken the Crown 340
65 *Śirase Mudrā: Mudrā* to Guide the Intellect 341

MUDRĀ THERAPY QUICK GUIDE 346
GLOSSARY(A) 354
GLOSSARY (B) 359
INDEX OF ILLUSTRATIONS 362

Acknowledgement

There are many who have made me push my own limitations. Thank you so much for your inspiration; I offer this work to each one of you. I express deep gratitude to my family and friends, who are my pillars of strength.

My Students

I thank the constant inspiration from my students globally; I cherish their presence in my life. For it is through them I learn to stay a student for lifetime.

Mentors and Masters

I am also thankful to my very first *Yoga* Guru Mrs. Shashi Khosla for sowing the seed of *Yoga* in me.

My gratitude goes out to my mentor and editor, Sunita Pant Bansal, whose creativity is contagious.

It is a blessing to have studied under many great masters and self-realized souls. I pay my respect to all of them for blessing me with their constant love and guidance.

I am very grateful for David Frawley (Vamadeva Shastriji) to offer his foreword to this piece of work. His works have inspired me for decades to refine my understanding of *Yoga, Ayurveda and Vedas*. A special mention also goes to Yogini Shambhavi for her kind reviews.

A special mention goes to Móni László for her timely presence in my life to give a me a new direction and insight.

Special Contributors

I thank Ṣiddhartha Krishna, who is an eminent *Vedādhyāyī* (knower of *Vedas*, the ancient-most texts of knowledge), for helping out generously with the glossary section and transliteration of the Sanskrit words in the book. Without him, it would not have been possible. He also offered his expert views on the Philosophy of *Mudrās* from a *Vedantic* point of view. I am so honored for him to be a part of this project.

My special thanks goes to Ágota Seszták for offering her insights into the psychology of body language. I deeply appreciate her professional contribution and hope that it will add to the perspective of the reader. Apart from this, she has been a source of inspiration to keep the message simple and short. As a partner she has given me strength and unconditional support.

I cannot forget to thank the place where I wrote this book: Swami Rama *Sādhaka* Gram, *Rishikesh*. I am thankful to the breeze that spreads the fragrance of freshly bloomed roses from its garden every day. I am thankful to the birds whose chirping woke me up every day and inspired me to speak what is pleasant to the ears. I am indebted to the eternal blessings present as subtle vibrations of the sages in *Rishikesh* for moment-to-moment inspiration.

Technical Team

I applaud the selfless support of my dear friend-photographer Gaurav Arora from India, who with utmost dedication, sincerity and expertise, took all the shots of the *Mudrā* for this book. I would also like to thank Mitchell Manz also for his readiness to do some last minute shots on meditation postures which were required to give a complete experience to the readers.

A special mention goes to Gurjit Kaur (Gogo) whose efforts made every step in this process smooth. Our discussions took hours, days and nights and her patience helped me bring out the best for the readers. I am indebted to the selfless offering of your time and presence throughout this project. I am ever thankful to your unconditional bond of friendship.

I offer my heartfelt thanks to Rina Tripathi who helped me to see things I could not and create a flow for the readers to enjoy. I would also like to mention of my friend Elizabeth Josh Hill, who supported me with her expert advice and immense love as I first began to jot my thoughts.

Thank you János Grāfl for the cover design of the book. Thank you Mady'sin Design for the book's overall presentation and design.

Textual Sources

The textual sources that inspired me were: *Mudrā* in Buddhist and *Hindu* Practices (Fredrick W. Bunce), *Mudrā Vijñāna*: Way of Life (Acharya Keshav Dev), Indian Classical Dance (KapilaVatsyayan), *Mudrā Vijñāna* (Pt Rajnikant Upadhyaya), Japa Yoga (N.C. Panda), *Mudrā Vijñāna:* Science of Postures (Vijay Bansal), *Mudrā: Vijñānaevam Sadhna* (Shyamkant Dwivedi Anand), "Sri Rudrabhayananda (Soul Searchers: The Hidden Mysteries of *Kuṇḍalinī)* and Cain Carroll & Revital Carroll (*Mudrās* of India)."

Readers

My humble *Namaskāras* and deep gratitude go towards all readers who have picked up this book. May you benefit from the knowledge of the sages and the ages, and may you share the light of this knowledge with the ones around you.

Most of all, I acknowledge the deep silence that is within each one of us. The richness, fluidity, and essence of this silence (*mauna*) that I soaked in during the writing of this book helped me find clarity. I pray and wish that you, as the reader, will be able to touch this silence and derive from this silence the strength, clarity, and immense potential that each one of us carries within.

Om Shantih Shantih Shantih
In Thy Name, At Thy Lotus Feet
Indu Arora
April 2015

Author's Note

I always try to stay aware of how much I do not know and how much more there is to know. This is my second book after *Yoga: 'Ancient Heritage, Tomorrow's Vision'* and like its predecessor, this book too is an inspiration from my students (whom I consider to be my teachers).

Let us start with the title of this book: *Mudrā: The Sacred Secret!*

What is so sacred about it, and why is it a secret?

The sacredness of the subject is due to the ability of the *Mudrā* to connect and bring forth communication in all the five layers *(pañca kośas)* of our being. It has been kept a secret since time immemorial due to the infinite powers that they bestow upon the practitioner; thus, the knowledge of the subject needs to be passed on with utmost care and precision. The secret is in the opening as well as the closing. As for me, opening and closing is the same thing. What is open outside is closed within, and vice versa. I am referring in particular to the *cakras* (psychic energy vortices). With the regular practice of *Mudrā* we open what is closed inside and close what is opened outwards. My focus in this book is on *Hasta Mudrā (hand Mudrā)* only, which clearly means that there is much more to *Mudrā* than just hand gestures. I hope that the introduction of *Mudrā* through this book whets your appetite to learn more...

For me, *Mudrā* is communication. The history of *Mudrā* dates back to the formation of the universe–or, what we may call the cosmos. None of it would have been possible without union and communication. Each living, non-living, animate or inanimate being in the cosmos communicates at many levels. Do not get confused about communication as just the ability to speak and gesticulate.

The five-element theory is based on *Sāṁkhya*. Every thing or being is made of five elements. The ratio and proportion of these five elements in that object or being gives it a particular shape, form, texture, color, and function. Five element are also present at the level of atoms and subatomic particles. What holds the subatomic particles together is the cohesive force of water; what keeps them moving is air; where they move/rotate is the space element; as they move, it creates friction and heat, which is the form of the fire element, and the combined weight of it forms the atomic mass that is the earth element. Even at the level of cells that the human body is made up of, the communication is at three levels: intracellular communication (communication within the nucleus, cytoplasm, and protoplasm of the same cell), intercellular communication (communication from one cell to another), and trans-cellular communication (communication of cell to the entire human body). Therefore, communication is the key and the particular position in which it happens is the *Mudrā*.

In today's world, where we have lost the ability to communicate at all three levels, *Mudrā* can prove to have a special purpose.

Having shared knowledge on this subject since 1999, I have been asked repeatedly: "Do you have a book on this subject?" My answer has always been, "No, but you are yourself like a book. Now that you have gained a basic understanding of the subject, practice it, and more shall be revealed to you."

Some get satisfied with this answer, and others still look for more material.

In most of the *Yoga* teacher-training programs, the only *Mudrā* touched upon is *Jñāna Mudrā* and that too in very little details. It is such an important aspect of *Yoga* and meditation, and yet, the least explored. I felt the need to bring this subject to light; I started conducting *Mudrā* teacher-training programs internationally. People have started approaching me thus: "Are you the *Mudrā* person?"

Students of *Yoga* as well as other people who do not have a background of *Yoga* seem equally interested, impressed, and happy to receive this knowledge.

I have personally seen the benefits of *Mudrā* in my body. I have felt its benefits during meditation as well as when used as therapy.

I planned to make this book a compilation of 108 hand *Mudrās* but I could not stick to this sacred number, as there are so many. I have skipped some and kept them aside for a book on advanced practice.

I have written this book with the intention that everyone should benefit from the precision, simplicity and clarity of content.

I would suggest you to practice the pronunciation of the name of the *Mudrās* as well as some Sanskrit terms using the Tranliteration Key provided in the first part of the book to master/be atuned to the correct vibrational frequency hidden in the name of the *Mudrā*/ Sanskrit term used. Additionally, you may look at the index with the name and the major benefit of specific *Mudrā* to find one that is suitable for you. However, I request you to go through the introductory chapter, which talks in detail about the guidelines regarding practice, history, science, and meaning of *Mudrā*.

I hope that each one of you enjoy it as much as I enjoy sharing my knowledge of this mystical art and science of communication.

With Namaskāra Mudrā
Indu Arora

EDITOR'S NOTE

I have always had a fascination for fingers…they are so small and yet do so much! They almost seem to have a life of their own. From the teachers, parents and grandparents gesticulating to explain things better, to finger puppet shows in school, to writing, cooking, stitching, painting and creating myriad creations, to eating and holding things, to dance…one can go on and on about the importance of fingers in our lives. I did not know about their role in *Mudrās*, at that time.

Mudrās or hand gestures have a therapeutic and spiritual quality, is something I became aware of in my own spiritual quest. I realizing that hand *Mudrās* lock and guide energy flow and reflexes to the brain. By bending, stretching and touching the fingers and hands, we can talk to the body and mind, as each area of the hand is connected to a certain part of the mind or body. This fact has been utilized in massages as well.

I was delighted and honoured to edit Indu's manuscript **- *Mudrā: The Sacred Secret.*** It was a tremendous learning experience as she peeled off layers upon layers and explained the origin, science, psychology and philosophy of *Mudrās* and went on to expatiate the types and benefits of the same with evocative pictures and beautiful illustrations. It was almost like listening to her talk! She is an experienced *yogini,* a fountainhead of knowledge, who endears her friends, followers, students and readers alike, with her deep-seated understanding imparted with utter humility.

When I met Indu first, she seemed a person deeply interested in *Yoga*, who had written a very comprehensive book about it too. But as I got to know her better, through her work, I realized that she is indeed a *Yogini* in the true sense.

Yoga is generally perceived as a combination of postures and breathing techniques for overall fitness and well being. While the postures are designed to affect all the body systems and breathing practices bring awareness of the relationship that exists between the body and the mind, there is still so much more to *yoga* – it has a subtle effect on our consciousness. This is done by the *Mudrās.*

Mudrās used in combination with breathing, enliven and enhance the flow of *prāṇa* in the body by stimulating the different parts of the body involved with breathing. Relating directly to the nerves, *Mudrās* create a subtle connection with the innate patterns in the brain influencing the unconscious reflexes in these areas. The internal energy is in turn balanced and redirected, affecting change in the sensory organs, glands, veins and tendons. It is an amazing power to be able to control our body in such a way – to focus our consciousness and manipulate our experience. The knowledge and experience of *Mudrās* techniques is so powerful! It adds a totally new dimension to the *yoga* experience.

The Universe is composed of five elements, earth, air, water, fire, and ether. Similarly, our body is also a composition of five elements, represented by our five fingers. According to *Ayurveda*, disease is due to an imbalance in the body caused by lack or excess of any of these five elements.The fingers are essentially electrical circuits. The use of hand *Mudrās* adjusts the flow of energy affecting the balance of air, fire, water earth and ether, bringing about healing. A daily practice ensures a healthy metabolism, glowing skin, active joints, focused mind and sharp senses.

The section on therapeutic *Mudrās* is one that should be read by all and applied when required. I feel that even the physicians should have knowledge of these *Mudrās*, as they would complement their treatment. In Indu's words, "What better tool can nature bless us with than we ourselves, who else has the ability to delve into the deepest core and secret of our being and dig out the reason for the conflict with our own body and mind?"

There are numerous *Mudrās*, many mysterious and others contemporary in nature.

The mysterious and important contribution of *Mudrās* in *Prāṇāyām* and *Gāyatri Mantra* discloses the amazing power of the combination of words and gestures in achieving miraculous results. The practice of *Prāṇāyām* redirects the *prāṇic* energy or life force into the appropriate energy pathway. *Mudrās* are used to avoid the leakage of *prāṇa* and intensify its force. Similarly, the thirty-two *Mudrās* for *Gāyatri mantra* are connected to thirty-two important vertebrae of our spine. It doesn't end here –the fascinating journey of connecting to self, unraveling and understanding the secret of *Mudrās* continues…

To conclude in Indu's words, "Do not lose any chance to connect to self…explore these *Mudrās*, one at a time, and practice for a few days to see the effect. Do not lose hope if you do not see any tangible result, be assured that each cell of your body is moving every time you are in practice and there is a subtle ripple effect building up…each cell is pregnant with dynamic energy, all you have to do is to connect."

Stay connected, stay healthy and happy!

Sunita Pant Bansal
2014, New Delhi, India

FOREWORD

Indu Arora has produced an excellent book on mudras that is likely the most comprehensive presentation yet available in the field. Several new publications on mudras have come out in recent years but hers adds additional yogic dimensions as well as subtle details of application. The variety of mudras and the explication of their usage is quite extensive, providing an abundance of approaches for the reader to explore for years to come.

Indu explores the usage of mudra as both a healer and as sadhaka, as one on the spiritual path. This makes her approach more experiential and reflecting of higher energies and intentions than those who look at mudras mainly at a physical or psychological level.

She highlights the healing power of different mudras making them relevant to everyone and easy to experiment with. Her explanations are clear and complete and she has adequate illustrations to explain each mudra and how to use it.

Mudras can be done simply and quickly when other Yoga practices may not be possible, such as when we are working during the day. Through holding our energy and awareness in the mudra, we can awaken the higher powers of our Yoga practice as needed.

Indu shows us many secrets of mudras and higher Yoga approaches that can help deepen our practice on whatever level that we choose to apply it. She unfolds inner dimensions to Yoga that add beauty, grace and energy to it. Her book is an important and innovative addition to the literature on mudras and on Yoga as a whole. It reflects a deeper understanding of Yoga than most of the available literature in the field.

No doubt Indu has such a deeper and thorough knowledge of many other aspects of Yoga. We hope that she addresses these in future publications.

Dr. David Frawley (Pandit Vamadeva Shastri) D. Litt.
Director, American Institute of Vedic Studies
Author of more than thirty books on Yoga and Vedic sciences

REVIEWS

"...so far, the most complete, practical, and authentic work on mudras. Clearly, Mudra: The Sacred Secret, is the fruit of Indu Arora's extensive studies and interaction with living teachers of the tantric tradition. With this work, Indu Arora has made a remarkable contribution to the field of yoga, tantra, and ayurveda, and has offered to the readers an opportunity to further enrich the healing modalities of their practices."

– Pandit Rajmani Tigunait, PhD
Spiritual Head, Himalayan Institute

"The Consciousness of Yoga as the Flow of Divine Grace rests upon a higher form of energy in order to manifest it. Indu Arora explores the deeper practices of Yoga through the dynamism of Mudra unfolding the powers of healing, rejuvenation and transformation. Mudra Jnana unlocks the yogic process revealing a secret force of Shakti hidden deep within our psyche. Indu awakens us to the grace and power of Mudra in our daily life, making our every gesture full of light."

– Yogini Shambhavi Devi
Author of 'Yogic Secrets of the Dark Goddess'

"This is a wonderful reference book. It is concise and relatable. Written with clarity and purpose, Indu will reach the beginner and the experienced Yogi, giving multifaceted material to satisfy every level of learner. I found the examples to be clear and concise, and the pictures are a wonderful guide into the gestures.

......hard to put it down. I will refer to this work over and over in my spiritual journey, and would recommend it to anyone who wants to expand their knowledge base."

– Beth Shaw
President and Founder: YogaFit Training Systems Worldwide

"In Mudra the Sacred Secret, Indu Arora has performed a remarkable work of scholarship and has made a valuable contribution to the study of yoga. Leaving seemingly no Mudra stone un-turned, Indu has dogged down the best-known and most obscure knowledge on the topic, creating the definitive work on this engaging and valuable topic. This is a very fine piece of work."

– Chris Kilham
Author: The Five Tibetans

"Indu Arora has chosen a very fundamental topic for presenting to a wider audience: the theme of mudra, which in the Indian tradition covers a wide range of meanings and practices, ranging from ritual to dance, to yoga, Tantra, iconography, and generally to the understanding of the human body and its infinite possibilities. Bringing together all these implications and applying them in the field of healing is her special contribution. Keeping in mind the spiritual background of mudra, she succeeds to bringing the hand poses into the practical field, which will be extremely helpful for therapists of different methods and traditions. In fact, mudra does not only include hand gestures and positions of the fingers, but also the whole body as an expression and attitude of the Divine, which in meditation and states of Samadhi assumes a spontaneous posture.

Her book will go a long way to overcome the dichotomy that is so widespread (especially in the West) between mind, body and spirit or self. The body is the best instrument for spiritual practice, and mudra is the most visible expression of a deep impression left on the soul (the original meaning of mudra also includes stamp, seal or impress).

I wish her a wide audience who can appreciate and use these insights in practice of healing and other ways of integration of body and self."

– Prof. Dr. Dr.h.c. Bettina Sharada Bāumer
Director: Samvidalaya at the Abhinavagupta Research Library, Varanasi, India

"Indu Arora has written an excellent book about the sacred art and science of Mudra. The book shares authentic information with simple scientific explanation about the ritual of Mudras. The most important being the intention and attention to align your individual spirit with cosmic spirit. It is a perfect addition to the vast library of modern day application of Vedic Sciences."

Thumbs Up (if that counts as a Mudra)

– Dr. Suhas Kshirsagar BAMS MD (Ayu)
Director: Ayurvedic Healing
Author: The Hot Belly Diet

"In Mudrā: The Sacred Secret, Indu Arora embarks on a journey to discover the esoteric history and meaning of Mudra (gestures), their profound spiritual effect and their therapeutic application. As readers, we are swept up in her enthusiasm and at times left stumbling in her footsteps. Her passion for the language of Mudra, takes her to the source—ancient Vedic texts and the wisdom of masters. Though I practice and teach Mudra and Mantra,

I am a novice in my understanding of the philosophical and spiritual foundation of these ancient practices, so Indu Arora's well-researched book will be my guide. In her quest for authenticity, the "Mudra Basics" section is anything but basic. Indu Arora explores the theories from ancient to modern, from religious and secular culture, from art, literature, dance and medicine to elucidate the science of Mudra. The sections that are the most beautifully photographed and explained are those that describe the individual Mudras themselves. Here, one need not be a scholar or even particularly drawn to the practice of Mudras to appreciate their beauty and their spiritual and therapeutic use. The book itself is art, and the philosophical and practical wisdom gathered here will provide an insightful reference for me and for students of Yoga and other spiritual traditions. "

– Amy Weintraub
Founder, LifeForce Yoga Healing Institute
Author of Yoga for Depression and Yoga Skills for Therapists

"Our ancient Indian yogic & artistic traditions are esoteric & mystical systems primarily designed to re-connect & re-align the microcosmic entity (human being) with its macrocosmic source (Cosmic Universe). Both these systems combine signs and symbols (mudras/ hastas), postures (asanas/sthanas) and sounds (mantras/shollus) to channelize the Universal life force (prana) in such a way that it balances, harmonizes and heals the body-mind. The body-mind then becomes a perfect vehicle, conducive to the flowering of a state of pure, serene and blissful awareness (Ananda).

Indian dance is yoga - a 'sacred communion of the Body, Breathe and Being moving in perfect harmony.' It is not surprising then that hastas (hand gestures) is one of the key elements of all Indian classical dance traditions and the purpose of Indian art is the aesthetic experience of Bliss (Rasananda).

In her book 'Mudra- The sacred secret', Indu compassionately shares her deep study, experience and wisdom of this sacred, esoteric science. The book is well researched, well-structured and beautifully illustrated with simple clear instructions that will enable its reader to deepen their understanding and practice of this vidya. It is a wonderful gift and guide for all sadhakas.

It is evident the effort and time Indu has spent on this wonderful encyclopedic book, to a dancer the vocabulary of hastas is an all- engaging process. Thank you Indu for this sharing."

– Dr. Prakriti Bhaskar
Indian Classical Dancer, Choreographer & Research Scholar
Director, Shiladhish Art & Research Institute, Mumbai- INDIA

"In Jyotisha (Vedic Astrology), the star constellation—Hasta—emits the power to place your heart's desire in the palm of your hand. Likewise, Indu Arora's latest book, Mudra: The Sacred Secret, reveals the profound powers within your own hand—to heal and awaken. Drawing from classical Yoga philosophy and Ayurveda, she enlivens the enlightening energy within your palms for your own benefit, as well as those whom you touch. Through textual references, inspiring examples, and beautiful images, Indu Arora breaks new ground with this never-before-explored topic. And you'll discover that as the eyes are the window to the soul, the hands are the doorway to the heart."

– Dr. Katy Poole, Ph.D.
Jyotishi (Vedic Astrologer) and Life Coach

"Indu Arora has no doubt written the most comprehensive book on mudras to date. Five fingers on each hand—who knew what powers they had! Rearrange them into one of the many mudras in this book, and you can release negativity, change your state of consciousness, heal yourself, transcend time, or become enlightened. Indu Arora provides clear instructions, diagrams, photos, and philosophy to make the practice of mudras easy and meaningful. This is an excellent book for healers, yoga teachers, yoga practitioners, and anyone who wants to add another dimension to their practice of yoga."

– Sharon Steffensen
Editor, Yoga Chicago magazine

"For years, Indu Arora has demonstrated a comprehensive knowledge of the interconnected traditions of Yoga and Ayurveda as well as the deep sincerity and dedication of a seeker and student. As a teacher, Indu Arora aptly demonstrates her mastery of mudra in her new book, Mudra: The Sacred Seed.

The science of mudra offers us a healing modality that can be used by anyone, at any level of ability, and is a powerful adjunct to multiple therapies as well as a stand-alone practice for anyone at any ability. In this elegant and user-friendly book, Indu Arora's comprehensive explanation of mudra advances our ability as teachers, students and practitioners to incorporate these techniques in classes and in therapeutic settings.

Indu Arora's combination of clear instruction and imagery as well as a synthesis of psychological and physical benefits of the mudra elevates our understanding of this essential component of yoga practice. Her new word advances the science of mudra as we understand it in the modern age and it is a must-have addition to any library for those interested in both personal practice as well as yoga as therapy."

– Felicia Tomasko, E-RYT 500, RN
Editor-in-Chief LA YOGA Magazine
President, the Bliss Network
Member of the board of directors, National Ayurvedic Medical Association

"Using the framework of five elements, five pranas, cakras and Gayatri mantra, Indu Arora takes the reader on an journey of mudrs in "Mudra: The Sacred Secret" for it's therapeutic and spiritual benefits. Each murda is beautifully illustrated with her own hands, describing general mudras, therapeutic mudras, five element mudras, five prana mudras, therapeutic mudras of touch, spiritual mudras, mudras of cakra and mudras in the practice of Gayatri mantra. The core qualities, formation, benefits, cautions of each mudras are described with proper illustrations. Highly recommend for yoga students, yoga teachers, yoga therapists, health care providers and scholars who are interested in the therapeutic and spiritual benefits of mudras and will find themselves coming back to the text time and time again for deeper study and practice."

– Dilip Sarkar, MD, FACS, CAP
Associate Professor of Surgery (Retired), Eastern Virginia Medical School, Norfolk, VA
President, International Association of Yoga Therapists

"Mudra is scared practice of the Rishis to instrument changes in consciousness and experience inner bliss. Mudra is an indispensable tool for sadhana, and assist in the experience of deeper states of meditation. However, a book detailing this great art and science was sorely missed. Indu Arora's book "Mudra the sacred secret" is perhaps the first book of its kind that dwells into this esoteric subject with depth of perception, insights and references form source literature. This book can be a companion for any sincere sadhaka in modern times."

– Acharya Shunya Pratichi Mathur
Founder, Vedika Gurukulam, School of Ayurveda and Vedic Studies, California
President, California Association of Ayurvedic Medicine (CAAM)

"As a young boy growing up in a traditional conservative family, I was introduced and taught the practice of Sandhyavandana (salutations to the Sun). Sandhyavandana drawn from the Vedas was performed thrice daily: morning (pratahsamdhya), noon (maadhyanika), and dusk (saayamsamdhya). The entire ritual involves invoking various deities, use of hand gestures (hasta mudras), breathing practice (pranayama), yoga sun salutations (surya namaskara) and mindfulness meditation (dhyana and dharana). The importance of this ritual was never understood; it was memorized and done perfunctorily. Later, during my doctorate and postdoctoral training in Neuroscience, I understood the importance of nerve connections and nervous stimuli especially in the skin and fingers. Touch is one of the five sensory potentials (pancha tanmatras) and is perceived by the skin. It is one of the gateways of the body through which we draw in impressions from the external environment.

The fingertips are richly endowed with nerve endings and are very sensitive to the touch stimuli. A set of specialized neurons transmit the touch signals (afferent impulse-role of samana vayu) to the cortical region of the brain where it is processed and experienced as a sensation and a suitable message gets delivered by motor neurons to the fingers for an appropriate action to be taken (efferent impulse-role of vyana vayu). In addition to the touch sensation, the fingertips and other areas of the body surface are also endowed with receptors that recognize pain (nociception) and temperature impulses (thermoception). For example: Bring the forefinger of one hand close to the center of the palm of the other hand. Try not to touch the palm with the forefinger but keep it very close to the palm and notice what sensations arise in the fingertip (commonly described sensations include among others pain, heat, a thin ray of energy or a jet stream of air moving in a clockwise direction). How do you explain this phenomenon?

Vedic texts describe the presence of numerous tiny chakras (reservoirs of energy) on the fingertips that either get energized or depressed depending on the stimulus received. This may also partly explain the phenomenon of phantom pains. Of interest, neuroscience does not have an answer to the chakras or the energy reservoirs in the subtle body (sukshma sarira).

So since the fingertips are richly endowed with receptors that recognize varied stimuli and since these are also the sites of subtle chakras, could the placement and position of the fingertips be manipulated for optimal health, wellbeing and prevention of health disorders? Interestingly, every movement of the body part (be it facial, hand, eyes or finger) denotes a Mudra. All types of emotions can be easily displayed through a specific mudra using one or more of the body parts. Furthermore, mudras have been used for centuries in vedic traditions for promotion of good health and could be used as a "stand alone" therapy or together with pranayama and meditation. Mudras were adopted to sustain optimal health, relieve stress, prevent illness, and to recover from a variety of physical, mental and emotional problems. The one advantage of mudras-it can be done with ease, it does not require any paraphernalia and it can be done just about anywhere and anytime.

As I started gaining further knowledge of Mudras through my Yoga and Ayurveda practice, I was able to realize the importance of these gestures as part of my daily Sandhyavandana that could serve as a valuable tool on the path of spiritual awakening. Unfortunately my knowledge of mudras was restricted to the dozen or so gestures that I use as part of my sandhyavandana ritual. Thus, I welcomed the book "Mudra-The sacred secret" written by Indu Arora.

The book opens with a detailed introduction to the vedic philosophy, the philosophy psychology, science, and benefits of Mudras, chakras and pressure points. Information is provided on nearly 140 hand mudras classified under three broad categories and is accompanied by full-color illustration of the hands and fingers, the proper placement, the Sanskrit name, transliteration and English translation. Additionally, Indu Arora has provided elaborate information on the technique, its applications, physical, mental and spiritual benefits of the mudra. Furthermore, information is also provided on health issues and alleviation of the health challenges with a specific mudra(s). It is a very insightful and informative book and I would highly recommend to anyone who wishes to understand subtle body energy systems, spirituality and mental wellbeing. Undoubtedly, the book will be of great interest to yoga and ayurveda practitioners, integrative and holistic teachers and students and all others interested in acquiring a comprehensive knowledge of mudras.

Finally, for those skeptical scientists, there are at least a couple of scientific studies that show the benefits of mudras in conjunction with meditation that results in down-regulation of the inflammatory process together with positive changes in mood, anxiety, and other neuropsychologic parameters. Needless to say Mudras are not only healing gestures but also holy gestures. With my hands folded into an Anjali mudra, I offer my pranams to Indu Arora for writing a book that offers us unlimited opportunities for growth, healing, and integration of the body, mind and intellect."

– Rammohan Rao PhD; CAS; RYT
Research Associate Professor of Neuroscience
Buck Institute for Research on Aging, Novato, CA
Faculty, California College of Ayurveda
Nevada City, CA, 95959

TRANSLITERATION KEY

VOWELS

अ *a* (but)	आ *ā* (palm)	इ *i* (it)	ई *ī* (beet)	उ *u* (put)	ऊ *ū* (pool)
ऋ *ṛ* (rhythm)	ए *e* (play)	ऐ *ai* (air)	ओ *o* (toe)	औ *au* (loud)	

CONSONANTS

Guttural	क *ka* (skate)	ख* *kha* (blockhead)	ग *ga* (gate)	घ *gha* (ghost)	ङ *ṅ* (sing)
Palatal	च *ca* (chunk)	छ* *cha* (catch him)	ज *ja* (john)	झ *jha* (hedgehog)	ञ *ña* (bunch)
Cerebral	ट *ta* (start)	ठ**tha* (anthill)	ड *da* (dart)	ढ**dha* (godhead)	ण**ṇa* (under)
Dental	त *ta* (path)	थ *tha* (thunder)	द *da* (that)	ध *dha* (breathe)	न *na* (numb)
Labial	प *pa* (spin)	फ* *pha* (philosophy)	ब *ba* (bin)	भ *bha* (abhor)	म *ma* (much)
Semi-vowels	य *ya* (young)	र *ra* (drama)	ल *la* (luck)	व *va* (vile)	

Sibilants	श *śa* (shove)	ष *ṣa* (bushel)	स *sa* (so)	ह *ha* (hum)	
Others	क्ष *kṣa* (ksatriya)	त्र *tra* (triśūla)	ज्ञ *jña* (jñānī)	ळ*ḷ (play)	ॢ* *ṝ*

अं (÷)*ṁ anusvāra* (nasalisation of preceding vowel) like *saṁskṛti*

अ: *visarga* = *ḥ* (aspiration of preceding vowel) like *prātah*

S *Avagraha* consonant #' consonant (like:- ime '*vasthitā*)

Anusvāra at the end of a line is presented by m (म) and not *ṁ*

* No exact English equivalents for these letters.

Mudrā Basics

Mudrā

The root of the *Sanskrit* word *Mudrā* is "*Mud*," which means to impart bliss, happiness, pleasure, joy, *ānanda*. *Mudrās* are the means for the achievement of *Ānanda-śrī*. *Ānanda* means "pure bliss," and *śrī* here symbolizes "feminine energy." The rising of the feminine energy to meet the masculine energy and the joy of this union is *Ānanda-śrī*. In other words, this bliss is attained through the divine powers of the *Mudrā* or hand gestures, which emphasize and intensify the concentration on the Divine and attract the blessings of the Divine.

In this connection, the *Tantrasāra* defines *Mudrā* as being a source of pleasure to the Gods worshipped and a cause of freedom from the defilements of sin and passion.

Another meaning of *Mudrā* is represented by the words 'seal,' 'gesture,' 'posture,' 'lock,' 'symbol,' and 'currency.'

As per Eastern philosophies, cultures and *Yogic* practices, *Mudrās* are systematic hand, body, and face gestures.

More closely, *Mudrās* are "closed electrical circuits" of the subtle channels in physical and etheric bodies.

> *Mudrās* are a combination of elegance and mysticism.
> They purify, energize, and Divinize the spiritual aspirant
> in a similar way as *mantra* recitation.

Definition of *Mudrā*

Mudrās are a non-verbal mode of communication and self-expression, consisting of hands, face, and body postures. They retain the efficacy of the spoken word. It is an external expression of inner resolve, suggesting that such non-verbal communications are more powerful than the spoken word.

It is certain that the word *Mudrā* has a deeper meaning than suggested by its mere translation or synonyms.

The word *Mudrā* is not merely a collection of letters; each letter relates to a particular vibration, and each vibration invokes a particular sensation, thought, and emotion. The sages and seers in their trance, or *śūnya*, state of mind as *parā* experienced these vibrations. The *parā* is a state where one receives the grace as an experience of the infinite, which is beyond any possible expression. One becomes the experience itself. The journey from *parā* to *paśyanti* gave birth to a meaning in their being through self-reflection. The *paśyanti* is the state of becoming a seer, a witness to the experience within, through *vimarśa*: self-reflection. When the meaning found a way out as speech through voice, it took the form of pure letters known as *akṣara*, or syllables as *vaikharī*. Each syllable is directed towards a specific vibration and a specific experience. The combination of all these experiences expressed as body and hand gestures is what we understand as *Mudrā*.

I would like to quote from Acharya Karunamoya *Sarasvatī's* foreword in Shyam Sundar Goswami's book *Laya Yoga* regarding the power hidden in the syllables…

"Yoga is hidden in the vedamantra (Ṛg-veda-saṃhitā, 10.114.9) as bīja which are its original form. The bīja are four: 'yang,' 'ung,' 'gang' and 'ah.' Again, 'yang' is composed of two bīja, 'ing,' and 'ang.' When the powers locked in the bīja are aroused and harnessed, the nāda-bindu factor is absorbed into the bīja aspect, and then the bīja, being arranged in order, constitute the shrouta word 'yogah,' which in that form, as well as in its complex spiritual forms, occurs frequently in the Saṃhitās of the Veda. The two matrika-letters 'ing' and 'ang' represent agni (fire) and soma (moon), or Piṅgalā and Iḍā. Piṅgalā and Iḍā cause respiratory motions which are based on yang bīja. When yang is roused, respiration is suspended because of the absorption of the Piṅgalā and Iḍā in the Suṣumṇā, and as a result kumbhaka is effected. At this stage, the yang-force is transformed into yama (control). The emergence of yama occurs in three stages: physical control in relaxation in āsana, vital control in kumbhaka, and sensory control in pratyāhāra. At the pratyāhāra stage, the bīja 'ung' is roused and radiates udāna force, by which concentration develops in three stages in the mental field: dhāraṇā, dhyāna and Samprajñāta Samādhi. At this Samādhi stage, yama (control) becomes sangyama (super-control). In Samprajñāta Samādhi, the bīja 'gang' is roused as concentration-knowledge-light (prajnaloka). Associated with the 'gang' is wisarga (ah); it is represented by the sign: Wisarga is Kuṇḍalinī. Kuṇḍalinī is aroused in Samādhi and illuminates the whole superconcentrated mind by her splendor. Then, Kuṇḍalinī absorbs superconsciousness by her absorptive power to effect a mind-transcendent stage in which Samprajñāta Samādhi is transformed into Asamprajñāta Samādhi. Finally, Kuṇḍalinī herself is absorbed into and united as one with Parama Śiva - Supreme Consciousness. This super absorptive yoga is layayoga. Ṛg-veda calls it the attainment of stage of Indra in yoga (Ṛg-veda-saṃhitā, 4.24.4)"

Each syllable uttered is a direct link to the cosmos and to the ultimate truth. If one meditates upon the word *Mudrā*, the complete knowledge of the subject shall be unveiled to that being. Each word is like a guided path to its source of knowledge in the *ākāśa*, the space. The word itself carries within it the entire DNA of that subject.

Here, I wish to mention *Sūtra* 1.4 (1st chapter, 4th aphorism) from *Śiva Sūtras* to shed some light on this, along with a poetic expression to the meaning of the *Sūtras.*

Jñānādhiṣṭhānaṁ Mātṛkā (1.4)

Bound in the *Karmic* body

I still saw the truth: *Parā*

I contemplated upon it: *Paśyantī*

I couldn't resist and uttered: *Vaikharī*

The vibration supreme

…As little mothers

They conceal the truth in its womb

Manifest the little (minimal truth as *akṣara*: letters: offspring of truth)

Back into womb, I have to go

To seek, to see and to know

The knowledge supreme

The mothers unknown* (countless forms of *Śakti*) shall illumine the path

For the truth of the vibration is, it is just the ***Vibration Of The Truth!***

*Here, it means the innumerable, countless forms of *Śakti* that are intangible, nameless, and formless, and from whose womb the universe continuously evolves from moment to moment.

Mudrā is communication. *Mudrās* are as old as human civilization, as old as the primeval living entity. There are as many *Mudrās* as living beings on earth, including human and other life forms. Each of them conveys who they are through communication of their silent body language, features, poses, language, sounds, and expressions.

Communication can be at three levels: Interpersonal, Intrapersonal, and Transpersonal. *Mudrā* is both an art and a science of communication at these three levels for erasing the difference between, and taking the veil off, *Antar-Ākāśa* (inner space) and *Bahir-Ākāśa* (outer space), to merge with the *Brahman* (ultimate abode). We communicate at all these levels: the communication between you and me is at the interpersonal level; the communication within the self is at an intrapersonal level; and the communication from oneself to the cosmos is at the transpersonal level. All these forms of communication without the use of words are *Mudrās*.

A smile on my face (form of *Mukha* [face] *Mudrās*) can communicate happiness to others and is non-verbal interpersonal communication, whereas a smile that is there in each pore of my being when I meditate is intrapersonal non-verbal communication, and we call it *Dhyāna Mudrā*. At the same time, my gazing at the quiet running river or a huge mountain, fixing my eyes on nature's glory with a sense of union is transpersonal communication, and is called *Trāṭaka Mudrā*.

The intention, as one practices the *Mudrā*, is to connect, unite, clear away blockages, and invite peace, love, and joy. As one holds the *Mudrā*, one invites the cosmic peace within.

This communication can also happen at a therapeutic level through *Mudrā* where holding a *Mudrā* allows for the balance and harmony between the five elements that constitute the *deha*, the physical body. By holding a *Mudrā*, the nine main organ systems (digestive system, respiratory system, excretory system, circulatory system, reproductive system, nervous system, endocrine system, skeletal system and the muscular system) start vibrating in a healthy rhythm, as the communication channels open with the practice of *Mudrā*. This communication is deeper than being just at the level of organ systems; it is actually the communication at the intracellular and intercellular levels. It is communication at the micro level to the macro level of our existence – between microcosm and macrocosm.

The ability to concentrate and assimilate the energies at such a micro level of existence, in order to seal it and to increase the energy without leakage, is a *Mudrā*. For example, *bandhas* are a concentrated form of *Mudrā*. Any practice in which you are filtering the energy and giving it a direction and avoiding a leak becomes a *Mudrā*.

Chogyam Trungpa

Mudrā is "a symbol in the wider sense of gesture or action... Also, it is a symbol expressed with the hands to state for oneself and others the quality of different moments of meditation..."

Sages *(ṛsi)* of ancient India have discovered that *Mudrās* change breathing (*Prāṇāyāma*) and direct air and *Prāṇā* to various parts of the body (via energy channels/meridians), hence balancing energy homeostatically, or opening and regulating energy channels, tonifying deficiency and sedating excess; breathing relates to the position of the hand. Mystic lore relates that *Mudrās* direct energy (*Prāṇā*) to certain parts of the brain.

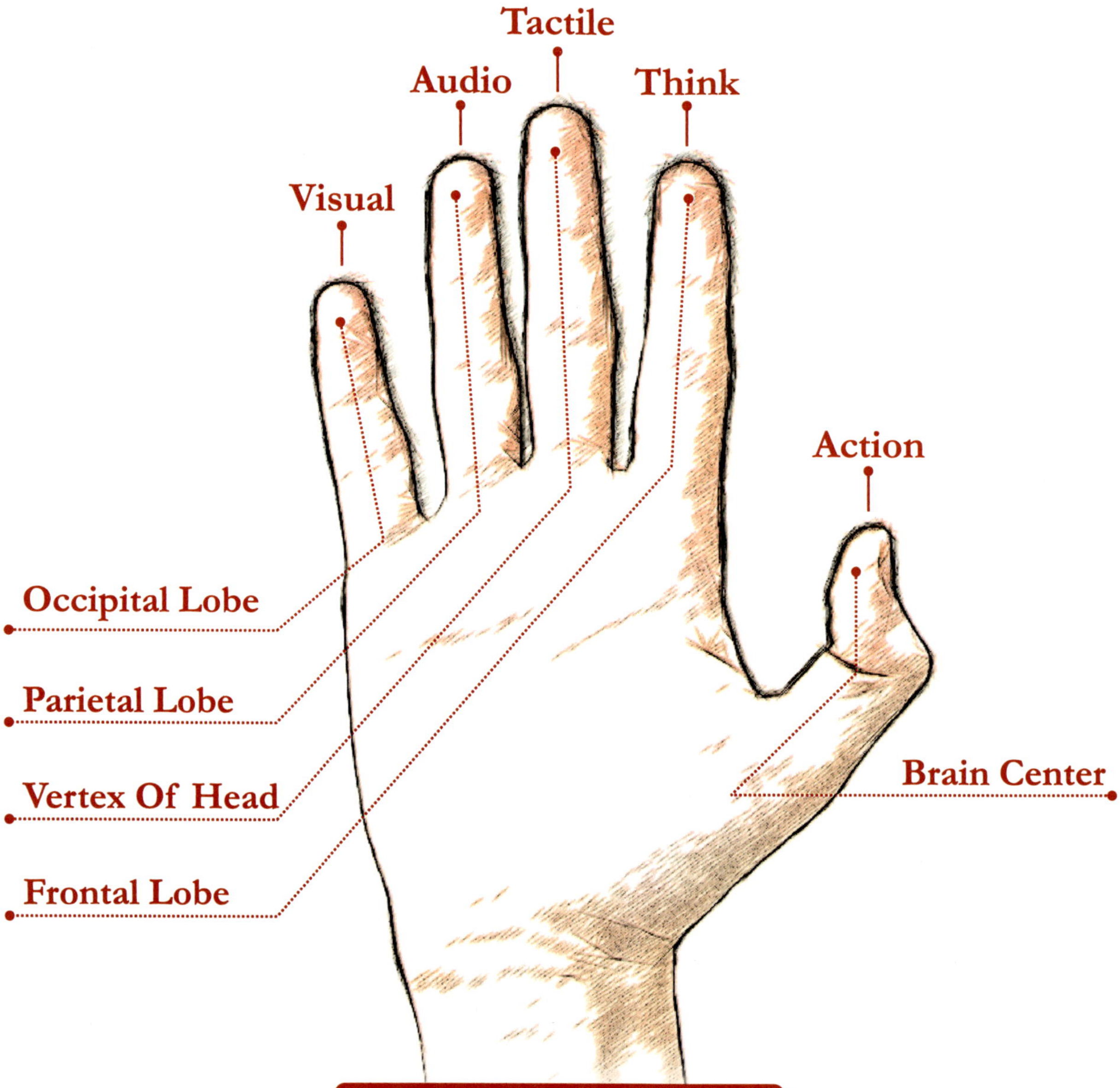

Fingers, Brain Areas And Tasks

Left Brain (Right Hand)

Right Brain (Left Hand)

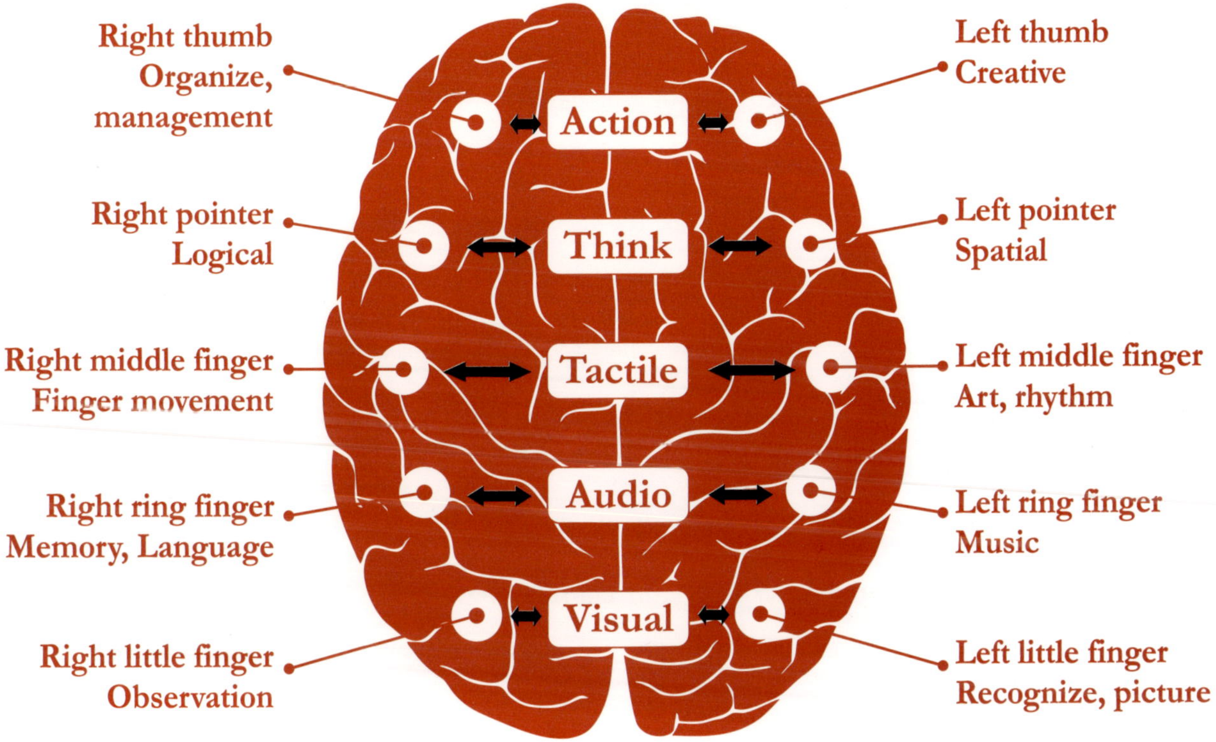

The Finger-Brain Lobe Connection

Application of *Mudrās* in spiritual practice

- The specific configuration of hands, feet, fingers, and other parts of the body is a *Mudrā* – for example,
  - – *Surabhī Mudrā* (*Mudrā* of the cow)
  - – *Ghaṇṭā Mudrā* (*Mudrā* of the bell)
  - – *Bhūmi-sparśa Mudrā* (*Mudrā* of touching the ground)
  - – *Abhaya Mudrā* (*Mudrā* of protection).
- The *Astras* (protective and annihilation tools) and *vāhanas* (carriers) of Gods and Goddesses – such as the conch, the discus, the flower, the mouse, and the lion, which are sported on their bodies or used as their seat – are also known as their *Mudrās* (refer to picture of Goddess *Durgā*).
- The secretive practices of *Hatha Yoga* like *Bhūcarī, Khecarī, and Agocarī* are all *Mudrās.*
- In secret *tantric* tradition, the woman is depicted with her spiritual partner in a special *Mudrā* of union.
- The science of dance was created by taking words from the *Ṛg-veda*, music from the *Sāma-veda, Mudrā* from the *Yajur-veda,* and emotion *(rasa)* from the *Atharva-veda.* In dance, dramatic representation plays a very important role. One form of that representation is the *Mudrā.*
- Specific hand and body gestures like *kara-nyāsas* and *aṇga-nyāsas*, performed during particular rites and rituals in the ritualistic worship called *karma-kāṇḍa*, are *Mudrā. Nyāsas* are the act of touching of the hands, fingers, and body parts as an act of cleansing and invocation of energy using *mantras.*

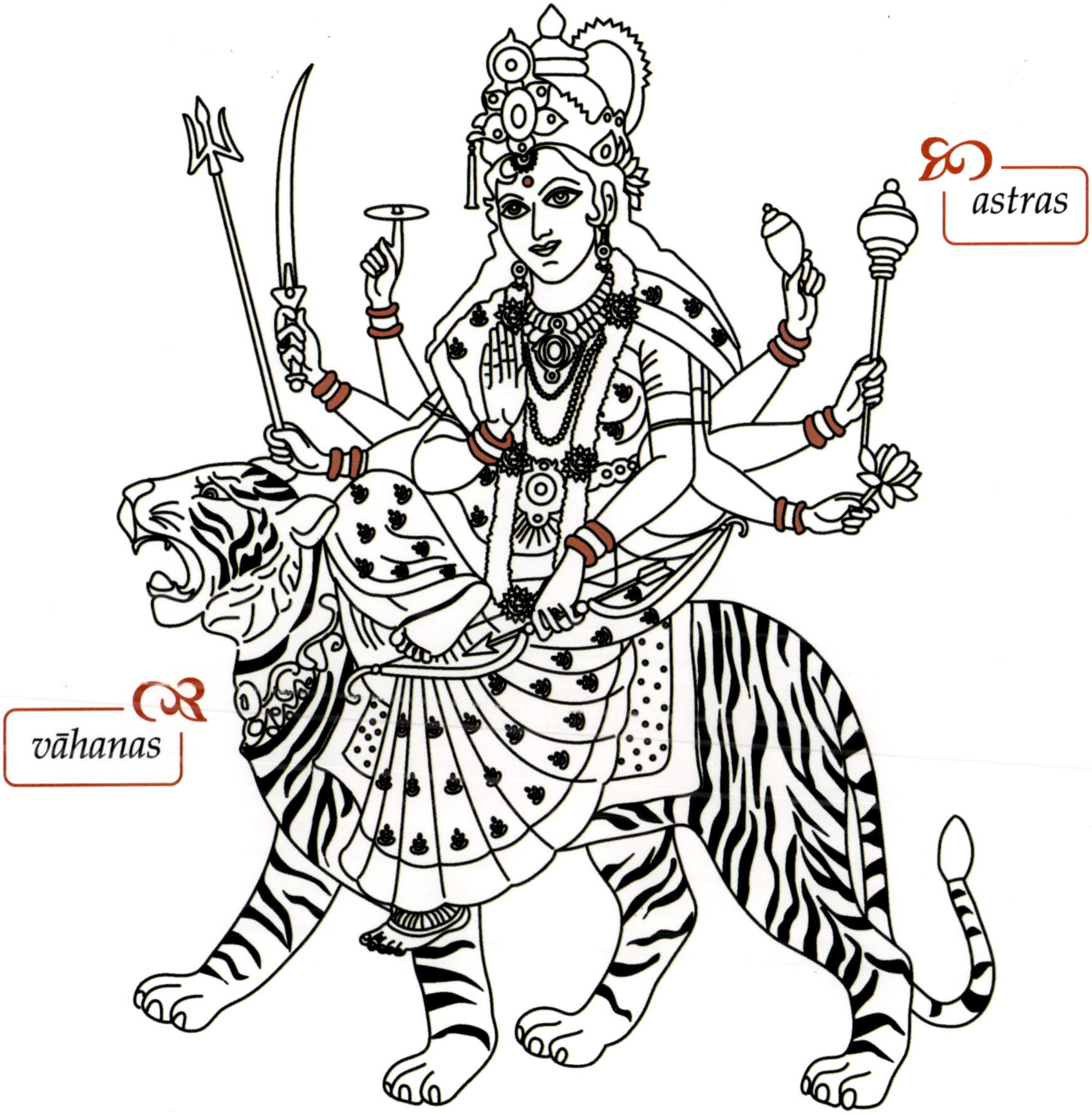

Durgā Depicting *Mudrās* In *Vāhanas* And *Astras*

Actions *(Mudrās)* are manifested thoughts

Thoughts are manifested emotions *(Rasas)*

Emotions are subtle and gross experiences

Experiences are a result of communication

Communication manifests at three levels

All of it starts with communication and ends with a *Mudrā*

The level of awareness will allow you to peel those layers

Chapter - I

Origin and History of Mudrā

Mudrā in various cultures, traditions, and countries

Sanātana Dharma

Sanātana Dharma shows the earliest recorded knowledge and analysis of *Mudrā*. The earliest documentations are found in *Mantra Śāstra* (the book of incantations), *Upāsanā Śāstra* (the book of worship and prayers), and *Nṛtya Śāstra* (the book of classical dances).

Islam

In Islam, the mystical whirling dervishes used hand signs or *Mudrā* for various rites and rituals.

Christianity

In Christian art, Jesus, John the Baptist and Virgin Mary are shown in various *Mudrās*. The Sign Language of the Mysteries by J.S.M. Ward is a book that can be taken as a reference in this case. The hand gesture used by priests in Catholic churches while blessing the devotees is known as *Mahā-jñāna Mudrā*.

Orient

In the Orient, *Mudrās* are a part of the rituals and rites of the rich cultural traditions of Hinduism and Buddhism in India, Tibet, China, Japan, Indonesia, etc. The paintings in the caves of Ajanta and the sculptures in the Ellora caves, dating back to the 2nd and 1st centuries BC, show innumerable *Mudrās*.

Babylon

The Babylonian Sun God Damuzi depicts *Mudrā* while descending into the underworld.

Egypt

Egyptian hieroglyphics are a virtual treasure house of *Mudrā*. The postures of their kings and queens even as mummies depict *Mudrā*.

Rome

Roman art is replete with *Mudrās*.

Yogic Tradition

Yogic texts like *Haṭha Yoga Pradīpikā, Yoga Vāsiṣṭha, Gheraṇḍa Saṃhitā, Pātañjala Yoga Sūtras,* and *Śiva Saṃhitā* talk about the *Mudrā* as very deep, secretive knowledge for the accomplishment of *turīya, nirvāṇa, kaivalya, and sādhanā.* All of it means realization of the true self and becoming one with the truth.

Tantra

Mālinī-vijayottara Tantra, Netra Tantra, Kulārṇava Tantra, and *Svacchanda Tantra* talk about the importance and usage of *Mudrā* in *tantric* rites and rituals.

Buddhism

Buddhas and *Bodisattvas*, and frequently other deities, are shown with their hands forming a number of different ritualized and stylized poses *(Mudrā)*. They may be holding different objects as well within these poses. Each, by itself and in combination with others, has specific meanings.

In the words of Rev. *Jñāna* – Zen *dharma* teacher:

"The earliest representations of the Buddha in human form did not appear until about the second century of the Common Era. At that time, the Mudrā of the first Buddhist statues in India had no precise iconographic meaning. The few symbolic gestures that initially were employed developed over time, acquiring a more specific nomenclature and a more exact iconographic significance. The mid-7th century CE Mahāvairocana-Sūtra Mahāvairocana makes note of over 130 separate Mudrās: 31 for the Great Buddhas, 57 for the great deities, and 45 for others."

Vajrayāna Buddhism

In *Vajrayāna* Buddhism, *Mudrā* also denotes the imagery used in any meditation or visualization practice to imprint certain qualities upon or to modify the practitioner, just as a seal leaves an impression on clay or paper.

Chapter - II

Textual References of Mudrā

Haṭha Yoga Pradīpikā

"The practice of *Mudrā* bestows upon the practitioner the eight *siddhis* (accomplishments) of *aṇimā, mahimā, garimā, laghimā, prāpti, prākāmya, īśitva,* and *vaśitva*. The knowledge of *Mudrā* is rare and not easily available to everyone."

"The knowledge of *Mudrā* should be treated like a treasure of fine jewels, only to be shared with the right person. It should be kept as a secret."

"To awaken the *Kuṇḍalinī Śakti*, which is sleeping/lying dormant at the *Brahma dvāra* (base of the spine), it is important for the sincere practitioner to practice the 10 main *Mudrās: Mahā Mudrā, Mahā Bandha, Mahā Vedha, Khecarī, Uḍḍīyāna Bandha, Mūla Bandha, Jālandhara Bandha, Viparīta Karaṇī, Vajroli, and Śakti Cālana.*"

"In this tradition, *Mudrās* are considered precious tools on the path of awakening. There are five classes on such *Mudrās* as taught in *Hatha Yoga Pradīpikā: hasta* (hand), *mana* (7 openings of the head: two eyes, two ears, two nostrils and one mouth), *kāyā* (postural), *bandha* (lock) and *ādhāra* (base or preineal)."

Siddhis	Meaning
Aṇimā	potential to reduce one to the size of an atom
Mahimā	ability to spread in space/reach out
Laghimā	ability to walk over water or ability to not be touched by water/ ability to make one's self as light in weight as possible
Garimā	ability to make the self as heavy as possible
Prāpti	the ability to achieve anything
Prākāmya	irresistible will – for example, the ability to make the self invisible
Īśitva	supremacy over body and mind
Vaśitva	supremacy over five elements

Eight Siddhis* of *Mudrās

Gheraṇḍa Saṁhitā

"There are 25 main *Mudrās*: *Mahā Mudrā, Nabho Mudrā, Uḍḍīyāna Bandha, Jālandhara Bandha, Mūla Bandha, Mahā Bandha, Mahā Vedha, Khecarī, Viparīta Karaṇī, Yoni, Vajroli, Śakti dhāriṇī, Taḍāgī, Maṇḍavī, Śāmbhavī*, five types of *Dhāraṇa Mudrās: Aśvinī, Pāśinī, Kākī, Mātaṅgī*, and *Bhujaṅginī*."

"What more shall I tell thee? In short, there is nothing in this world like *Mudrā* for giving quick success (in spiritual path)." Verse 100

Śiva Saṁhitā

"With the practice of *Mudrā*, what is impossible becomes possible. The dormant *Kuṇḍalinī Śakti* is awakened and rises up."

Mantra Śāstra

Etā Mudrā na jānāti gāyatrī niñphalā bhavet

Etā Mudrā kartavyā gāyatrī supratiñohitā

"One who does not know the *Mudrā*, the chanting of *Gāyatrī mantra* to that person does not bring results."

Upāsanā Śāstra

"During the rites and rituals, in the offering to deities, specific *Mudrās* should be used."

"*Mudrā* plays a most important role in *Śrī Vidyā*, the worship of the Supreme Divine Mother, *Śrī Lalitā Mahā-tripura-sundarī*, the Goddess of Infinite Love, Infinite Purity, Infinite Beauty, Power, Sweetness, and Tenderness. One worships and invokes the Goddess through special *Bīja mantras* and corresponding hand *Mudrās* (gestures). This sacred *Mudrā* multiplies the effects of the *Bīja mantras*. The combination of *mantra* recitation and simultaneous performance of the corresponding *Mudrā* helps the sincere and pure-hearted devotee to progress on the spiritual path."

Mudrā	**English Name**
Añjali Mudrā	Seal of Honoring
Āvāhanī Mudrā	Seal of Invitation
Sthāpana Karmāṇi Mudrā	Seal of Fixing Action
Saṁnidhāpanī Mudrā	Seal of Bringing Close
Saṁnirhodhinī Mudrā	Seal of Full Control
Dhenu Mudrā / Amṛtī- Karaṇa Mudrā	Cow Seal/ Seal for Creating the Nectar of Immortality
Matsya Mudrā	Fish Seal
Kūrma Mudrā	Tortoise Seal
Padma Mudrā	Lotus Seal
Yoni Mudrā	Seal of the Womb/Vulva

Ten *Mudrās* of *Śrī Vidyā*

In the practice of *Śrī Vidyā Tantra,* in *Śrī Vidyā* tradition the 10 gestures/ *Mudrās* correspond to the 9 triangles of the *Śrī Yantra* (or *Śrī Cakra*), and the tenth relating to the inclusive whole (Goddess); they are used to invoke the Goddess *Tripura Sundarī*. (Refer to the picture below)

Śrī Lalitā Mahā-Tripura-Sundarī

Nṛtya Śastra

"Various stories, characters, objects, animals, and situations are described by the use of *Mudrā* of hands, eyes, body, and face."

The four forms of expression (*abhinaya*) in Indian classical dance and drama are:

1. ***Vācika*** – verbal (song, dialogue)
2. ***Āṅgika*** – body language basically *Mudrās*
3. ***Āhārya*** – costume and makeup
4. ***Sāttvika*** – moods, emotions, sentiments expressed through face

Classical Indian dance technique views the joints are the initiators of movement and shapes the performance. Instead of initiating movements from the muscles of the hands or arms, every *Mudrā* is articulated and intitated from the wrist. This change of focus imbues each *Mudrā* with a certain connectivity that carries the impact of the gesture deep into the dancer's core and the spectator's heart. The *Mudrās* in dance are the focal point around which everything else revolves. The verse below, from the *Abhinaya Darpaṇa (Nandikeśvara)*, poetically describes the importance of *Mudrās*:

Yato hastas tato drishtih, Yati drishitis tato manah
Yato manas tato bhavo, Yato bhavo tato rasah

"Where the hand goes, the eyes follow. Where the eyes go, the mind follows.
Where the mind (awareness) is, mood or emotion *(bhāva)* is created.
Once *Bhāva* is created, sentiment *(rasa)* arises."

Nṛtya Mudrā

Śiva Sūtras

In the *Śiva Sūtras*, one of the most important texts of Kashmir *Shaivism, Mudrā* is mentioned in two contexts: as *Mudrā-virya* and *Mudrā-karma. Mudrā-virya* refers to the innate power that serves as the foundation of our experiences as *Turiya* (pure awareness). *Mudrā-karma* refers to the state in which mind alternates between internal awareness of "self" and external awareness of the "world" and is not able to discern the difference between the two. In this context *Mudrā* is the sense of having united with something larger, while simultaneously knowing that such a union is primordial."

Ārya Mañjuśrī Mūla Kalpa

"If an undertaken task appears impossible to accomplish, then it can be achieved with chanting accompanied by certain *Mudrā*."

Sangīta Śāstra

"During the vocal expression of various stories, *Mudrā* is also used."

Mālinī-vijayottara Tantra

"*Mudrā* is *Śiva-Śakti* itself!"

"*Mudrā* is a means to attain *Mantra-Siddhi*." (*Mantra-Siddhi* means accomplishing or fructification of a *mantra*.)

Kulārṇava Tantra

"*Mudrā* are not merely a means of *sādhanā* (meditation), they are also highly therapeutic, beautiful, as well as a great means of communication."

"It traces the word *Mudrā* to the root *Mud* and *dru* (to draw forth). This hints as an ecstatic state of non-duality or union with the deity."

Svacchanda Tantra

"*Mantras* are energetic of wisdom (*Jñāna Śakti*), but *Mudrā* are energetic of the energy (*Kriyā Śakti*) of the supreme consciousness."

Netra Tantra

"There are three ways/means to attain self-realization: *mantra*, meditation, and *Mudrā*."

"*Mudrā* symbolizes *Śakti* itself."

Abhinaya Darpaṇa (Nandikeśvara)

There are 28 single hand gestures and 24 united hand gestures. All these different hand gestures or *Mudrās* are frequently used in Indian classical dance forms, especially in *Bharata-nāṭyam*. There are special hand gestures or *Mudrās* that denote all the Gods and Goddesses (*Brahmā, Viṣṇu, Śiva, Sarasvatī*, and *Lakṣmī*, to name a few), the four different castes *(Brāhmaṇa, Kṣatriya, etc.),* different relationships (mother, daughter, etc.), the nine planets (Mars, Jupiter, etc.), rivers *(Gaṅgā, Yamunā,* etc.), animals (lion, deer, etc.), and so on.

Book of Changes *(Yijing)*

The classical *Mudrās* are representative of ancient symbols, and carry and transmit ancient knowledge to us. In this context, it is more accurately translated as the Classic of Symbols.

Research: Science Daily

A brain-focused research paper published in the National Academy of Sciences in November 2009 demonstrated that hand gestures stimulate the same regions in the brain as language.

Chapter - III

Psychology of Mudrā

"One cannot not communicate." *(P. Watzlawick)*

When we talk about *Mudrā*, the first thing that we have to make clear is the meaning of the word: *Mudrā* itself means gesture or seal. Gesture is a form of non-verbal communication… and here is the key: communication.

What is communication, then?

Communis, the root of the word, means, "share."
For communication, we need a sender, a receiver, and the content.
How we communicate depends upon the type of *Mudrā*…

In the case of therapeutic *Mudrā* the "sender" is the physical body who performs the *Mudrā*; the "content" is the energy field that we form during the practice of that particular *Mudrā*; and the "receiver" is the self. In the case of *Mudrā* in Indian classical dance: the "sender" is the dancer; the "content" is the meaning of the *Mudrā*; and the "receiver" is the audience. During interpersonal communication, 93 percent of the message is communicated non-verbally (38 percent is through vocal tones, 55 percent through facial expressions) and only 7 percent is verbally communicated.

Basically, all *Mudrā* help us to get in touch with ourselves... in the process of healing ourselves, in communication with others (to express what is going on inside), or in getting in touch with the One by performing spiritual *Mudrā*. In all of these cases, the goal is to make the connection stronger with our true nature, with the Self, by optimizing and balancing the energy field. It is not possible to not communicate. We are constantly interacting with ourselves and with the ones around us, whether we speak or not.

Ever since Darwin's work (related to the expression of emotions in man and animals), we know that expressions of some basic emotions are not only similar in every culture but we also share these with animals. The facial expression of emotions like anger, disgust, fear, happiness, sadness, and surprise is the same in every single culture! Even if we do not understand the complexity of dance *Mudrā*, and even if we do not understand the whole meaning of an Indian dance performance, we can still get the core meaning, the core story of a performance, because we can get these emotions through their universal expression. There is one theory that is more interesting, called facial feedback... meaning that if you perform a facial movement of a special emotion (for example, happiness => smile), you will actually find yourself happier…

Ágota Seszták is a Psychologist and a Yoga therapist/instructor from Budapest, Hungary. In her own words, "The essence of my teachings is "To Be." My intention is to create a 'space', where everyone can come and find themselves, where the heavy loads of expectations and goals can be lifted, where silence exists and everything else fades. It is possible to stay relaxed in tense situations. It is possible to keep the inner center still while there is chaos around. It is possible to BE when there is pressure to BECOME." She stands by the philosophy of Nisargadata Maharaj: Love says, "I am everything." Wisdom says, "I am nothing." Between the two, my life flows.

Chapter - IV

Philosophy of Mudrā

"ॐ इदं नम ऋषभि्यः पूर्वजेभ्यः पूर्वेभ्यः पथकृिद्भ्यः ॐ"

The relationship of body and mind is indeed a very mysterious one, very little is understood even today. Modern psychologists often refer to it as the "mind-body problem". However, *Vedic* traditions have explored this mysterious connection since millennia, as part of their quest for inner purity, peace and bliss. To rise above the perpetual suffering of this world, the *Vedic* traditions seek to purify the mind from its impurities. Mental impurities *(citta malā)* include hatred, anger, pride, greed, envy, ignorance and selfish lust etc. They are considered impurities because they are at the root of all suffering, and also because they are obstacles to the experience of inner bliss when they render the mind extrovert by constantly disturbing and agitating it. After purification the mind becomes introvert and peaceful. An introvert and peaceful mind has the potential to know and understand itself, and also to experience its deeper blissful nature – the Self *(ātman)*.

On the way in this voyage into the inner world it became evident to the *Vedic* mystics that like the mind and its functions influence the body in everything it does: ranging from simple acts such as raising our hand to the most complex interpersonal or social behaviors; similarly, the body and its actions can also influence the mind and its functions by casting long-lasting effects upon them. They discovered the secret – the mind cannot only be affected from within, but also from without. Even though as a conscious willful observer I have direct internal control over my mind, which is evident from the fact that I can willfully direct my mentation, nevertheless, there are situations where I fail to control the mind directly from within; for example, there is no way I can instruct from within the mind to become completely peaceful. In such cases, reaching the mind through its two external layers is more effective. These two layers are the breath and the physical body[1].

In a sense, approaching the mind from without is even more effective than approaching it from within, because, while we can only control from within the part of mind of which we are conscious, which is not more than the tip of the actual iceberg that the mind is, affecting it from outside allows us to control and alter even some of the unconscious part of the mind. Success in affecting some of the unconscious mind means that we can also control and alter some physical processes or behaviors over which we have otherwise no conscious control.

In this journey of approaching the mental through the physical, *āsana* (*yoga* posture) is the very first step. With an ardent practice of *āsanas*, awareness starts to expand into parts of our body of which we otherwise remain unaware. After awareness is allowed to spread throughout the body up to the very tip of the toe, the spreading of awareness is taken a step further – awareness of breathing through *Prāṇāyāma*. Breathing is a natural process of which we generally remain unaware. Becoming aware of breathing was found to be so effective in purifying the mind, that the practice of *Prāṇāyāma* is often compared to a furnace that burns away all impurities of a metal ore. This is because breath-control has a calming effect on the mind, and most of the impurities are products of a restless and agitated mind. After purification, the mind becomes ready for meditation.

---

[1]Kṛṣṇa Yajur Veda Taittiriya Aranyaka (8.2 etc.) mentions five kośas (pañca kośas), sheaths or layers, within this body. Like the scabbard of a sword or the cocoon of a silkworm, they envelope the innermost Substance, the Self, the Supreme Being (ātman) – annamaya (physical body), prāṇamaya (breath or life force), manomaya (mind), vijñānamaya (intellect) and ānandamaya (bliss).

But, how to acquire constant awareness of a mystical thought during meditation without allowing any other thought to intervene? Indeed, not an easy task, because, like a monkey, the mind is accustomed to jump from one thought to another, incessantly. Can we solve this problem also through a physical approach? Yes, *Mudrā* is the answer.

Mudrā is a hand gesture that mimes the abstract idea expressed by a *mantra* (mystical verse or sentence from the *Vedas* or other mystical texts) such as *OM* etc. The hand gesture has the capability to make the meditator aware of all esoteric ideas explicitly stated or symbolized by the *mantra*. It is well known that during meditation a *mantra* is very helpful in focusing the mind upon a mystical thought. However, a *Mudrā* allows a meditator to further sharpen the focus of his single-pointed awareness by allowing him to drop away the words of the *mantra*, and only retain the abstract idea expressed by those words.

For example, during meditation on *Aham Brahma Asmi* (I am Brahman, the omnipresent Consciousness) a gesture known as *Jñāna Mudrā* allows the meditator to transcend the words, and yet retain the idea of his oneness with the Omnipresent within his conscious awareness. *Jñāna Mudrā* presents the same idea of oneness through depicting a circle, which symbolizes a zero or emptiness, formed by joining the index finger with the thumb, which symbolizes the union of the individual with the Omnipresent. In this case, the index finger denotes the individual, the meditator, who has transcended the three [2]*Guṇas* (nature's constituent qualities) denoted by the rest of the fingers; and the thumb denotes the Omnipresent Absolute. The detailed explanation might sound complex, but its essence, the universal oneness and transcendence from the world of emotions and plurality, is extremely simple. This simple quintessence is retained and reinforced in the mind during the entire session through the help of the gesture. Indeed, such gestures are a wonderful means of intra and inter-personal communication in the realm of mysticism, which transcends the mental limitations created by words. Therefore, according to the *Siddha Tantras* the word *Mudrā* itself denotes the nameless *(anākhyā)* supreme *Ṣakti* (power).

---

[2]*The three Guṇas are – Sattva Guṇa (the quality of knowledge), Rajo Guṇa (the quality of action) and Tamo Guṇa (the quality of inertia).*

In short, *Mudrā* is a *Mantra* with no words, or even letters!

In other words, a *Mudrā* works like a prop for the mind to support itself in the realm of the nameless and formless reality. It helps the mind to retain the awareness of an idea even without the aid of any verbal representation or *mantra*. Even in the highest state of meditation, where the meditator has transcended his limited identification with the physical body and has entered the limitless identification with the universal existence, the *Mudrā* remains like an authoritative seal in his hands. For a person standing outside, it is the only way to know the internal state of the meditator. Many enlightened masters leave their bodies while retaining a *Mudrā* in their hands. I have seen this happening with my own teacher – H.H. Swami Vidyananda Giri Ji Maharaj, the tenth master in a highly respected lineage of masters from Kailas Ashram Brahma Vidya Peetha. The thumb and the index finger of his right hand remained interlocked in *Jñāna Mudrā* throughout the last months of his life, even during the last two weeks when he had to be put on ventilator. Quite astonishingly, the *Mudrā* remained in place even after he left his body.

Due to their effectiveness, *Mudrās* form the most mystical component of worship rituals in *Vaidika Sanātana Dharma* (Hinduism). Worship rituals are a primary form of meditation meant to prepare a devotee for more advanced mental worships *(mānasa pūjās)* and internal rituals *(upāsanās)*, and ultimately for meditation on the highest essence – the Self. A devotee makes use of a complete array of *Mudrās* to bring the sublime ideas of *Vedic* mysticism into his awareness during such worships. These *Mudrās* awaken and bring forward into awareness some of the most divine and virtuous ideas already present within the devotee's mind, either inherently or due to earlier training received from the masters. The external form of the deity that is being worshipped by the devotee is a personified form of these inspirational divine virtues and benevolent thoughts of universal well being which help a person to evolve further on the path of inner evolution. Therefore, it is said that *Mudrās* awaken the deity within our heart.

Mudrās that are used in worship rituals can be divided into three categories. The first category consists of purificatory gestures *(Saṁskāra Mudrās)* used at the beginning of worship. This is associated with purification of the worshipper's person, of the place of worship, and of the ingredients of worship. The second category is known as *Āvāhana Mudrās* (gestures of invitation). In this sequence of *Mudrās* the worshipper envisages a sequence through which the omnipresent divinity gradually assumes a personal form essential for communication and takes up residence in the worshipper's innermost core – the heart. The heart is conceived as a lotus *(Hṛdaya-kamala)* that becomes the seat of the deity. The lotus depicted as a seat of a deity in Indian iconography symbolizes this purified heart. Then the worshipper invites the deity to emerge from his lotus-heart to sit upon the pedestal set up in front of the worshipper, so that offerings of flowers and fruits etc. may be made. Usually a statue or a picture is placed on that pedestal to symbolize the presence of the deity. In their absence, any other symbol (*Pratīka*), such as an areca nut, a mystical diagram *(Yantra)*, a crude piece of stone or even a small ball of cow-dung is used. The third category of *Mudrās* is called *Pūjā Mudrās* (gestures for worship). These are used when the worshipper makes offerings of flowers and fruits etc. The final offering is of the worshipper's own self, which symbolizes his complete surrender to the divine will by giving up his own limited ego. Finally, the ritual ends with the worshipper envisaging the deity taking leave *(Visarjana)* and being reabsorbed in the heart of the worshipper.

Therefore, *Āgama* texts define a *Mudrā* as that which "delights *Devas* (*Mu* = to delight) and puts to flight the offspring of bad deeds (*Dra* = to put to flight)." According to Shankaracharya *(Chāndogyopaniṣad Bhāṣya) Devas* (radiant beings) stand for mind's thoughts and inclinations that slant towards the resplendent path leading towards wisdom. Such thoughts and inclinations are instilled into the mind when a person studies, meditates upon and lives by the teachings of the *Vedas*. *Mudrās* strengthen these uplifting and inspiring thoughts. As they get strengthened, the *Asuras* (demons), the bad subliminal impressions impressed upon our mind by deeds that have caused pain and suffering to others, lose their strength, and hence are said to "put to flight" by the *Mudrās*. This inner battle between good and evil has been going on within us since time immemorial. It is only through this inner battle that we can realize our highest human potential. *Mudrās* work like weapons that assist us in winning this internal battle.

Not only the meditator, the devotee, but even the deities are sculptured or pictured holding various *Mudrās* in *Vedic* iconography. We find Lord *Rāma* in *Jñāna Mudrā* (gesture of wisdom) while imparting wisdom to his closest devotee Hanuman *(Rāma Pūrva Tāpinī Upaniṣad 31)*. Similarly, we see *Lord Kṛṣṇa* in the same *Mudrā* while imparting the wisdom of the *Gītā*, the very essence of the *Vedas*, to his closest devotee and friend *Arjuna (Gītā Dhyānam 3)*. We see Lord *Śiva* holding the same *Mudrā* while teaching about *Brahman*, universal Consciousness *(Bhagavata Purāṇa* 4.6.38). Lord *Dakṣiṇāmūrti*, another form of Lord *Śiva* and personification of the ultimate master of *Vedic* wisdom, who is well known for imparting his mystical teachings only in complete silence without using any word at all, is always depicted in *Jñāna Mudrā*. Similarly, most of the forms of the divine worshipped in *Vaidika Sanātana Dharma* (Hinduism) are seen holding at least one *Mudrā*. Not only deities, but also various great masters are portrayed holding *Mudrās*. The great master of *Yoga* and the author of the *Yoga Sūtras*, Maharshi Patanjali, obtained his name from *Añjali Mudrā* (gesture of salutation). The *Mudrās* of the *Buddha*, the Bodhisattvas, the Jain *Tirthankaras* and *Arhats* are well known and can easily be seen in their respective statues or pictures. Even some of the ten Gurus of Sikhism are depicted holding *Mudrās*. Indeed, *Mudrās* held by the deities express their purposeful work of granting fearlessness, blessings and mystical wisdom etc.- "The Lord exhibits His serviceability to His devotees through *Mudrās*." *(Bhagavata Purāṇa* 12.11.16)

Not only in eastern traditions, but we find that the fundamental idea of the *Mudrās*, that the functioning of the body has a profound effect on the mind, apparently, also was important in early Christianity. C.S. Lewis puts it rather amusingly in his Screwtape Letters (1960), in which he has an older devil advising a younger devil on how to tempt humans. The old devil advises that it is important to tempt humans to think that they can pray in any old comfortable position, because this will keep them out of positions which actually make a prayer more effective. Furthermore, Christianity, Consecration, Baptism, Eucharist and Benediction involve sacred gestures somewhat comparable to *Mudrās*. Various icon paintings, such as that of Jesus Christ Pantokrator, show Him making the gesture of teaching or benediction with his right hand, somewhat similar to a *Mudrā*.

Finally, even though *Mudrās* like *Mantras*, are beneficial even if performed without an understanding of their deeper meaning, yet, when we perform them with complete understanding, they become most effective and fruitful. Then they truly have the capacity to heal our heart and mind. After all, they are symbols, and unless we don't understand what they symbolize, their effect over the mind cannot be fully realized. "What, indeed, one performs with knowledge, faith and meditation; that, indeed, becomes most powerful", says the *Sāma-veda Chāndogyopaniṣad* (1.1.10).

Today, as more and more people are introducing esoteric practices, such as *yoga*, meditation and Vedanta, into their lives, interest in the science of *Mudrās* has also multiplied. However, there are not many books available that deal authoritatively with this vast esoteric subject. I am sure that this book by Indu Arora will fill the gap and allow us to have an insight into the mystical depths of the science of *Mudrās* by providing a comprehensive understanding of the mystical gestures.

May the *Abhaya Mudrās* (gesture of fearlessness) held in the hands by various deities and masters make us fearless, and also inspire us to grant fearlessness to all beings by abandoning any thought, word or deed that could cause any harm or suffering to them!

Siddhartha Krishna was raised in the family tradition of Yoga. He was educated at the Kailas Ashram Brahma Vidya Pitha, a monastery focusing on the teaching of Vedanta, whose name is related to well known scholars and Masters such as Swami Vivekananda (founder of the Ramakrishna Mission), Swami Ramatirtha (founder of the Ramatirtha Mission), Swami Tapovan (Master of Swami Chinmayananda, founder of the Chinmaya Mission), and Swami Sivananda (founder of the Divine Life Society). Later, he taught courses on Sanskrit grammar and Indian philosophy at the same monastery, and also edited their publications on Vedanta. In his further study he has specialized on Veda and Yoga philosophy as well and has published translations of and commentaries on Sanskrit texts. Siddhratha also writes two columns in the quarterly magazine Australian Yoga Life. Currently, he teaches at Swami Rama Sādhaka Grama (SRSG) and Omkarananda Patanjali Yoga Centre in Rishikesh, India, and as a guest instructor abroad. Omkarananda Asharam Himalayas has produced CDs of some of his philosophical discourses in which he discusses the ancient texts in a way which supports more universal understanding of the Yogic wisdom and its source, the Vedas, in accordance with modern intellectual thought.

Chapter - V

Sacred Science Of Mudrā

Like the physical body, the subtle body has its own nervous system, or channels conveying *Prāṇa*. In *Yogic* tradition, these channels are *Nādīs*. *Mudrās* help in clearing some of these channels of impurities of psychic, emotional origin.

Mudrā attracts cosmic energy into the microcosm. They arouse the subtle body's latent energy into awakened activity. All the dormant and passive nerve cells of the brain are awakened and stimulated into action. *Mudrās* bring efficiency in the functioning of the organs and organ systems of the physical body. These energies that a *Mudrā* awakens, manifest as magnetic and electrical forces, depending on their form.

"Spin theory in Mudrā energetics, explains the movement of the spirit through reality,

or the opening of an envelope (kośa) of consciousness [similar to dissolution of the elements (pralaya mahābhūta)].

Mudrās are like bridges enabling the journey of the spirit to more subtle levels/dimensions of awareness.

Mudrās generate specific energetic signatures on vortices of healing (aura fields),

according to their intended function, which is determined by form (or finger connection formula)."

–Michael Hamilton

There are atleast ten different ways to understand how a *Mudrā* works to balance and harmonize the life current in the body, so as to maintain a healthy state of mind and body.

Let us explore Sacred Science of *Mudrās*.

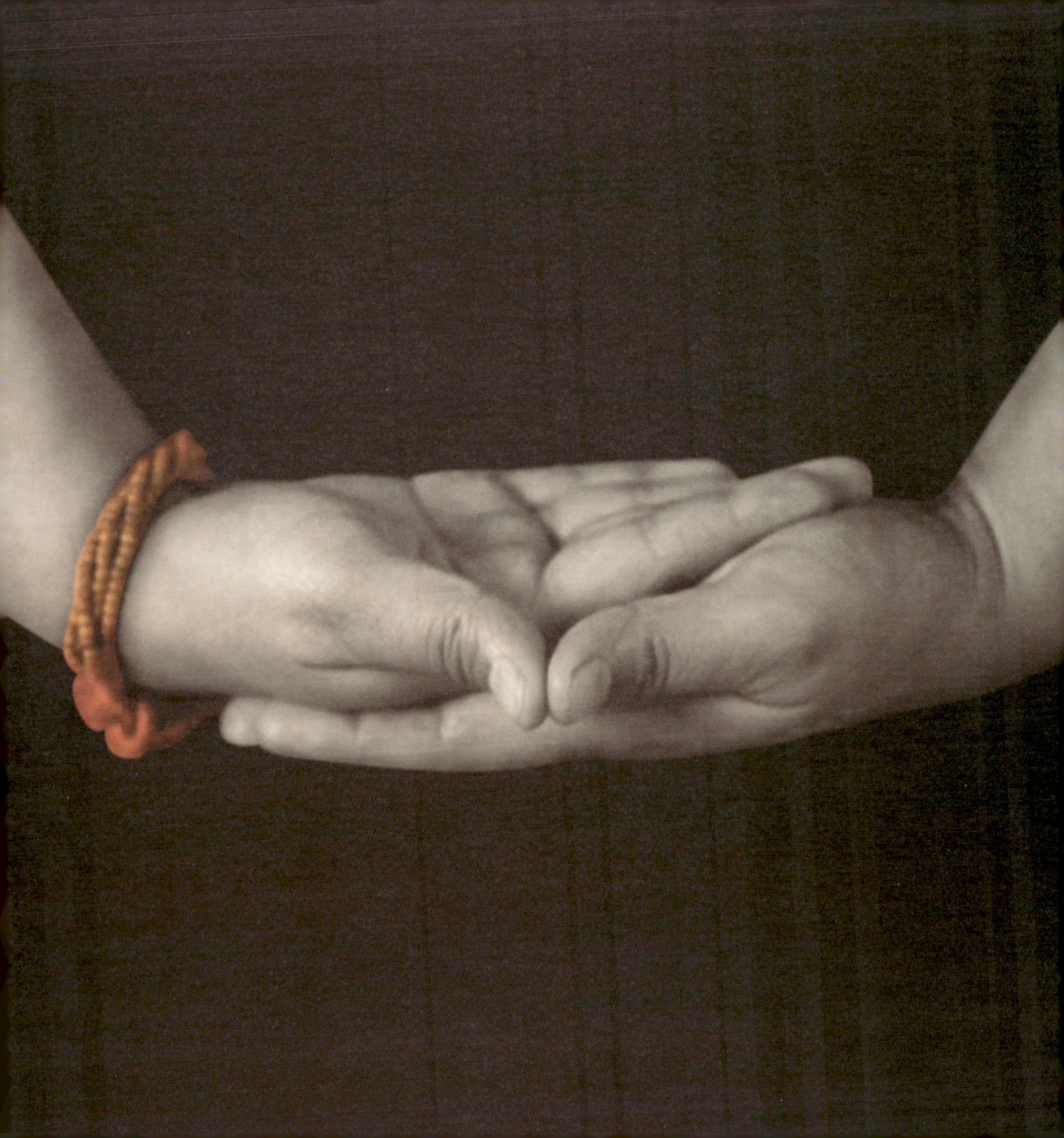

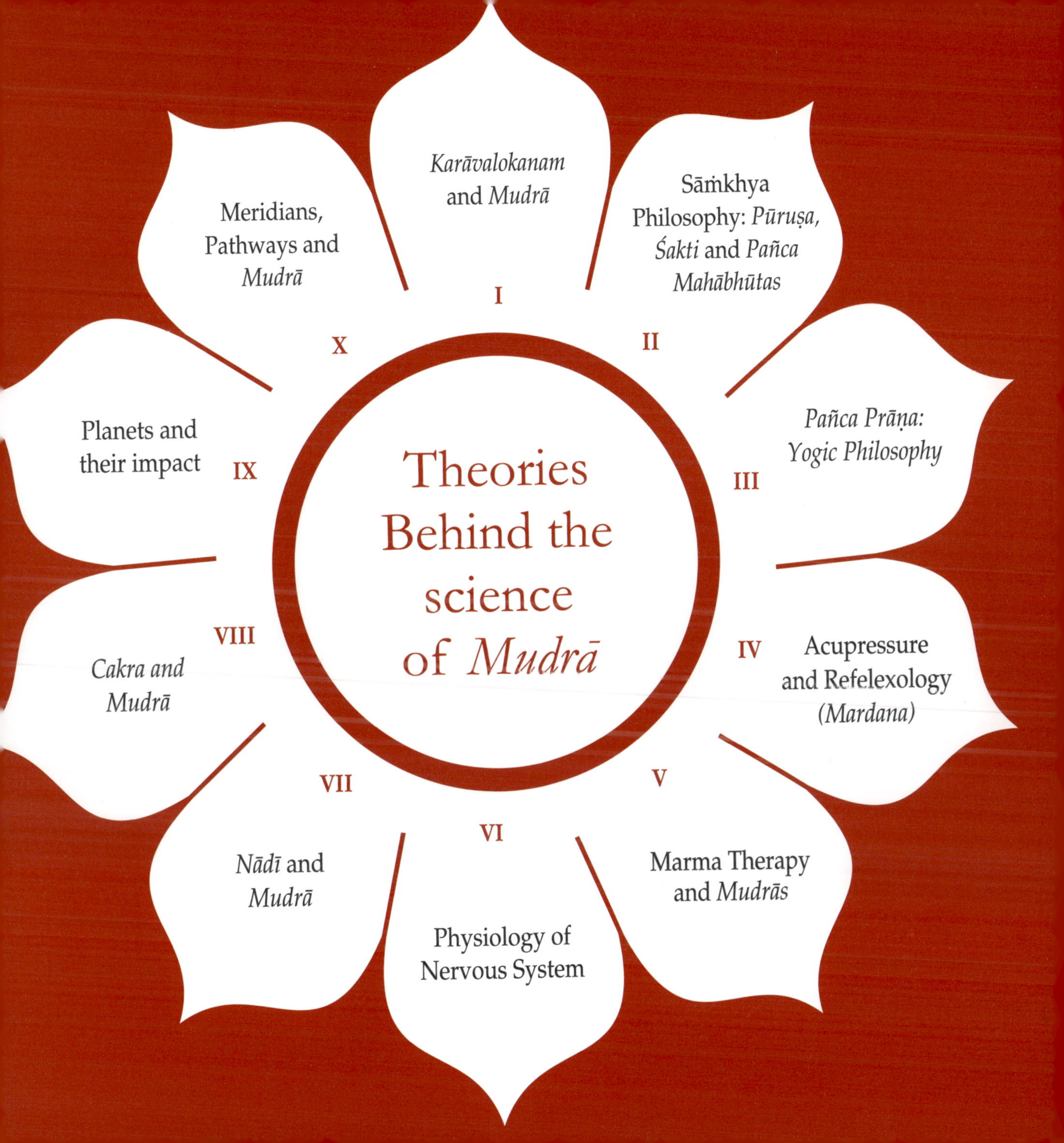
Theories Behind the science of *Mudrā*
I
Karāvalokanam and *Mudrā*
II
Sāṁkhya Philosophy: *Pūruṣa*, *Śakti* and *Pañca Mahābhūtas*
III
Pañca Prāṇa: *Yogic Philosophy*
IV
Acupressure and Refelexology *(Mardana)*
V
Marma Therapy and *Mudrās*
VI
Physiology of Nervous System
VII
Nādī and *Mudrā*
VIII
Cakra and Mudrā
IX
Planets and their impact
X
Meridians, Pathways and *Mudrā*

I. *Karāvalokanam* and *Mudrā*

Karāgre vasate lakṣmiḥ kara-madhye sarasvatī;
kara–mūle tu govindaḥ prabhāte kara-darśanam.

कराग्रे वसते लक्ष्मीः करमध्ये सरस्वती ।
करमूले तु गोविन्दः प्रभाते करदर्शनम् ।।

Meaning:

The front part of the hands (the fingertips: *karāgre*) is ascribed (*vasate*: residence, home) to *Lakṣmī*, the Goddess of Wealth; the middle part (the palm proper, *kara-madhye*) to *Sarasvatī*, the Goddess of Learning; and the root (the part of hand near the wrist, *kara-mūle*) to *Govindaḥ* (God).

Therefore, every morning (*prabhāte*), one should have a respectful look (*darśanam*) at one's hand, to invoke and invite such characteristics in one's persona and life. This is called *karāvalokanam* (worshipping the energy hidden in one's hands).

kara = hand; *agra* = tip; *agre* = at the tip; *vasate* = lives; *Lakṣmī* = Goddess of wealth and consort of *Lord Viṣṇu*; *madhye* = in the middle; *sarasvatī* = Goddess of education and learning; *mūle* = at the base/corner; ; *Govindaḥ* = (go + *vinda*) go = cattle; *vinda* = friend); *prabhāte* = early in the morning; *darśanam* = appearance (seeing).

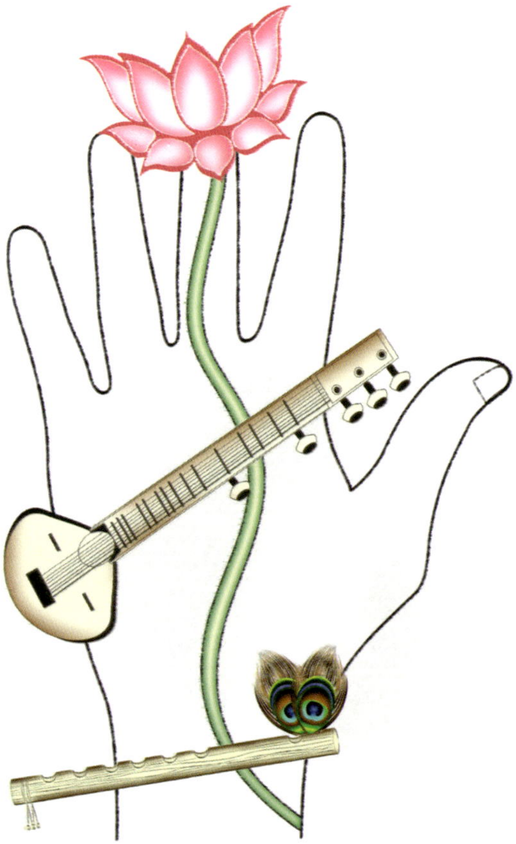

This *Śloka* can be understood in many different ways:

As per the understanding of *Karma:-*

The tip of the fingers is said to be the seat of *Kriyā Śakti*, the power of action. It is our finger and thumb tips which propel us in action so here in this *Śloka* they are compared to Goddess *Lakṣmī*, the goddess of wealth and abundance. She represents *Artha* and *Kāma*. The abundance replies on our *Karma* and by worshipping our fingertips we divinize the connection to our inner source.

The center of the palms is said to be the seat of *Jñāna Śakti*, the power of wisdom. It is the center of the palms which helps us in understading what we hold in our hands, body and minds so here in this *Śloka* it is compared to Goddess *Sarasvatī*, the Goddess of wisdom and guidance. *Sarasvatī*, holds the *Vedas* in the hands, it represents the *Dharma*.

The base of the wrist represents *Icchā Śakti*, the power of willing consciousness or desire.

Helena Petrona Blavatsky in her 'The Secret Doctrine (1888)' introduces the concept of "*Icchā Śakti*" by saying:

"Its most ordinary manifestation is the generation of certain nerve currents which set in motion such muscles as are required for the accomplishment of the desired object."

It is from the wrist that the motivation and desire to act begins followed thus by the fingers with the right use of tissue in the palm. In this *Śloka* this region is compared to Lord *Govindaḥ*: The lord of all desires, motivations and inclinations.

By worshipping these three areas in our hands, with our awareness of what they uphold and represent we divinize and nourish the three *Śaktis*. This is called *Karāvalokanam* (worshipping the energy hidden in one's hands).

II. Sāṁkhya Philosophy: *Puruṣa, Śakti* and *Pañca Mahābhūtas*

In the un-manifested universe (*Brahman*), the attributes (*guṇas*) are stable, *puruṣa* and *prakṛti* are in union. The pulsations of the cosmic life force (*Spanda*) cause the *Guṇas* to destabilize and the first principle of manifestation occurs. *Prakṛti* is the first principle of manifestation. *Prakṛti* contains all the knowledge of the universe. In the light of *puruṣa*, *prakṛti* becomes aware of *puruṣa*, and it is from this awareness that the second principle of manifestation known as *mahad* occurs. *Mahad* is supreme universal intelligence and stores the blueprint for all manifestation. *Mahad* puts all things in their proper place, whether in the cosmos or in the individual. From *mahad*, the third principle of creation known as *ahaṅkāra* manifests. *Ahaṅkāra* is the "I-ness" or feeling of self that is created the moment identification with an object of perception occurs. In the human being, *ahaṅkāra* is defined as the ego. The moment the "I" is formed, *mahad* is reflected in the individual as *buddhi* (wisdom faculty).

Once *puruṣa* and *prakṛti* separate, and *mahad/buddhi* and *ahaṅkāra* are established, the individual mind and body manifest. From the movement of *rajas* upon *sattva*, the *manas* (cognitive function), the *jñānendriya* (sensory faculties), and the *karmendriya* (motor faculties) manifest. The five senses of *jñānendriya* are to hear, feel, see, taste, and smell. The five motor faculties of *karmendriya* are speaking, grasping, moving, procreating, and eliminating.

In order for *manas*, *jñānendriya*, and *karmendriya* to function, they need a body and the five senses. From the movement of *rajas* upon *tamas*, the *tanmātra* (sense qualities) and the *mahābhūtas* (five elements) manifest.

Each element has a *jñānendriya* (organ of knowledge), a *karmendriya* (organ of action), and a *tanmātra* (sense quality) associated with it. The organs of knowledge are what the five senses use to perceive the world, and the organs of action are what the five senses use to act upon what they perceive.

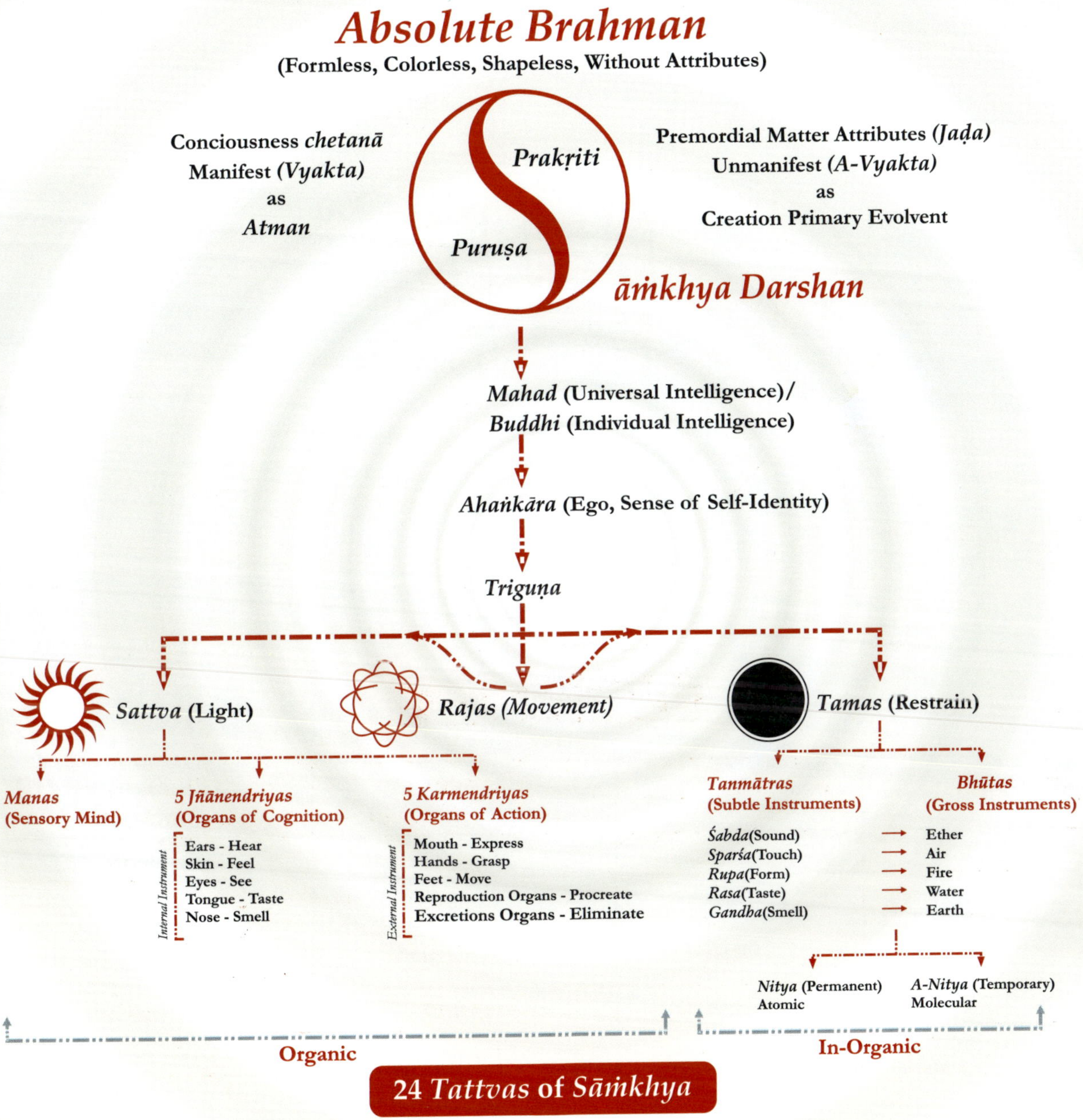
Absolute Brahman
(Formless, Colorless, Shapeless, Without Attributes)
Conciousness chetanā
Manifest (Vyakta)
as
Atman
Prakṛiti
Puruṣa
Premordial Matter Attributes (Jaḍa)
Unmanifest (A-Vyakta)
as
Creation Primary Evolvent
āṁkhya Darshan
Mahad (Universal Intelligence)/
Buddhi (Individual Intelligence)
Ahaṅkāra (Ego, Sense of Self-Identity)
Triguṇa
Sattva (Light)
Rajas (Movement)
Tamas (Restrain)
Manas
(Sensory Mind)
5 Jñānendriyas
(Organs of Cognition)
Internal Instrument
Ears - Hear
Skin - Feel
Eyes - See
Tongue - Taste
Nose - Smell
5 Karmendriyas
(Organs of Action)
External Instrument
Mouth - Express
Hands - Grasp
Feet - Move
Reproduction Organs - Procreate
Excretions Organs - Eliminate
Tanmātras
(Subtle Instruments)
Śabda(Sound)
Sparśa(Touch)
Rupa(Form)
Rasa(Taste)
Gandha(Smell)
Bhūtas
(Gross Instruments)
Ether
Air
Fire
Water
Earth
Nitya (Permanent)
Atomic
A-Nitya (Temporary)
Molecular
Organic
In-Organic
24 Tattvas of Sāṁkhya

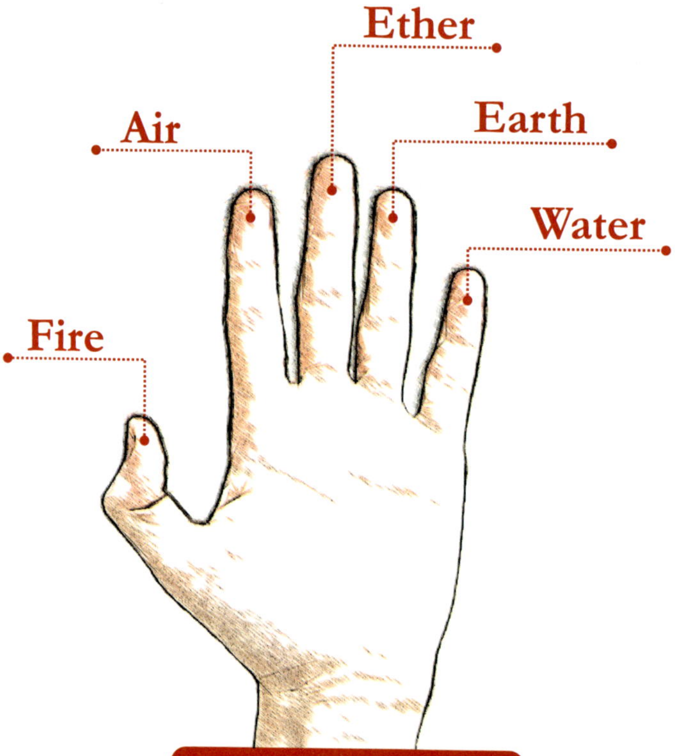

Fingers and *Tattvas*

Finger	Param *Tattava*	Finger (*sanskrit name*)	Element (*bhūtas*)
Thumb	*puruṣa*	*aṅguṣṭha*	fire (*agni*)
Index	*prakṛti*	*tarjanī*	air (*vāyu*)
Middle	*prakṛti*	*madhyama*	ether/space/ sky (*ākāśā*)
Ring	*prakṛti*	*anāmikā*	earth (*pṛthivī*)
Little	*prakṛti*	*kaniṣṭhikā*	water (*jala*)

Fingers, Tattvas & Bhūtas

24 Tattvas of Saṁkhya (23+1)

Primary Evolvent (1) - *Prakṛti*

Evolvents (23) -

Mahad (1), *Ahaṅkāra* (1), *Manas* (1), *Jñānendriya* (5), *Karmendriya* (5), *Tanmātra* (5), *Bhūtas* (5)

The *jñānendriya* are the ears, skin, eyes, tongue, and nose, and these perceive the world through the senses of hearing, feeling, seeing, tasting, and smelling, respectively. The *karmendriya* are the vocal cords, hands, feet, genitals, and anus, and these act upon the world through speaking, grasping, walking, procreating, and eliminating, respectively. The *Mahābhūtas* (five elements): either, air, fire, water, and earth have the *tanmātra* of sound, touch, form, taste and odor, respectively.

Thus, human body is made of five elements represented by four fingers and thumb. The ratio, proportion, and harmony of these elements in the cells determine the physical, mental, and emotional health of a person. These four fingers and thumb are the trigger areas of these five elements, each governed by a particular element.

Any activity in these *Tattvas* (elements) is possible by the union of *puruṣa* and *prakṛti (Śakti)*. The thumb represents *puruṣa* and the four fingers are symbolic of *Śakti*. For the energy to flow, the union of *puruṣa* and *prakṛti(Śakti)* is very important.

The effects of pressure on different areas of the thumb and fingers as per *Yoga Tattva Mudrā Vijñāna* are summarized thus:

- By pressing or squeezing the sides of the fingers, according to the needs, one can affect both the emotion and the corresponding organ.
- By touching the thumb tip to the tip of a finger, we can balance the element.
- By touching the thumb at the base of the finger, we can cleanse/increase the element.
- By curling the finger in the center of the palm and pressing it on the top with the thumb, we can decrease the element.
- By curling the finger at the base of the thumb, we can neutralize the element.

III. *Pañca Prāṇa* - Yogic Philosophy

Prāṇa is the primal life force, the subtle energy behind all mind-body functions, and the catalyst for all matter to manifest. It is responsible for coordination of breath, senses, and mind. *Prāṇa* is the vital energy taken in through liquids and breathing, and is carried through the liquids in our bodies (blood and plasma) as well as absorbed through the senses of hearing and touch. *Prāṇa* in the mind allows it to move and respond to the challenges of life. *Prāṇa* is also responsible for enthusiasm and expression in the psyche. *Prāṇa*, at the deepest levels of consciousness, governs the development of higher states of consciousness. This *prāṇic* force resides in the *prāṇic* body *(Prāṇamaya Kośa)* as five vital air currents: *Prāṇa, Apāna, Samāna, Vyāna, and Udāna,* each carrying its own function, in its own seat where it operates. A disturbance in their flow (more, less, or blocked) affects the corresponding organs, organ systems, and functions of the physical body. A specific thumb-finger(s) combination helps to reduce, increase, or release the blockage of a particular air current.

An imbalance or malfunction of these vital currents may cause a hindrance, inefficacy, and a lack of harmony in the organs and organ systems in the region of these currents, thus affecting the health at the level of *Annamaya Kośa* and *Prāṇamaya kośa* (the first two layers as per the *Taittirīya Upaniṣad* veiling the true self). Specific *Hasta Mudrās* help in restoring the balance, distribution, and communication of these five vital airs.

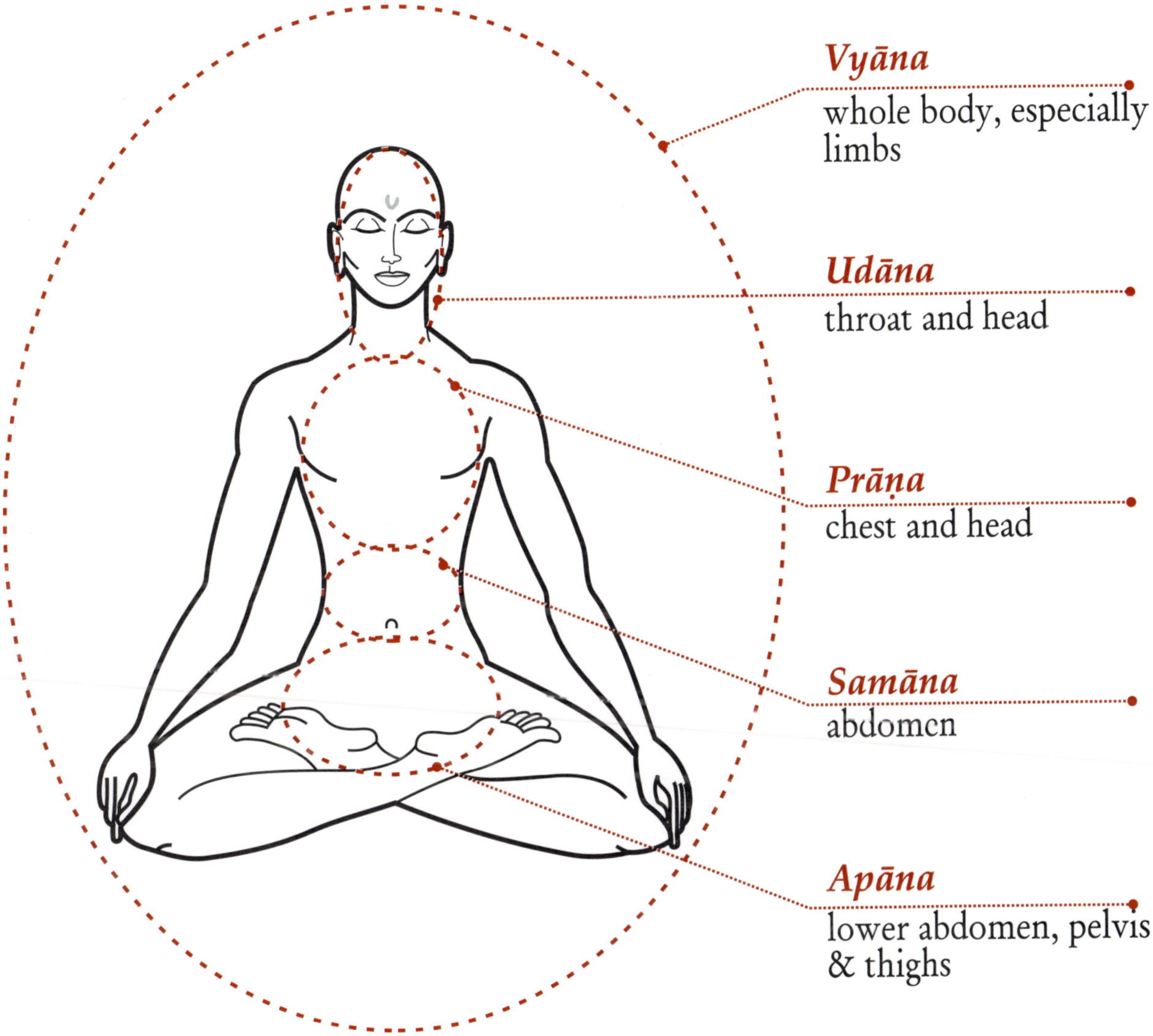

Pañca Prāṇas

Prāṇa	Location and function
Apāna	*Apāna* is located in the genitals, anus, and lower extremities. It is responsible for the downward and outward movement of matter through defecation, urination, menstruation, ejaculation, release of reproductive fluid, birthing and exhalation. It relates to the earth element.
Vyāna	*Vyāna* is located all over the body. It is the vital current that is the cause of movement, enables circulation, and relates to the water element.
Samāna	*Samāna* is located in the navel. This centripital energy regulates digestion and metabolism. It relates to the fire element.
Prāṇa	*Prāṇa* is located in the chest and lungs. It is the inward and forward movement of energy. It is responsible for the absorption of the vital life force from inhalation. It relates to the air element.
Udāna	*Udāna* is located in the throat region. It is the energy of expression and creativity; it draws energy upward for the higher functions of cognition and perception. It relates to the ether element.

***Pañca Prāṇas* Location and Function**

IV. Acupressure and Refelexology *(Mardana)*

Acupressure, known as *mardana*, is an ancient healing art using the fingers to gradually press key healing points, which stimulate the body's natural self-curative abilities. Acupressure developed in Asia over 5,000 years ago. Using the power and sensitivity of the hand, acupressure therapy is effective in the relief of stress-related ailments, and is ideal for self-treatment and preventive healthcare for boosting the immune system.

Mudrās are self-acupressure. When we hold the hands in a particular *Mudrā* by exerting a minimal pressure for a certain amount of time, we activate nerve endings in the palms related to different organs and organ systems. This self-acupressure exerted by the practice of *Mudrā* is rooted in the innate wisdom of the body. Each person has palms and fingers of unique size, shape, and strength. This unique formation puts a specific end nerve tension required by our body. This nerve tension at the end of the fingertips is the just the right amount of pressure/tension required by the body, which helps in clearing up the energy blockages in the particular area.

Mudrā practice, or this form of self-acupressure, releases tension, increases circulation, reduces pain, releases endorphins (natural painkiller), and ensures vibrant health. The advantage in *Mudrā* is that the pressure to be applied on the nerves is automatic and controlled by the shape and size of the fingers and not by external agencies. The diagram given here helps to understand how different reflexology regions affect different organs and organ systems.

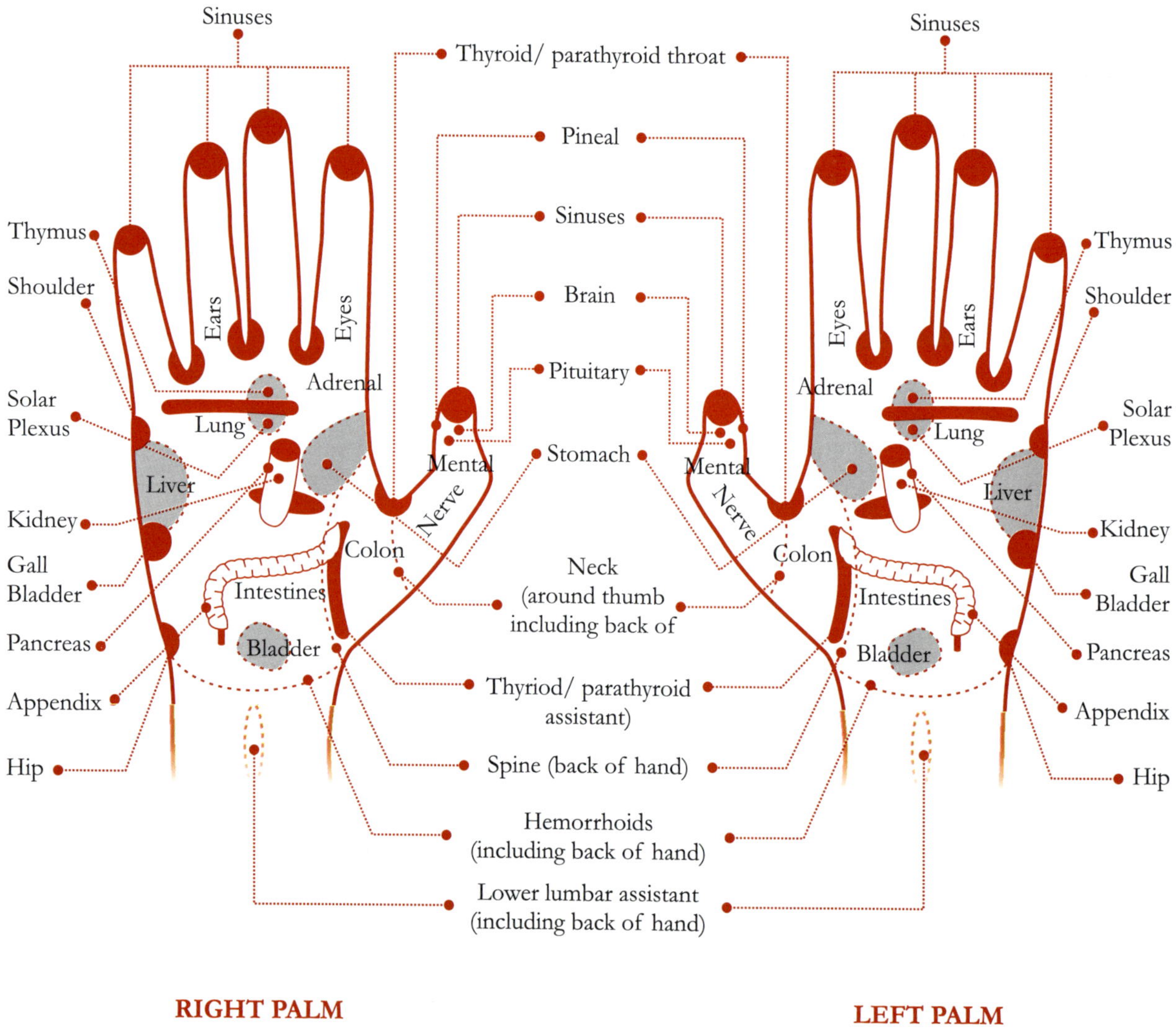

Acupressure Points In Hands

Eating food with hands is rooted in the practice of *Mudrā* and refelexology in India.

Eating food with hands is a part of tradition, culture, ritual and health based on the concept of *Pañca Karma Indriya* (five organs of action) and *Pañca Jñāna Indirya* (five organs of senses)

Indian *Thāli*

Traditionally, the six tastes (sweet, salty, pungent, astringent, sour and bitter) and varied food items are served all together on one platter (called *Thāli*) which immediately pacifies the sense of vision, smell, taste and touch.

Silence is observed, in order for the sense of hearing to be as less stimulated as possible and take the stimulus from the sub vocalization of the sound of chewing. All of this helps in the activation of salivary glands and salivary amylase (enzyme responsible for aiding in the catabolic action on

Traditional posture of Eating Food in *Sukhāsana*

Skin (use of hands)	touch the food and feel all consistencies bread, rice, soup, salad etc, feel the temprature
Eyes	see all colorful food items
Nose	smell the food
Tongue	taste the food
Ears	hear the sound of chewing/ eating/ gulping

Co-Relation of Five Senses & Eating Food with Hand

the food). All the five sensory organs when engaged in the activity of eating food in the above said traditional method, have minimal outgoing tendencies and the senses go into the anabolic or energy conservation mode so that this energy is utilized for digestion.

Now let us talk about the five organs of action - hands, feet, organs of reproduction, organs of elimination and vocal cords. These five organs of action have the tendency to respond according to the information collected by the five sensory organs and are generally catabolic in nature.

In order for the body to keep in the optimum state of metabolism, the outgoing tendencies of these organs should be minimized, which is done by crossing the legs (minimalizing the locomotion). Crossing the legs also redirects the *prāṇic* energy away from the organs of reproduction and elimination, which do not have a role yet to play during the intake of food. The hands are engaged in eating food and vocal cords are relaxed by observing silence.

- As we sit cross-legged, the spine attains its natural curve, which allows the abdominal organs to relax and receive maximum blood supply.

- When we use hands to eat food, we tend to bring the fingers and thumb close to each other, which forms *Samāna Mudrā* (refer to the picture). It is a therapeutic hand gesture, which activates the *Samāna Mudrā*. If we see the diagram, we see that the reflexology region of all the abdominal organs is in the center of the palms. When we form this *Mudrā* we are naturally putting an acute but controlled pressure to these organs – which is required to keep the digestive system strong, healthy, and active, thus controlling/balancing the metabolic rate.

Samāna Mudrā

The food intake is not merely a way to satisfy the hunger, but to sublimate the senses and infuse satisfaction. It is a way to nourish the inner Self and not merely a physiological activity.

- The use of hands allows one to feel the texture and temperature of the food, which further stimulates the salivary glands using the sense of touch, smell and sight. It also prevents one from eating very hot or very cold food as these extreme temperatures are not pleasing to the human body and neither is good for the digestive fire.

- The center of the palm is the seat of digestive organs as per acupressure. When we use hands for eating food, we naturally trigger these pressure points, which help in the release of digestive juices from the liver and gall bladder.

- The center of the palm is also one of the most therapeutic *Marma* points that activate the release of *prāṇic* energy in the entire body, which is triggered in the use of hands.

- The use of cutlery blocks the senses to directly communicate with the body, mind and breath.

- The general habit of using dining table for having meals may lead to overeating, as when we sit cross-legged on the floor to eat food, every time we bend forward to break a morsel it puts pressure on the stomach and once the stomach is $3/4^{th}$ full it leads to burping. Burping while eating is a natural sign of the stomach being happily full and anything more would be over eating. While sitting completely straight we suppress this natural urge/ sign from the body's innate intelligence. As per *Ayurvedic* principles, the stomach should be only $3/4^{th}$ filled with food and the rest $1/4^{th}$ space should be allowed for the free movement of gases and for the process of digestion.

The practice of *Mudrā* not only controls and maintains the health of an organ but also works deep on the *manomaya kośa* (the sheath of emotions) to release and heal the deep-seated emotions from the layers of the subconscious. During the practice of *Mudrā* for a specific time, the coordination and use of breath peels layers within layers of our being to allow such a release to happen.

Thumb	The thumb represents the stomach and worry. The thumb is the symbol of divine energy – energy that flows through our vehicle unconditioned by our subconscious patterning or karmic complexities. The thumb is the symbol of will power, that can be drawn upon by our willing (not willful) consciousness. At an emotional level it represents emotional pain, tears and worry.
Index Finger	The index finger represents the lungs, the large intestine, and the emotions of depression, sadness, terror and grief.
Middle Finger	The middle finger represents the heart, the small intestine, and the circulatory and emotion of rage and resentment. and respiratory systems; the emotions associated are impatience and hastiness.
Ring Finger	The ring finger relates to the liver, the gall bladder, the nervous system, and corresponds to anxiety, pre occupation.
Little Finger	The little finger corresponds to the kidneys and lack of self esteem.

Relationship between the organs, fingers and emotions

As an exercise to experience this connection, gently hold each finger with the opposite hand for two to five minutes until they feel a steady, rhythmic pulse. This will help move and drain blocked energy, and bring back a sense of balance and harmony to the body mind relationship. As you hold the finger, breathe in deeply; recognize and acknowledge the strong or disturbing feelings or emotion that may rise and fade. Breathe out slowly and let go. Imagine the feelings draining out your finger into the earth. Breathe in a sense of harmony, strength and healing. And breathe out slowly, releasing past feelings and problems.

Pratyakṣe kiṁ pramāṇam: What proof does a direct experience require?

Taste me in silence

For in silence I am closest to you

Do what thy will is

And I shall enjoy

There is a charm

When u can see but not taste

Taste but not see

We are one forever in spirit

What can the five senses do to separate us

For I am beyond taste fragrance touch sound and sight

I am in you, with you beyond all…

V. *Marma* Therapy and *Mudrās*

The word *marma* comes from the *sanskrit* "*mṛ*" and means "hidden, secret, and vulnerable." The *Sanskrit* phrase *mārayanti iti marmāṇi* means "there is likelihood of death or serious damage to health after infliction at the places in the body that are *marma* regions."

The word *marma* is used at least seven times in the *Ṛg Veda*, which is the most ancient and the most holy text of India. There is also a mention of this word in *Yajur Veda*.

By definition, a *marma* point is a juncture on the body where two or more types of tissue meet, such as muscles, veins, ligaments, bones, or joints. *Marma* points are the sensitive energy points in the body, which are the openings to the subtle body (*cakras* and *nāḍīs*). These are the meeting points of energy of the five elements, *tri-guṇas* (*sattva, rajas, and tamas*), *prāṇa, tejas, and ojas*, and the meeting points of masculine and feminine energy in the body. There are 108 classical *marma* points all over the body.

As sensitive zones, *marmas* can hold various emotions like fear *(vāta)*, anger *(pitta)*, or attachment *(kapha)*, as well as the *guṇas* or primary qualities of *sattva* (calm), *rajas* (aggression), and *tamas* (inertia).

The *Mudrā* is used as self-*marma* therapy. To use them as *marma* therapy, the only prerequisite shall be to relax and then focus the *prāṇic* awareness on the *marma* points in the hands while practicing a *Mudrā*. These *marma* points are the key in all forms of hand *Mudrā*: general (*vyāvahārika*), therapeutic (*cikitsaka*), and spiritual (*ādhyātmika*).

Marmas serve as "*prāṇic* control points" or "*prāṇic* switches" to the level that these points are compared to mini brains in various parts of the body, controlling and governing the functions of the body at all the five levels - physical body *(annamaya Kośa)*, energy body *(prāṇamaya kośa)*, emotional body *(manomaya kośa)*, intellectual body *(vijñānamaya kośa)*, and bliss body *(ānandamaya kośa)*.

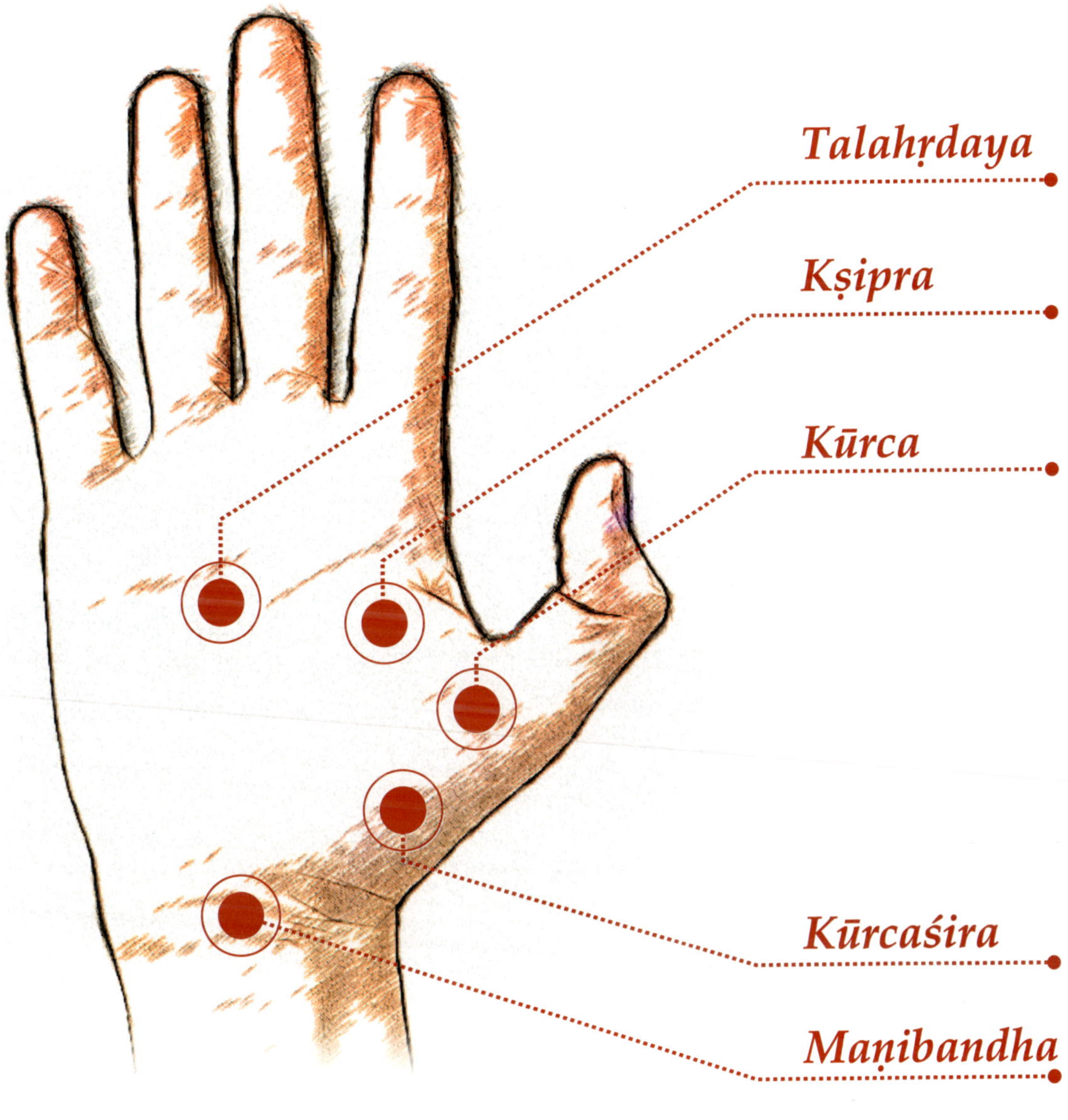

Five Main Marma Points

Tālahṛdya Marma

Meaning: *Tāla* means "flat surface" and *hṛdaya* means "heart" – the center of a surface, which in this case is the palm.

Number: 2 (one in each hand)

Location: Center of the palm under the middle finger

Size: ½ *aṅgulī* (finger unit)

Type: Junction of muscle: muscle-based *marma*

Benefits: It is one of the most therapeutic and healing *marmas* in the entire body. It is an important *marma*, controlling the circulation of blood and *prāṇa* (energy). It regulates the respiratory system, the heart, and the lungs, and maintains the thermostat of the body by temperature regulation through skin and lubrication in the heart and the lungs. It also controls the hands as a motor organ; any injury to this *marma* can affect the 2nd, 3rd, and 4th fingers. Its main region is the circulation around the navel.

This marma transmits energy from the healer to the client in massage therapy, reiki, and prāṇic healing, and in the case of blessings given by a Guru to a disciple, through Abhaya Mudrā, Vitarka Mudrā, and Jñāna Mudrā. All the hand Mudrās benefit due to the trigger of this marma, including Namaskāra Mudrā, Saṇkalpa Mudrā, the five element Mudrās, the five vital air Mudrās, and all seven cakra hand Mudrās.

Kṣipra Marma

Meaning: *Kṣipra* means "quick, fast, and instantaneous (in effect)."

Number: 2 (one in each hand)

Location: Between the thumb and the index finger (the web region); minor/secondary *Kṣipra* regions are in-between fingers as finger-web regions and toes as toe-web regions.

Size: ½ *aṅgulī* (finger unit)

Type: Ligament (*snāyu*)

Benefits: This *marma* region controls the two main vital airs: *prāṇa* and *vyāna vāyus*. *Prāṇa* is the main energy current in the entire body and *vyāna* is responsible for bringing about the distribution of the filtered energy in the peripheral body through the movement of arms and legs. It also regulates the respiratory system and plasma circulation.

This marma point helps in conditions of restricted movement in limbs, like gout, arthritis, and Parkinson's disease, as well as in conditions like asthma, bronchitis, and arrhythmia, with Mudrā like Liṅga Mudrā, Apāna Vāyu Mudrā, Vāyu Mudrā, Kāleśvara Mudrā, and Garuḍa Mudrā.

Kūrca Marma

Meaning: *Kūrca* means "knot/bundle."

Number: 2 (one in each hand)

Location: The entire mount region of the thumb, but the core region is the bundled/elevated, rounded root joint region of the thumb

Size: 4 *aṅgulīs* (finger unit)

Type: Ligament (*snāyu*)

Benefits: This *marma* point is responsible for the sensory acuity, especially the vision. This point also controls the *prāṇic* energy in the head region.

Certain Mudrās like Mahāśīrṣa Mudrā, Garuḍa Mudrā, Prāṇa Mudrā, Vyāna Mudrā, Liṅga Mudrā, Śaṅkha Mudrā, and Uttarabodhi Mudrā are especially helpful in triggering this marma.

Kūrcaśira Marma

Meaning: *Kūrca* means "knot/bundle" and *Śira* means "head/head of the knot."

Number: 2 (one in each hand)

Location: At the root of the thumb just above the wrist, the head of the bundle of ligament

Size: 1 *aṅgulī* (finger unit)

Type: Ligament (*snāyu*)

Benefits: This *marma* point controls mainly the digestion, all kinds of fire required for metabolism, vision, luster and glow, color of skin, perception, and cognition. It also helps in the filtration of the energy as *samāna vāyu* through the interaction of *prāṇa* and *apāna Vāyus* in the abdominal region. Further, it helps in calming down the ailments pertaining to any imbalance of the energy of air and ether elements.

The main Mudrās that help in the triggering of this marma are Namaskāra Mudrā, all the Sparśa Mudrās(the 10 Mudrās of touch), Padma / Paṅkaja Mudrā, Saṅkalpa Mudrā, Śaṅkha Mudrā, Samāna Vāyu Mudrā, and Añjali Mudrā, to name a few.

Maṇibandha Marma

Meaning: *Maṇi* means "jewel," *Bandha* means "lock" or "clasp" and *Maṇibandha* means a "bracelet" or "wrist jewelry."

Number: 2 (one in each hand)

Location: Between the four bones in the wrist, at their junction points. The core point is lateral to the center of the wrist joint (both front and back). *Maṇibandha Marma* lies in the inter-carpal ligaments and nerves.

Size: 2 *aṅgulīs* (finger units)

Type: Joint (*sandhi*)

Benefits: *Maṇibandha* regulates *apāna vāyu*, is related to the reproductive organs, rectum, prostate, and cervix, and is useful in the treatment of sexual dysfunction, hemorrhoids, as well as emotional disturbances. Most of the therapeutic hand *Mudrā* put pressure in this region of the palm, naturally helping in boosting the body's immunity, easing the breath and pain. It is a *marma* point that works on the skeletal system, lubrication in the joints, and the reproductive system.

The main Mudrās triggering this marma point are Yoni Mudrā, Mātaṅgī Mudrā, Śakti Mudrā, Surabhī Mudrā, Liṅga Mudrā, and Bhairava / Bhairavī Mudrā.

VI. Physiology of Nervous System

The fingertips of every living being have many concentrated nerve root endings that are free energy discharge points. Science also confirms that around every tip there is a concentration of free electrons. By touching together the tips of the fingers or the fingertips to other parts of the palm, this free energy (*prāṇa*) is redirected back into the body along specified channels, back up to the brain. The redirected energy traveling through the nerves stimulates the various organs and organ systems. Keeping the hands on the knees stimulates the *Gupta Nāḍī* (secret nerve channel in subtle body) and makes the energy rise from the *Mūlādhāra Cakra*.

Thus, the tension applied to the nerve(s) and/or the neural or psycho-neural circuits formed by the *Mudrā* for specified periods tones up the nervous system.

Such a lock, clasp, or seal created by *Mudrā* helps in intensifying the electromagnetic field around the body by building the inner circuit. This inner circuit created by the redirection of the free electrons inwards, reduces the oxidation and neutralizes the free radicals in the body, keeping the body healthy and afresh.

Thus, all the *Hasta Mudrās* are energy conservation systems. Fingertips have a negative charge and thumbs have a positive charge, and hence, joining the fingertip with the thumb tip is the union of positive (+) with negative (-). Positive charge symbolizes masculine energy and negative charge symbolizes feminine energy. Once again, here is a union of opposites.

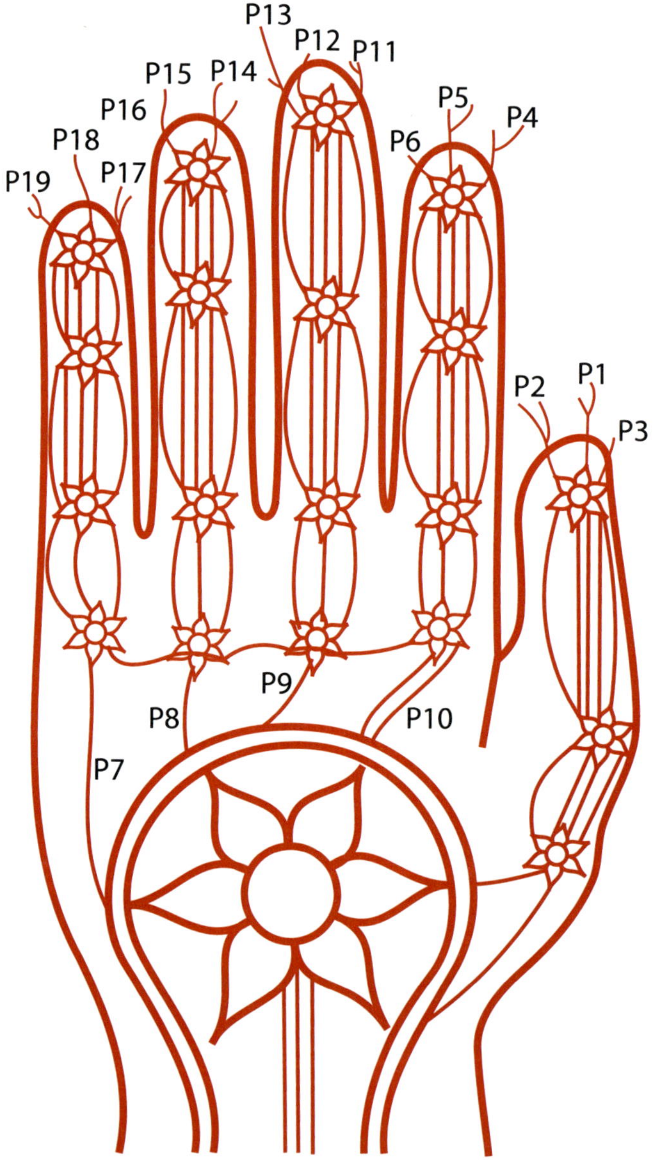

Minor *Nāḍīs* In The Palms

VII. *Nādī* and *Mudrā*

Nāḍī is a *Sanskrit* word, which finds its root in the word "*nāda*", which means "sound". It is a tubular organ through which the *prāṇa* flows. The origin point of the *Nāḍī* is called the "*kanda*," located just above the *Mūlādhāra* (root) *Cakra*. This place is the origin point of 72,000 to 3, 50,000 *Nāḍīs*. All the vibrations in the universe are simultaneously echoed in the subtle system of the ethric body, which in turn affects the physical body. This in turn afftects the *Prāṇa* flowing through the *Nāḍīs*.

The major and minor *Nāḍīs* in the palms play an important role in the stage of *Sādhanā* to purify the subtle body and connects us to deeper ethric currents. Here is a list of major and minor *Nāḍīs* of palms so that you can connect it with the study of *Mudrās*

- P1: *Madhyama Śūnya Nāḍī*: The work of this channel is similar to *Suṣumṇā* channel. It is physically very active. Its etheric energy can be activated using *Mudrās* which gives pressure to the middle tip of the thumb.

- P2: *Agni Śūnya Nāḍī*: This channel is similar to *Piṅgalā Nāḍī*. The basic nature of this channel is to heat. Thus, when there is leakage of heat in the body this channel is the one to be sealed.

- P3: *Chandra Śūnya Nāḍī*: This channel is similar to *Iḍā Nāḍī*. It works like a thermostat maintaining the optimum heat in the body. It also works as a coolant by relasing sweat from the palms.

- P4 (*Dhyāna Nāḍī*), P11 (*Mukta Nāḍī*), P14 (*Vimukta Nāḍī*), P17 (*Śīlā Nāḍī*): The concept of *dhyāna* (meditation) requires various *Mudrās* and each one of them acts in a unique way to affect the physical body. *Dhyāna Nāḍī* gets activated with *Dhyāna Mudrā*, *Mukta Nāḍī* with *Hṛdaya Mudrā*, *Vimukta Nāḍī* with *Apāna Mudrā*, *Śīlā Nāḍī* with *Yoni Mudrā*.

- P5 *(Omkār Nāḍī)*, P12 (*Shalina Nāḍī*), P15 (*Shipra Nāḍī*), P18 (*Swaha Nāḍī*): These *Nāḍīs* work during the initial phase of concentration and pass on the sensory stimulus to various other channels in the vicinity.

- P6 (*Sheena Nāḍī*), P13 (*Mādhavī Nāḍī*): These channels work on conjunction with P5, P12, P15 and P18.

- P16 (*Urvaka Nāḍī*), P19 (*Pavana Nāḍī*): These two channels allow the inflow of energy (***prāṇa***) into the body and seal it as in case of ***Prāṇa** Mudrā* and *Samāna Mudrā*.

- P7 (*Vaidehi Nāḍī*), P8 (*Viplaksha Nāḍī*), P9 (*Vimohi Nāḍī*), P10 (*Vacha Nāḍī*): These channels work as correlation channels between the minor *Cakra* and *Nāḍīs* P4, P11, P14, P17, P5, P12, P15, P18, P6, P13, P16 and P19. Movement of the four fingers is controlled by the *Vaidehi* (index), *Viplaksha* (middle), *Vimohi* (ring) and *Vacha* (little finger) *Nāḍīs* respectively.

Based on the therapy and principle of the *Pañca Tattvas* in hands, each finger is a control center for the five main energy centers or vortices.

Thus, the practice of the *Mudrā* controls not only the elements but also the energy distribution in each energy center. There are specific *Mudrās* to control the energy flow in each *cakra*, as mentioned in the *Ādhyātmika* (spiritual) *Mudrā* section of this book.

VIII. *Cakra* and *Mudrā*

Every *Cakra* is nothing but a vibration, in order to connect to this vibration there are many pathways and practices. One of the unique practices to connect to the main energy plexuses is *Mudrā*. *Mudrā* is the vibration and wave of bliss. Every *Mudrā* has an innate impact in our inherent vibratory field and the practice of it slowly aligns the mental vibratory field to its innate vibration and energy.

In this section of the book, an attempt is being made of connecting *Mudrā* with *Cakras*. Refer to the table ahead to understand the connection between elements, fingers, *Cakras* and *Mudrā*. In this practice the contemplation on a particular *Cakra* is practiced along with the practice of its corresponding *Mudrā*. The *Mudrā* is held for as long as one feels connected and can stay focused on that particular energy field. The basic foundation of this understanding is that each finger connects to a particular endocrine-exocrine gland through reflexology as well as each finger represents the energy of an element. In order to connect, reflect, radiate and absorb the energy of a particular *Cakra* the corresponding *Mudrā* is practiced to invoke the element and through acupressure (*Mudrā*) specific nerve endings related to the gland.

The practice can be focused on a particular *Cakra* or may be practiced as a journey from *Mūlādhāra Cakra* to *Sahasrāra Cakra* by staying for atleast few minutes at a particular *Cakra* field.

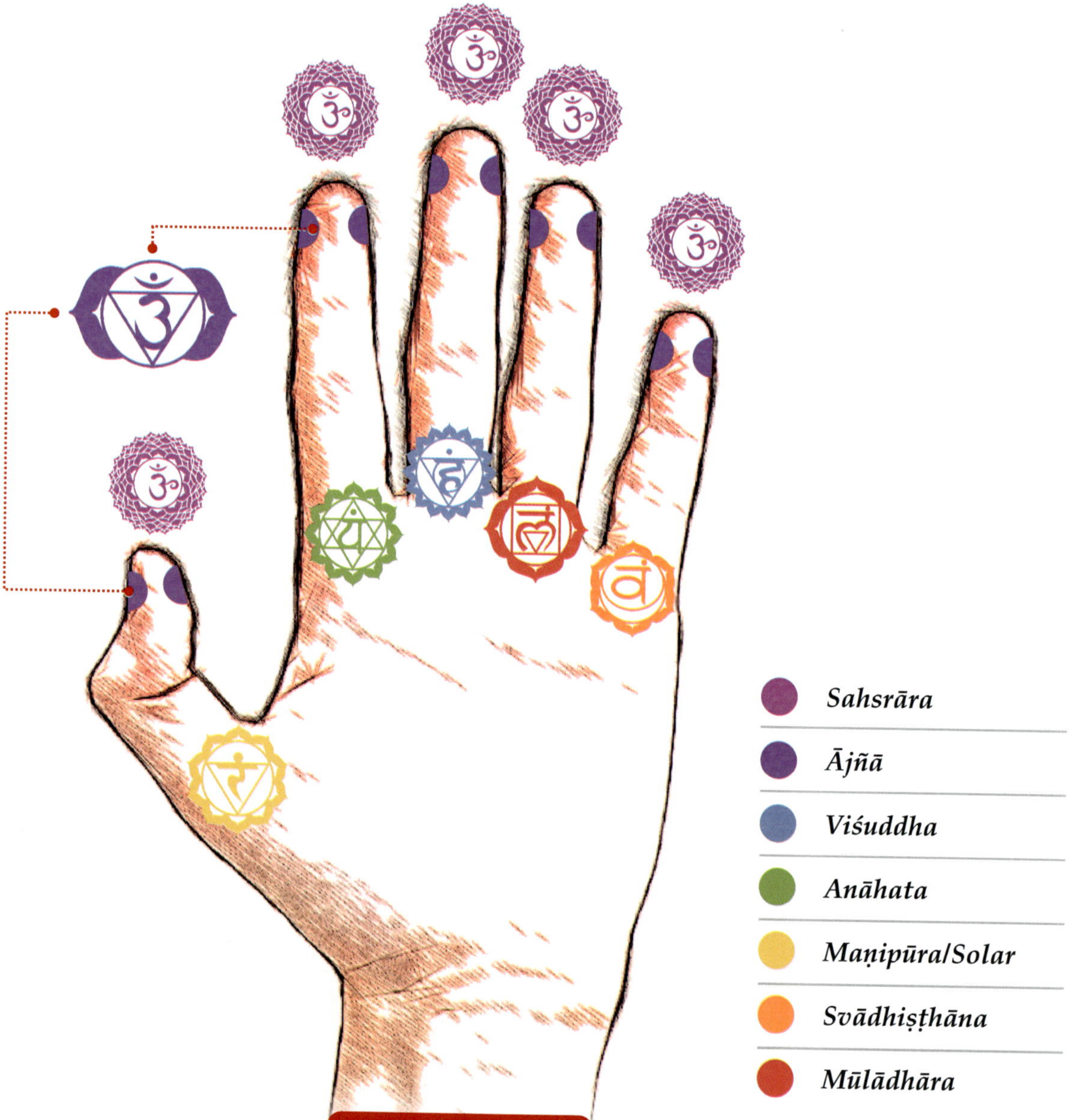

Cakra In Hands

Cakra/Plexus	Location	Fingers	Seed Syllable/ Mantra	*Prāṇa*/ Air	*Kośa*/Sheath	Organ of Action	Organ or Sense	Element/ Color
Mūlādhāra/ Coccygeal Plexus	Base of the Spine	Ring Finger	*Laṁ*	*Apāna Vāyu*	*Annamaya*/ Food Sheath	Elimination	Smell	Earth/Red
Svādhiṣṭhāna/ Sacral Plexus	Below Navel	Little Finger	*Vaṁ*	*Vyāna Vāyu*	*Annamaya*/ Food Sheath	Procreation	Taste	Water/ Orange
Maṇipūra/ Solar Plexus	Above Navel	Thumb	*Raṁ*	*Samāna Vāyu*	*Prāṇamaya*/ Emotional Sheath	Movement	Seeing	Fire/ Yellow
Anāhata/ Cardiac Plexus	Heart	Index Finger	*Yaṁ*	*Prāṇa Vāyu*	*Manomaya*/ Mind Sheath	*Grasping*/ Holding	Feeling	Air/Green
Viśuddha/ Pharyngeal Plexus	Throat	Middle Finger	*Haṁ*	*Udāna Vāyu*	*Vijñānamaya*/ Intellectual Sheath	Speaking	Hearing Speech	Ether (*Ākāśa*)/ Blue
Ājñā/ Cavernous Plexus	Third Eye	Side of all fingers	Om		*Vijñānamaya*/ Intellectual Sheath	Mind	Mind	Indigo
Sahsrāra/ Cavernous Plexus	Crown	Tip of all Fingers	Silence		*Ānandamaya*/ Bliss Sheath	Consciousness	Consciousness	Violet

Comprehensive Study of *Cakras*

IX. Planets and Their Impact

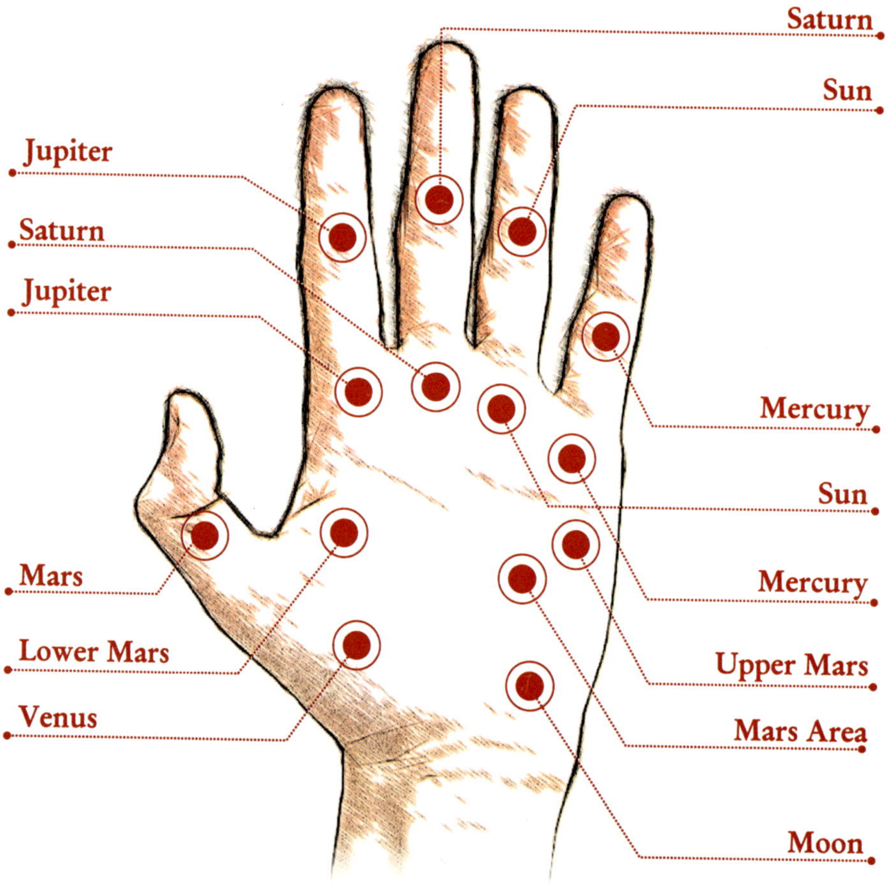

Location of Planets as per Astrology

As per the science of palmistry, the lines in your hands depict your past, present, and future. Each region of the palm along with the four fingers and thumb represent a planet, and each planet governs a certain aspect of your health (to the point that each planet governs a particular organ and organ system) and your personal, professional, emotional, and financial states.

Finger	*Mudrā* and Planet
Thumb	***Liṅga Mudrā*** The thumb is the Mars. The thumb is the symbol of divine energy, energy that flows unconditioned by our subconscious patterning or karmic complexities. The thumb is the symbol of willpower.
Index Finger	***Jñāna Mudrā, Pūrṇa Jñāna Mudrā*** The index finger is the Jupiter finger and is the symbol of our ego and personality; it symbolizes energies controlled by subconscious mind patterning. Its energies produce expansion.
Middle Finger	***Śūnya Mudrā, Ākāśa Mudrā, Kāleśvara Mudrā*** The middle finger symbolizes the Saturn force and is the most karmic or the most conditioned of energies.
Ring Finger	***Sūrya/ Agni Mudrā, Śakti Jāgaraṇa Mudrā*** The ring finger symbolizes the Sun energies. These energies relate to the strength of an individual.
Little Finger	***Jala Mudrā, Girivara Mudrā, Jala Surabhī Mudrā*** The little finger is the Mercury finger. It emanates energies that are important in the unfolding of the intellect and of business.
Center of Palm	***Abhaya Mudrā*** The earth

Finger and Corresponding *Mudrā*

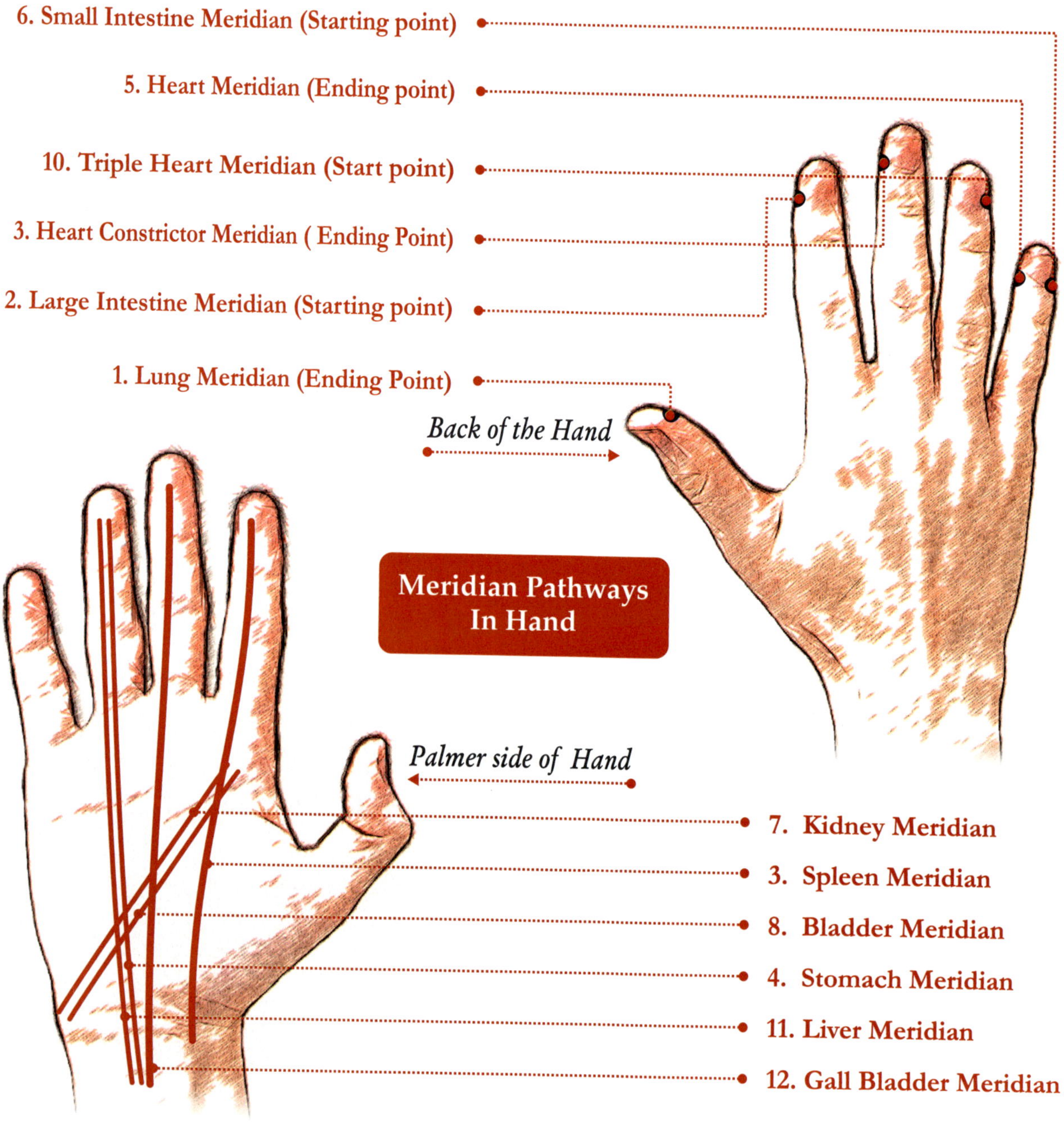
6. Small Intestine Meridian (Starting point)
5. Heart Meridian (Ending point)
10. Triple Heart Meridian (Start point)
3. Heart Constrictor Meridian (Ending Point)
2. Large Intestine Meridian (Starting point)
1. Lung Meridian (Ending Point)
Back of the Hand
Meridian Pathways In Hand
Palmer side of Hand
7. Kidney Meridian
3. Spleen Meridian
8. Bladder Meridian
4. Stomach Meridian
11. Liver Meridian
12. Gall Bladder Meridian

X. Meridians, Pathways and *Mudrā*

Meridians are "energy channels" – or, "rivers of energy" – flowing freely in the body. Just like any other energy channel, these are also invisible and have a physical presence like that of organs. Along these channels, there are certain high-energy points known as meridian points that may help clear off the blockages and increase/decrease the energy flow going to a particular organ.

In the practice of *Mudrā* through self-acupressure, the meridian channels and their important points are triggered in a gentle and effective manner to release, increase, or block the excess energy passing through the particular meridian. The practice of *Mudrā* is like practicing self-*shiatsu* or Chinese massage.

There are 12 main energy meridians, and their locations and the main *Mudrā* affecting these meridians arc explained as follows:

1. **The Lung Meridian:** This meridian helps in the intake of Qi energy from breath to build up resistance against any external intrusion.

   Location in Hands: Ending point is on the inner side of the thumb tip at the back of the hands.

Main *Mudrās*

Liṅga Mudrā, Jñāna Mudrā, Saṅkha Mudrā, Yoga Mudrā, Hākini Mudrā, Vitarka Mudrā

2. **The Large Intestine Meridian:** This meridian helps in the function of lungs. It also eliminates the stagnation of Qi energy. This energy meridian along with the spleen and pancreas meridians improve the functioning of the abdomen, relieving symptoms such as cramping, pain, diarrhea, and constipation.

   Location in Hands: Starting point is on the inner side of the index fingertip (close to the thumb), at the back of the hands.

Main *Mudrās*

Vāyu Mudrā, Apāna Vāyu Mudrā, Vitarka Mudrā, Sūcī Mudrā

3. **The Spleen Meridian:** It is involved in digestion and the process of fermentation. Mental fatigue has a negative effect on the spleen.

   Location in Hands: In the palmer side of the hand, it runs from base of wrist (close to the thumb) all through the index finger.

Main *Mudrās*

Muṣṭi Mudrā, Tse Mudrā, Kāyākalpa Mudrā, Samāna Mudrā, Surabhī Mudrā

4. **The Stomach Meridian:** This meridian is involved in the healthy functioning of the stomach, esophagus, and duodenum, as well as the functioning of the reproductive, lactation, ovary, and appetite mechanisms. It is also involved in the menstrual cycle.

Location in Hands: In the palmer side of the hand, it runs from center of wrist all through the ring finger.

Main *Mudrās*

Bidāla Mudrā, Muṣṭi Mudrā, Samāna Mudrā, Udāna Vāyu Mudrā, Sūrya Mudrā, Mahāśīrṣa Mudrā

5. **The Heart Meridian:** This governs emotions. It is responsible for the circulation of blood in the entire body through the brain and the five senses.

Location in Hands: Ending point is at the inner side of the little fingertip (closer to the ring-finger side), from the back of the hand.

Main *Mudrā*

Apāna Vāyu Mudrā

6. **The Small Intestine Meridian:** The small intestine governs the total body through the displacement and digestion of food. Anxiety, anger, nervous shock, and emotional excitement can affect the circulation of blood, and the small intestine can actually cause blood stagnation that affects the body as a whole.

   Location in Hands: Starting point is at the outer side of the little fingertip, from the back of the hand.

Main *Mudrās*

Tse Mudrā, Muṣṭi Mudrā, Samāna Mudrā

7. **The Kidney Meridian:** This meridian controls the energy of the body and governs resistance against mental stress by controlling hormone secretions. It also detoxifies and purifies blood.

   Location in Hands: It runs from the base of wrist (closer to the little finger) to the center of the palm in the palmer side of the hand.

Main *Mudrās*

Jala Mudrā, Pṛthivī Mudrā, Prāṇa Mudrā, Mahājñāna Mudrā

8. **The Bladder Meridian:** This is related to the mid-brain, which cooperates with the kidney system and the pituitary gland. It is connected to the autonomic nervous system related to the reproductive and urinary organs. It is also responsible for expelling urine.

   Location in Hands: It runs parallel to the kidney meridian, from the base of wrist (closer to the center of the hand) to the center of the palm, in the palmer side of the hand.

Main *Mudrās*

Jala Mudrā, Girivaraa Mudrā, Jala Surabhī Mudrā

9. **The Heart Constrictor (Pericardium) Meridian:** This meridian acts as a supplemental function of the heart related to circulatory system, which includes the heart sac, the cardiac arteries, and the system of arteries and veins. It is also responsible for total nutrition. This energy meridian helps to relieve thoracic symptoms such as ribcage pain or straining of the muscles in the upper and mid-back, and guards against nerve damage in all parts of the body.

   Location in Hands: Ending point is on the inner side of the middle fingertip (closer to the thumb), at the back of the hands.

Main *Mudrās*

Apāna Vāyu Mudrā, Prāṇa Mudrā, Vyāna Mudrā

10. **The Triple Heater Meridian:** This meridian acts as a supplemental function of the small intestine, and controls the visceral organs that circulate energy to the entire body. It also protects the function of the lymphatic system. The upper heat is related to the chest, the middle heat to the solar plexus, and the heat above the navel and below is related to the peritoneum as well as circulation to the extremities. Disharmony in the energy through this meridian may relate to abdominal distention, urinary problems, and issues with the ear, nose, and throat.

    Location in Hands: Starting point is on the inner side of the ring fingertip (closer to the little finger), at the back of the hands.

Main *Mudrās*

Apāna Vāyu Mudrā, Agni Namaskāra Mudrā, Sūrya Mudrā, Pṛthivī Mudrā, Prāṇa Mudrā

11. **The Liver Meridian:** This meridian stores nutrients and energy for physical activities. It also helps resist against disease and supplies, analyses, and detoxifies blood in order to maintain physical energy.

    Location in Hands: In the palmer side of the hand, it runs from center of wrist all through the ring finger.

Main *Mudrās*

Samāna Mudrā, Prāṇa Mudrā, Apāna Mudrā

12. **The Gall Bladder Meridian:** This meridian distributes nutrients throughout the body and balances the total energy through the help of internal hormones and secretions including bile, saliva, gastric acid, insulin, and intestinal hormones.

Location in Hands: In the palmer side of the hand, it runs from center of wrist all through the middle finger.

Main *Mudrās*

Apāna Mudrā, Bidāla Mudrā, Mṛga Mudrā, Samāna Mudrā, Muṣṭi Mudrā

Chapter - VI

Benefits of Hand Mudrās

The regular practice of *Mudrā* benefits the mind, body, psyche, and biomagnetic fields. *Mudrā* is intrinsically related to union and connection. Union is oneness, and oneness is reverberating in everything in this universe. It is the most non-violent, inexpensive, and available source of health and well being for all. Anyone who can breathe can practice *Mudrā*.

1. **Health:** The power of *Mudrā* clears the subtle channels (meridians, *nāḍīs*) and psychic centers (*cakras, marma* points) in the etheric body, allowing life force to flow unhampered to the organs and all parts of the body.

2. **IQ Improvement:** As the physical cleansing process takes place, the mind becomes clear and the mental faculties are enhanced, making it possible for the innate soul intelligence to express itself with greater intensity.

3. **Enhancing and Expanding the Aura:** The magnetism produced by the *Mudrā* cleanses the biomagnetic field of the body and empowers it with greater vitality, thereby also forming a protective shield against negative forces.

4. **Expansion of Consciousness:** As a result of the cleansing process and the activation of *Śakti* in the form of *Kuṇḍalinī*, one's consciousness is transformed, transcending ordinary awareness.

5. **Acquisition of *Siddhis*/Powers/Attainments:** Along with the transformation of one's consciousness, certain powers and virtues of the soul would unfold and dormant spiritual senses would awaken, according to *Haṭha Yoga Pradīpikā*.

6. **Transformation and Regeneration of the Physical Body:** The overall effect of the constant practice of *Mudrā* is the complete transformation and regeneration of the mind-body principle, a spiritual expansion of the consciousness stylized in the Mystery Schools as the "second birth."

7. **Stability and Stillness:** The *Mudrā* imparts stability–just like postures.

8. **Respiratory System:** The various types of *Mudrā Prāṇāyāmas* (*Sparśa Mudrā*) have effects on various parts of the lungs.

9. **Experience of Bliss:** A *Mudrā* causes vital energy (*Prāṇa Śakti*) to flow through a specific channel, thus increasing the effect of the vital energy on oneself or others. This vital energy is the real bliss or *Ānanda*.

10. **Balance of Elements:** As per *Yoga Tattva Mudrā Vijñāna*, the practice of *Mudrā* brings harmony and balance in the five elements (earth, water, fire, air, and ether) within the body.

11. **Restores the Innate Rhythm of Organ Systems:** The regular practice of hand *Mudrā* revives the cellular pathways, forming new communication channels between the organs and the organ systems. All this helps in restoring the innate rhythm of the organs and the organ systems. This restoration of the rhythm brings about a state of well being and good health.

The three basic effects of *Yoga Mudrās*

1. **Balancing**: When the tip of the thumb joins the tip of any finger, it will bring the associated element into balance. As in case of Air element gesture where the index finger tip joins the thumb tip to balance the air element in the body.

2. **Sedating/ reducing:** When any finger rests at the root of the thumb and the thumb cover the finger and presses its second phalange, the associated element is reduced or sedated. For example in case of ether element gesture when the middle finger is covered by the thumb then the space element is sedated.

3. **Cleansing/ tonifying:** When the thumb touches the root of any finger then it brings a cleansing/ detoxifying/ toning effect of the element. As in case of detox gesture, the placement of thumb tips at the root of ring finger, tones and cleanses the earth element.

Chapter - VII

Guidelines for the Practice of Mudrās

General (*Vyāvahārika*) *Mudrā* and Therapeutic (*Cikitsaka*) *Mudrā*

To maintain the efficacy of therapeutic *Mudrā*, one should follow the guidelines below:

1. **Time:** The ideal timings are the *prabhāta sandhyā* (morning), *madhyāhna sandhyā* (afternoon), and *śyāma sandhyā* (evening). These are the transition timings and, so, the best to reach the inner realms of one's being. These times are when the cosmic energy is at its peak. It symbolizes the transition of the subconscious to the conscious and of the conscious to the subconscious. On the other hand, *Mudrā* is not bound by anything and can be practiced at any time of the day.

2. **Place:** It is best to practice at the same place every day, but in case of hand *Mudrā* as therapy, one may practice them anywhere at any time.

3. **Diet:** *Mudrās* are generally practiced empty stomach. Therapeutic *Mudrā* should not be practiced after meals, especially the ones that interfere with metabolism.

4. **Duration:** It takes 30 seconds for the *Mudrā* to form the electromagnetic circuit. However, a *Mudrā* should be practiced for a minimum of 2 to 5 minutes in each practice cycle. As you advance, it is good to keep in mind that one should practice *Mudrā* for 45 minutes daily. The 45-minute duration can be split into 15 minutes, 3 times a day. To begin, you may start with 2 to 5 minutes, 3 times a day. Let your intuition function here. It will tell you when you are ready to stop or continue with a *Mudrā* if required.

5. **Body Position:** The maximum benefits of *Mudrā* are derived when they are practiced in a meditative state of mind. Such a state of mind acts as a catalyst, but one may practice *Mudrā* also while walking, reading a book, or sitting, or even during *āsana* practice, as long as one keeps the spine straight. One should not practice *Mudrā* while eating and working. It is suggested that *Mudrā* be practiced in one of the meditative poses like *Sukhāsana* (easy pose: simple cross-legged position); *Padmāsana* (lotus pose); *Siddhāsana* (adept's pose); *Vajraāsana* the thunderbolt pose or diamond pose) or *Maitriāsana* (friendly pose or seated on a chair). In case of therapeutic *Mudrās,* it is important to keep the arms externally rotated in a way that inner corner of the elbow is slightly pushing the rib cage to open up the chest cavity. By doing so, the breath becomes deeper and there is complete engagement of the diaphragm. Keep the other fingers (straight ones) stretched slightly to activate the meridian flow of energy. It is not advisable to keep the fingers limp, although, in case of Spiritual *Mudrās* it is suggested to keep the hands completely relaxed.

Sukhāsana (Easy Pose)

Cross your legs comfortably as per your capacity without exerting pressure on any part of the leg or spine. Maintain a steady posture keep the spinal column in slight "s" shaped curve by marinating the normal arches in lumbar and cervical regions. You may choose to use a triangular cushion or blanket under the seat for relaxing the knees and lower back. Rest the hands on the knees with palms facing up/down in a *Mudrā*.

Padmāsana (Lotus Pose)

Practice this posture only if you have enough flexibility and strength in your hip, knee and ankle joint. To attain this posture, sit on the floor with legs extended in front of you, then cross your legs in a way that the heels rest close/ touch the ovary regions in female or the groin areas in case of males. It is important that your knees touch the floor, if the knees do not comfortably touch the floor it is a sign that more work is required to open up the body before you attempt this posture. Rest the hands on the knees with palms facing up/ down in a *Mudrā*.

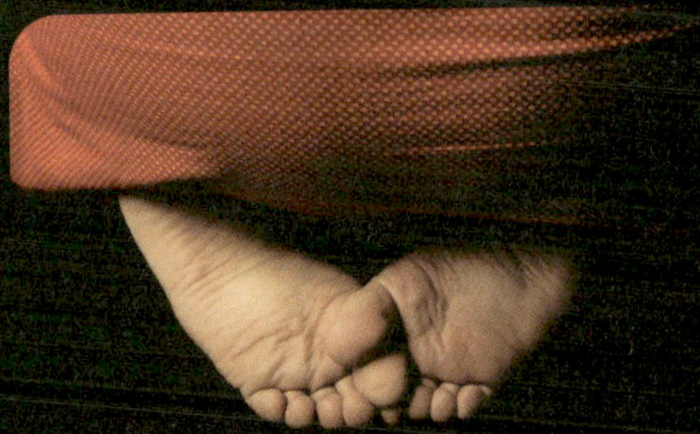

Feet Position

Vajraāsana (Thunderbolt Pose/Diamond Pose)

Fold your legs in a way that big toes resting over each other and heels are spread out to create a swing, rest the buttocks between the swing of the two heels. Keep both the knees joined and back straight. Rest the hands on the knees with palms facing down in a *Mudrā*.

Siddhāsana (Adept's Pose)

Cross your legs so that one heel (left heel in case of women and right in case of men) is brought to the perineum, then the opposite ankle (right in case of women and left in case of men) placed with the toes and heel of the second foot resting in the fold between the thigh and the calf of the first leg beneath it. Rest the hands on the knees with palms facing up/down in a *Mudrā*.

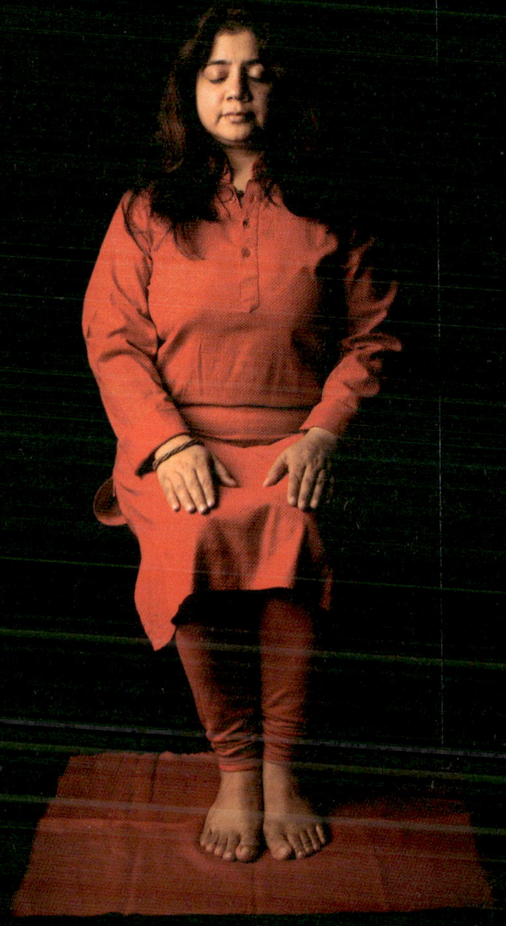

Maitriāsana **(Friendly Pose)**

Sit on a chair with the back straight, trying not to sit a little ahead of the back support of the chair; choose a chair without arm rest and rest the hands on the knee; keep a woolen blanket under the feet, and keep the feet, knees and thighs together.

6. ***Asaṁyukta/Saṁyukta*:** For the therapy of the organs in pairs, one may practice *Asaṁyukta* (single hand) *Mudrā* or *Saṁyukta* (both hands) *Mudrā*. For the organs that are not in pairs, the opposite hand is held in *Mudrā*. For example, when practicing the *Mudrā* for the heart, practice it with right hand. In some cases, both hands attain a separate *Mudrā*.

7. **Pressure:** A minimal pressure is applied at the point of contact. When held for longer durations, a natural nerve-ending tension is created which helps in opening up the blocked channels/meridians.

8. **Awareness:** During the practice of a *Mudrā*, let your awareness be at the point of contact made by the *Mudrā* in order to experience the subtle communication and vibrations.

9. **Observation:** Every *Mudrā* changes the energetic pathway represented as breath pattern, and it is important to observe the subtle changes in the breath pattern, the taste in the mouth, and the body temperature. If the taste in the mouth changes to anything (sour, bitter, dry, sticky, metallic, absurd, etc.) except for sweet (sweet taste denotes the activity of earth element which is symbolic of repair process in the body), then one should practice tongue rotation. In tongue rotation, one rotates the tongue around the teeth (under the lip and over the teeth) in clockwise direction until one experiences the sweet taste.

10. **Signs from the Body:** If one feels nausea, heartburn, dizziness, discomfort, overheated, or cold, one should stop the practice of the *Mudrā*. With focus, one can feel a subtle pulsation at the points of contact between thumbs and fingers, between two palms, as you join the palms in certain *Mudrā*, in the center of palm when you make a fist in certain *Mudrā*, etc. Such a pulsation is a positive sign of the energy circulation and formation of the electromagnetic circuit in the body.

11. **Age Group:** Anybody of any from the age of 5 years can practice *Mudrā* independently or with assistance.

12. **Children, Special Population (Physically and mentally challenged):** In case of children and special population, external help can be provided to hold the *Mudrā*. I personally have used *Mudrā* as therapy for cerebral palsy, Down's syndrome, autistic and attention deficit hyperactive cases by helping people practice certain *Mudrās* (by using my hands to help them hold the *Mudrā* for the required time period), and witnessed results in the form of calmness and an improved range of motion.

13. **Menstruation:** Only certain *Mudrās* (like *Apāna, Prāṇa, and Samāna Mudrās*) should be practiced during menstruation.

14. **Seniors and Bedridden People:** Seniors and bedridden persons may practice *Mudrā* in laying-down position.

15. **Position of Hands:** In almost all the *Mudrās* except for *Bhūmi Sparśa Mudrā* and *Cin Mudrā*, the hands are kept on the knee facing up – pointing them down drains the energy. Resting the hands with the palms facing up is also symbolic of the openness to receive.

16. **Purity:** To receive the true benefits of this mystical science, *śarīra śuddhi* (physical cleansing), *āhāra śuddhi* (intake of pure and healthy food), *manah śuddhi* (mental cleansing through meditation), *vāk śuddhi* (purity of speech through chanting as well as practicing mindful speech and *mauna*), and *karma śuddhi* (purity of actions) are essential. Practice *Mudrā* with a relaxed state of body and mind. When using *Mudrā* as therapy, eat simple , easy to digest and cooked food.

17. **Use of Breathing Pattern:** For additional benefits, one may choose to synchronize the breathing patterns as 1:1 or 1:2 while practicing a *Mudrā*, although each *Mudrā* generates its unique breathing rhythm.

18. **Use of Affirmation:** Affirmation and resolution act as catalysts in any practice. One may choose to use the affirmation quoting them in the present tense, keeping the sentences short and clear.

19. **Visualization:** One may internally visualize the burning of toxins, the clearing up of the blocked pathways, the absorption of white light, the release of black light, and many such other visuals that may help bring additional results.

Spiritual *Mudrās*

1. Spiritual *Mudrās* are practiced during meditation and certain rites & rituals.

2. The Spiritual *Mudrās* should be practiced in meditative poses like *Sukhāsana, Padmāsana, Siddhāsana, or Maitriāsana,* to allow the *Kuṇḍalinī Śakti* to rise up.

3. The best times to practice *Mudrā* are between 4 am and 6 am in the morning, and between 5 pm and 7 pm in the evening.

4. Keep the same place for meditation as for the practice of *Mudrā*.

5. Practice *Yoga-Nidrā* or *Śavāsana* before the practice of these *Mudrās*.

6. Spiritual *Mudrās* may be accompanied by internal chanting of specific *mantras* for specific *Mudrā*. If you are not aware of the specific *mantra*, chant *OM or SO-HUM*. Chant "*SO*" as you inhale and "*Hum*" as you exhale, and continue the rhythm.

7. There is no fixed time duration to hold a Spiritual *Mudrās*; one may choose to do it as long as one can maintain the meditative state or stay in the meditative state.

8. The pressure applied at the point of contact in hands in case of Spiritual *Mudrās* is minimal.

The intention is just to redirect the energy to form a circuit.

9. One should not practice Spiritual *Mudrās* while eating, talking, lying down, and defecating. Seniors and bedridden people are not bound by any of these rules; they can practice these *Mudrās* in the laying-down position also.

10. While practicing Spiritual *Mudrās*, the hands should be above the level of the lower abdomen, in most cases at the level of the heart or on the knee with palms facing up.

11. One should face the east or northeast direction while practicing the *Mudrās* to gain the maximum benefit from the earth's magnetic field alignment.

12. The practice should preferably be done on empty stomach or with very light refreshment/fruit/water/tea intake. Since the best time to practice them is in the early morning or evening, one is generally not bothered about this guideline.

Chapter - VIII

Types of Mudrās

Every position of the body is a *Mudrā*. The very moment we speak through our body, that very moment we communicate. Each and every possible position is a *Mudrā* of one of the Nine Emotions (*Nava Rasas*). The highest of the these emotions is the one that takes us to *Ānand Śri*, the emotion of *Śāntī*. These nine emotions or *Rasas* that *Mudrās* evoke are:

Emotion	Meaning	Color
Śṛngāram	Love, Attractiveness	Light Green
Hāsyam	Laughter, Mirth, Comedy	White
Raudram	Fury	Red
Kāruṇyam	Compassion, Tragedy	Grey
Bībhatsam	Disgust, Aversion	Blue
Bhayānakam	Horror, Terror	Black
Vīram	Heroic Mood	Golden
Adbhutam	Wonder, Amazement	Yellow
Śāntam	Peace or Tranquility	White

Rasas, Meaning and Color

The *Nātyasāstra* identifies eight *rasas* with eight corresponding *Bhāva* (mood)

Ratī :	Love	*Hāsya* :	Mirth
Śoka :	Sorrow	*Krodha* :	Anger
Utsāha :	Energy	*Bhaya* :	Terror
Jugupsa :	Disgust	*Vismaya* :	Astonishment

Categories of Mudrās as per varied applications.

- Classification as per expression and time of usage
- Classification as per parts of the body used to express
- Classification as per benefits
- Classification of *Hasta Mudrā*
- Classification as per their use in rites, rituals and *tantrik* worship

Classification as per expression and time of usage

As per the *Tantrāloka* by Abhinava Gupta, the practice of *Mudrā* is expressed at three times:

Āvāhane: At the time of invocation

Pūjanānte: At the commencement of a ritual

Visarjane: At the time of immersion of the energy invoked

At these three times, *Mudrās* are expressed in three different ways:

Kāyika: through body

Mānasika: through intention

Vāṇigata: through speech

Mudrās can also be expressed in the follwing three ways:

Manojaa Mudrā: The *Mudrā* expressed though intention (*manas*)

Vāgbhāva Mudrā: The *Mudrā* expressed through speech (*vāg*)

Dehobhāva Mudrā: The *Mudrā* expressed through physical body (*deha*: hands, eyes, body, touch, etc.)

Classification as per parts of the body used to express

1. ***Mukha Mudrā:*** *Mukha* means "face," and these are *Mudrās* that are expressed using emotions on the face, as in classical dances.

2. ***Cakṣu Mudrā:*** *Cakṣu* means "eyes." These are *Mudrās* that are practiced by focusing the vision externally or internally on an object, a body part, breath, *cakra*, etc. as in *trāṭaka, nāsāgra dṛṣṭi, bhrū-madhya dṛṣṭi, anāhata dṛṣṭi*, etc.

3. ***Jihvā Mudrā:*** *Jihvā* means "tongue." These are *Mudrās* in which the tongue is locked in different positions, as in *Śītalī Prāṇāyāma, Jihvā Bandha, Khecarī Mudra*, etc.

4. ***Adhara Mudrā:*** *Adhara* means "lips," and these are *Mudrās* in which the upper and lower lips are locked/ sealed in a position during *Prāṇāyāma*, *Mantra* chanting, *Āsana, Dhyāna* (meditation), etc., as in *Kākī Mudrā*, *OM* chanting, and *Śītalī Prāṇāyāma*.

5. ***Grīvā Mudrā:*** *Grīvā* means "neck." These are *Mudrās* in which the neck is moved in different directions with or without chanting, as in *Brahma Mudrā*, *Mayūra Mudrā*, and *Jālandhara Bandha*.

6. ***Hasta Mudrā:*** *Hasta* means "hands," and these are *Mudrās* in which fingers, thumb, and palms unite in different positions like *Namaskāra Mudrā* and *Prāṇa Mudrā.*

7. ***Kāya Mudrā:*** *Kāya* means "skin" or "body," these *Mudrās* are practiced using the entire body; like in *Gomukha Bhujaṅginī Mudrā*, *Vajrolī Mudrā, Viparīta-karaṅī Mudrā*, etc.

8. ***Sparśa Mudrā:*** *Sparśa* means "touch," and these are *Mudrās* where palms rest at various locations on the body, especially around the chest, like in *Madhyama Sparśa Mudrā.*

9. ***Pāda Mudrā:*** *Pāda* means "feet," and these are *Mudrās* where foot soles join or rest at different positions, like in *Baddha-koṇāsana*, *Vṛkṣāsana*, etc.

Classification as per benefits

1. **General (*Vyāvahārika*) *Mudrā*:** These are *Mudrā* used in everyday communication, classical dances, rites, rituals, and ceremonies.

2. **Therapeutic (*Cikitsaka*) *Mudrā*:** These are *Mudrās* of *Yoga Tattva Mudrā Vijñāna* used as therapy by balancing the ratio of the five elements (*Pañca -Tattvas*) as well as building harmony among them.

3. **Spiritual (*Ādhyātmika*) *Mudrā*:** These are *Mudrās* used in meditation, *bandhas, sādhanā, mantra* chanting, connecting to *cakras* and subtle body, to impart truth, etc.

Classification of *Hasta Mudrā*

1. ***Saṁyukta* (both hands) *Mudrā:*** *Saṁyukta* means "together," and these are *Mudrās* that are practiced using both hands together or in isolation.

2. ***Asaṁyukta* (single hand) *Mudrā*:** *Asaṁyukta* means "separate" or "not together," and these are *Mudrās* that are practiced with one hand only.

Classification as per their use in rites, rituals and tantrik worship

1. ***Japa Mudrā:*** Used in repetition of chants using (*mālā* beads made of stones, seeds, woods or root, *kara-nyāsa, anga-nyāsa* etc.)

2. ***Avahana Mudrā:*** *Mudrās* used in invocation.

3. ***Kāmya-karma Mudrā:*** Used in the rites of abundance.

4. ***Naivedya Mudrā:*** Used in offering foods.

5. ***Snana Mudrā:*** Used in bathing of deity.

Hasta Mudrā

Chapter - I

VYĀVAHĀRIKA HASTA MUDRĀ

GENERAL MUDRĀS

Vyāvahārika Hasta Mudrā are the ones used in day-to-day life as an extended version of expressing self through body language as posture, hand gestures and expression of eyes. *Sumudraka Śāstra* is the science of reading an individual's character through such configurations of the body. In addition, they are also used in *Hindu* and Buddhist ritualist worship. These are the miracles of everyday life, the beauty of expression.

Abhiśeka Mudrā: Mudrā of Anointing an Idol with Water via Conch

Type: *Saṁyukta* (both hands) *Mudrā*

Meaning: *Abhiśeka* is a part of the worship of Lord *Śiva*.
It is the ceremonial bathing of the *Śiva Liṅgam* in temples.

Usage: *Hindu* rituals, worship

Acalāgni Mudrā: Mudrā of Eternal Fire/ Flame

Type: *Saṁyukta* (both hands) *Mudrā*

Meaning: Never-dying/eternal fire

Usage: *Hindu* and Buddhist rituals during worship, chanting

Agrā Mudrā: Mudrā of Salutation to the Teacher Outside and Within

Type: *Saṁyukta* (both hands) *Mudrā*

Meaning: Forward, surrender

Usage: As greeting in *āsanas* of *Hatha Yoga*, meditation

Añjali Mudrā: Mudrā of Salutation/ Gratitude to the Guru and the Six Higher Cakras

Type: *Saṁyukta* (both hands) *Mudrā*

Meaning: Handful, palms full of offering

Usage: Meditation (surrender), *Guru-śiṣya paramparā* (greeting), *Hatha Yoga* (*āsanas*)

Arcita Mudrā: Mudrā of Greeting and Salutation

Type: *Asaṁyukta* (single hand) *Mudrā*

Meaning: Prayers

Usage: *Hindu* and Buddhist rituals (prayer, worship)

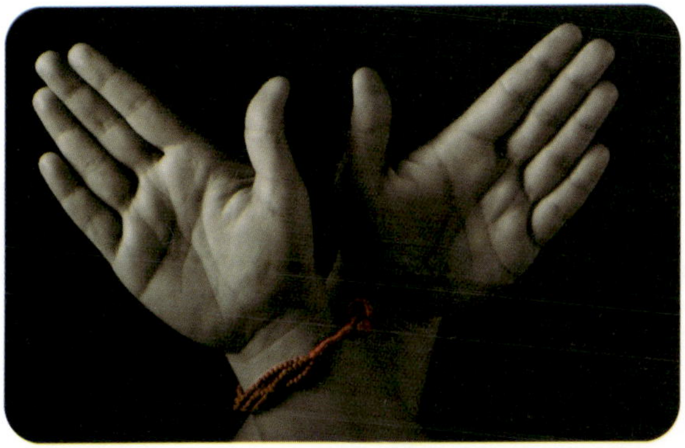

Aśoka Mudrā: Mudrā depicting a moving Aśoka Tree

Type: *Saṁyukta* (both hands) *Mudrā*

Meaning: Without sorrow/name of a tree

Usage: Classical dances and art forms

Ātmāñjali Mudrā: Mudrā of offering from the Soul

Type: *Saṁyukta* (both hands) *Mudrā*

Meaning: Offering from the soul

Usage: *Guru-śiṣya paramparā*, *Hindu* rituals, general greeting, surrender

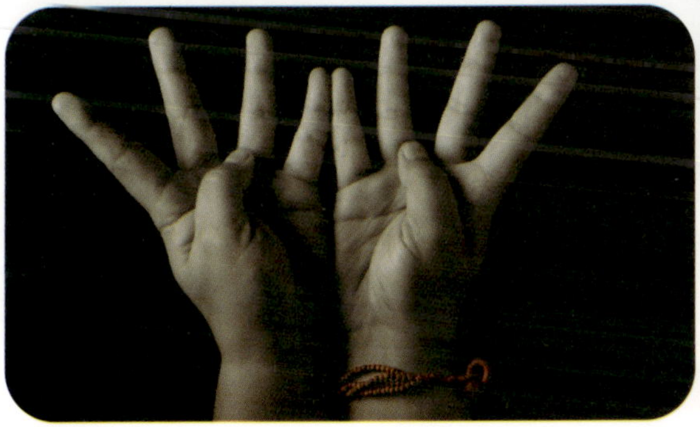

Āvāhana Mudrā: Mudrā of Invocation

Type: *Saṁyukta* (both hands) *Mudrā*

Meaning: Invocation, calling upon, invitation

Usage: *Hindu* rituals (prayers, chanting, and worship)

Bhramara Mudrā: Mudrā depicting Silence, Bee, Crane, or Sexual Union

Type: *Asaṁyukta* (single hand) *Mudrā*

Meaning: Humming bee

Usage: Buddhist and *Hindu* rituals, prayers, chants

Buddha-pātra Mudrā: Upholder of Law

Type: *Saṁyukta* (both hands) *Mudrā*

Meaning: *Buddha's* or a monk's begging/alms bowl

Usage: Buddhist tradition to depict the teachings, morals, laws

Haṁsa Mudrā: Mudrā of Inner Rhythm

Type: *Saṁyukta* (both hands) *Mudrā*

Meaning: Swan

Usage: *Hatha Yoga āsanas*

Hansi Mudrā: Mudrā of Peace and Restoration

Type: *Asaṁyukta* (single hand) *Mudrā*

Meaning: Joy, peace

Usage: Expression of joy, wisdom, peace, prosperity

Hṛdayāñjali Mudrā: Mudrā of offering from the Heart

Type:	*Saṁyukta* (both hands) *Mudrā*
Meaning:	Offering from the heart
Usage:	*Hatha Yoga āsanas*, *Hindu* rituals, meditation, worship

Kailāsa Mudrā: Mudrā of Contemplation and Salutation to the Sahasrāra Cakra

Type:	*Saṁyukta* (both hands) *Mudrā*
Meaning:	Name of Himalayan peak in India, precious jewel of snow, precious crystal
Usage:	*Hindu* and Buddhist rituals, *Hatha Yoga āsanas*

Kaśyapa Mudrā / Kacchapa Mudrā (Turtle Mudrā): Mudrā of Liṅga with Yoni

Type: *Asaṁyukta* (single hand) *Mudrā*

Meaning: Turtle/name of a *ṛṣi* (seer) in India

Usage: Buddhist and *Hindu* tradition for depiction of union

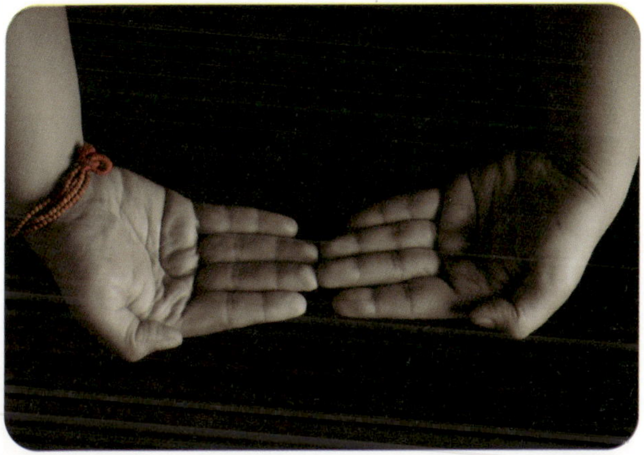

Latā Mudrā: Mudrā of Union and Entwinement

Type: *Saṁyukta* (both hands) *Mudrā*

Meaning: Creeper-like, one who clings to God, slender and entwining

Usage: In *Hindu* rituals and worship

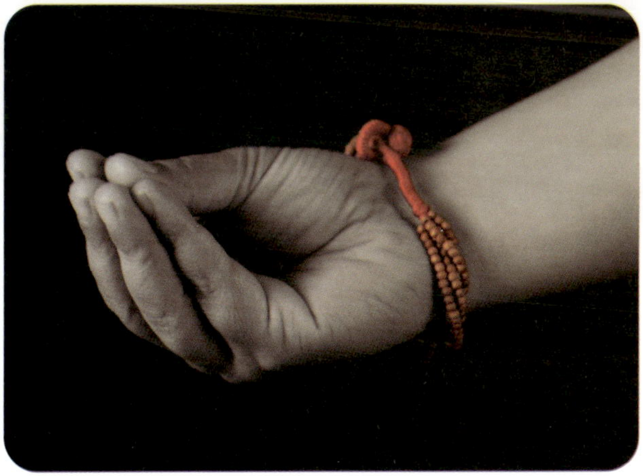

Mukula Mudrā: A gesture of Virginity/Unbloomed Flower Bud

Type: *Asaṁyukta* (single hand) *Mudrā*

Meaning: Unbloomed flower, a bud, inner self

Usage: *Hindu* rituals, prayers

Namaskāra Mudrā: Mudrā of Salutation and Acknowledgement of Divinity in Everyone

Type: *Saṁyukta* (both hands) *Mudrā*

Meaning: Greeting, acknowledgment, salutation, bowing, surrender

Usage: General social greeting, prayers in *Hindu* and Buddhist tradition

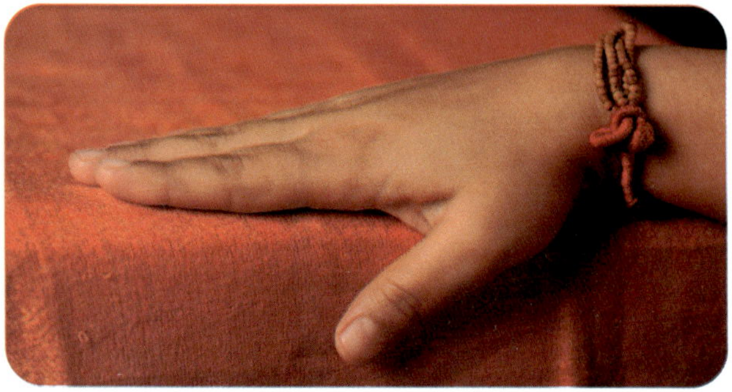

Nidrā-hasta Mudrā: Mudrā of putting One to Sleep

Type: *Asaṁyukta* (single hand) *Mudrā*

Meaning: Calming hands for putting one to sleep or relaxation

Usage: For cajoling a child to sleep

Nidrā Mudrā: Mudrā for Deep Sleep

Type: *Asaṁyukta* (single hand) *Mudrā*

Meaning: *Mudrā* of sleep

Usage: For invoking sleep in case of insomnia

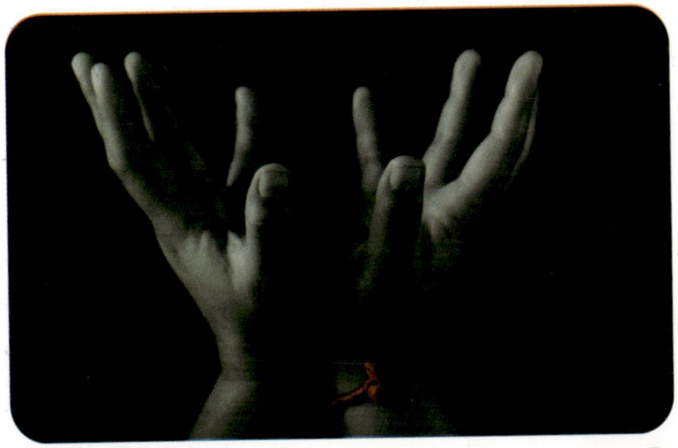

Paṇkaja/Padma Mudrā: Mudrā of offering Flowers to Deity/Mudrā of Full-bloomed Lotus

Type: *Saṁyukta* (both hands) *Mudrā*

Meaning: Lotus flower

Usage: In *Hindu* and Buddhist rituals, Indian classical dances

Padma-kośa Mudrā: Mudrā of Blossom, Lotus Bud, Brilliance

Type: *Asaṁyukta* (single hand) *Mudrā*

Meaning: Heart of lotus, lotus bud

Usage: Indian classical dances, Buddhist tradition

Puṣpāñjali Mudrā: Mudrā for Holding Flowers

Type: *Saṁyukta* (both hands) *Mudrā*

Meaning: Handful of flowers

Usage: Offering flowers to deity, *Hindu* rituals

Puṣpa-puṭa Mudrā: Mudrā for offering flowers, rice, water, alms

Type:	*Saṁyukta* (both hands) *Mudrā*
Meaning:	Offering flowers, water, alms, rice
Usage:	*Hindu* traditional rituals, classical dances

Śakti Mudrā: Mudrā for honoring the energy flow

Type:	*Saṁyukta* (both hands) *Mudrā*
Meaning:	Feminine energy
Usage:	Invocation of the feminine energy in *Hindu* rituals, classical Indian dances

Śikhara Mudrā: A gesture of strength and steadiness

Type: *Asaṁyukta* (single hand) *Mudrā*

Meaning: Tip/peak of a mountain

Usage: Indian classical dances, *Hindu* rituals, worship, prayers

Sūcī (Needle) Mudrā I: Elephant tusk, universe, or transgression

Type: *Asaṁyukta* (single hand) *Mudrā*

Meaning: Needle, something pointed, sharp

Usage: Indian classical dances

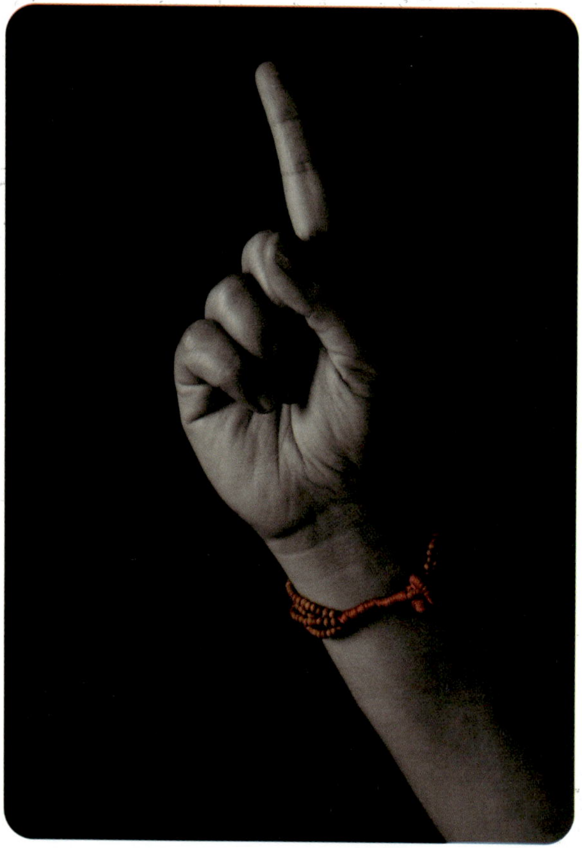

Sūcī (Needle) Mudrā II: Astonishment, anger, threat, turning the potter's wheel

Type: *Asaṁyukta* (single hand) *Mudrā*

Meaning: Direction, threat, strong message, guidance

Usage: In imparting teachings in *Hindu* and Buddhist tradition

Sūcī (Needle) Mudrā III: Concentrated energy: Healing Mudrā

Type: *Asaṁyukta* (single hand) *Mudrā*

Meaning: Concentration like that of a laser beam

Usage: In healing therapies, meditation

Sūrya Prāṇa Mudrā: Mudrā for soaking in Solar Energy

Type: *Saṁyukta* (both hands) *Mudrā*

Meaning: *Prāṇic* energy of the sun

Usage: *Yoga* practices, meditation, Indian classical dances

Tattva Mudrā: A gesture of Truth

Type: *Asaṁyukta* (single hand) *Mudrā*

Meaning: Basic element, principle

Usage: *Hindu* and Buddhist rituals, classical Indian dances

Vajrapradama Mudrā: A gesture of Unshakable Trust

Type: *Saṁyukta* (both hands) *Mudrā*

Meaning: Diamond

Usage: Buddhist and *Hindu* traditional rituals

Vajra Mudrā: Mudrā of Thunderbolt or Unshakeable knowledge from Emptines

Type: *Saṁyukta* (both hands) *Mudrā*

Meaning: Thunderbolt

Usage: Buddhist tradition, Indian classical dances

Vitarka Mudrā: A gesture of discussion/preaching of Buddhist Philosophy

Type: *Asaṁyukta* (single hand) *Mudrā*

Meaning: Fruitful discrimination, contemplation, thought conception

Usage: Buddhist tradition

Yoga Mudrā: Gesture of Union

Type: *Saṁyukta* (both hands) *Mudrā*

Meaning: *Mudrā* of union, peace, harmony

Usage: *Yogic* tradition, meditation

Summary

There is a beauty in acting with awareness; there is a miracle in every moment. All we need to do is pause and observe the self, the interaction process and how the body expresses itself without the use of words, millions times a day. Next time you move or stay still, I urge you to allow for a rising for curiosity to understand and introspect your own gestures and postures. If you have witnessed a *Hindu* or Buddhist ritual before, next time observe them with new sight… Be watchful of the communication process with the subtle energies. Every moment is a miracle…

Not this mind
and neither the spirit
I am you
and
I am THAT
You are me
And
You are THAT

Give and ask not
Receive and get none
Give…receive…enjoy all at once
Give not…receive neither…
Enjoy still the silence pure.

Chapter - II

Cikitsaka Hasta Mudrā

Therapeutic Mudrā

When all the other conventional therapies are failing to impart and regain health, *Mudrās* are still unexplored as alternate method of regaining balance in the body through the balance of *tattvas, pranās, gunās and doshās.* Let us explore how *Mudrās* can be used as therapy for various conditions as a precaution as well as an adjunct to other therapeutic modalities.

Apāna Vāyu Mudrā

Mṛta Sañjīvanī Mudrā

First Aid to Cardiac Issues

Mṛta means "death," *Jīvana* means "life," *Sañ* means to "bring along," *Jīvanī* means "life giving." The meaning of *Apāna Vāyu Mudrā* (also known as *Mṛta Sañjīvanī Mudrā)* is "one that brings along life from death."

This *Mudrā* is the most powerful therapeutic *Mudrā* in the *Yoga Tattva Mudrā Vijñāna*.

FORMATION

Fold the index finger at the base of the thumb and press the second phalange of the index finger with the thumb. Join the tip of the thumb with the tips of middle and ring fingers simultaneously. Rest the hands on the knees keeping the elbow straight. Keep the little finger extended. Perform it with both hands to receive more benefit. Left side of the body represents cooling and feminine energy, and by embracing it with the right hand, we trigger the activation of the right nostril – that is, masculine solar energy. It can be practiced as both *Saṁyukta* (both hands) *Mudrā* and *Asaṁyukta* (single hand) *Mudrā*.

BENEFITS

1. The regular practice of this *Mudrā* helps prevent heart attacks and their recurrence.
2. It balances the *tri-doṣas* in the body: *vāta*, *pitta*, and *kapha*. It is a *Tridoṣa Nāśaka Mudrā*.
3. It rekindles the digestive fire and increases the lung capacity.

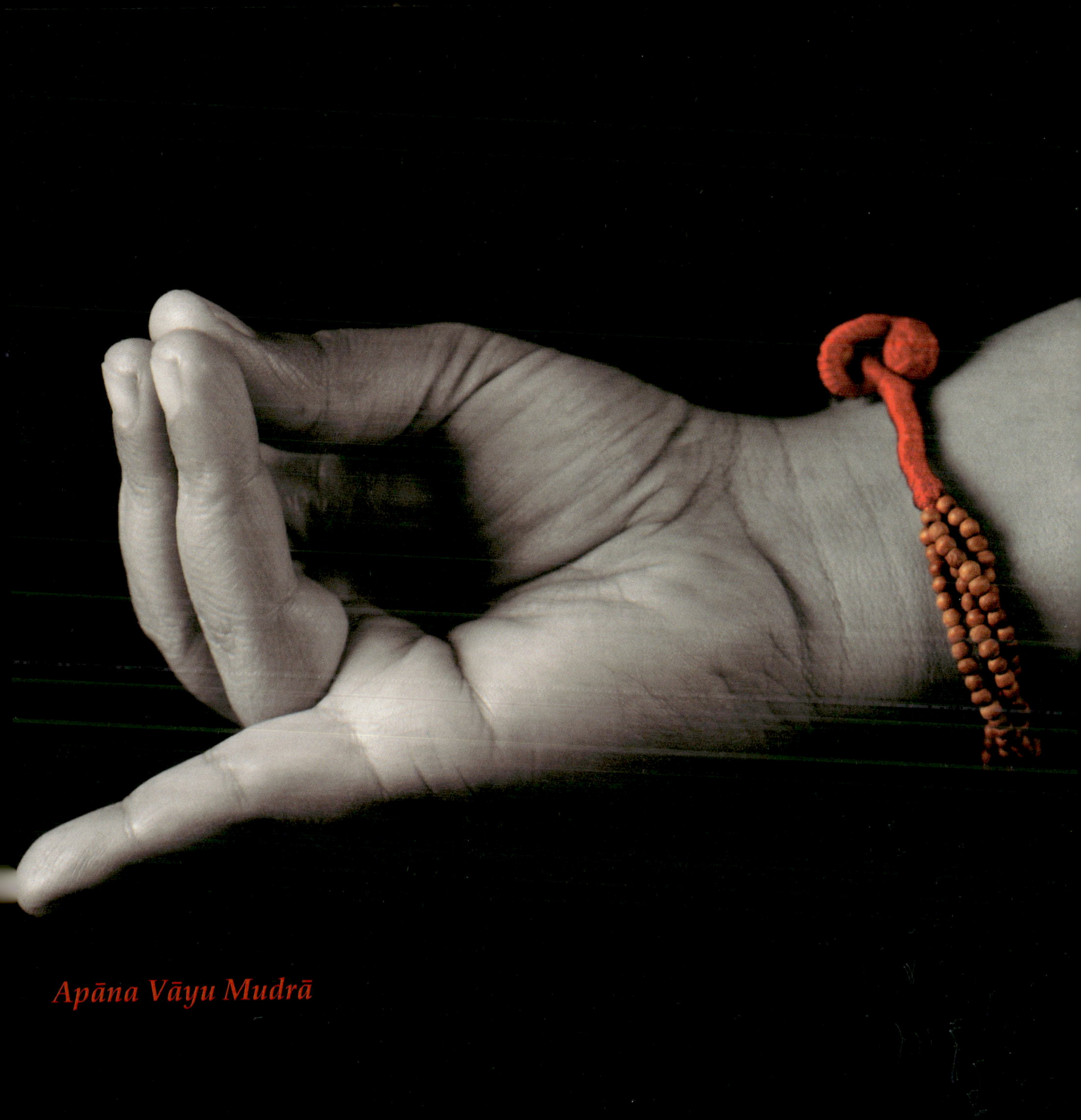

Apāna Vāyu Mudrā

DAṆḌA SVĀSTHYA MUDRĀ

Mudrā for Spinal Health/ Healthy Back

Daṇḍa means "spinal column," *Svāsthya* means "established in self" / "established in well being." This *Mudrā* is especially for maintaining the flow of energy, blood circulation around the vertebrae. It is a *Saṁyukta* (both hands) *Mudrā.*

FORMATION

1. **Right Hand:** Join the middle, the little finger tip with the tip of the thumb, keep the index and ring finger extended. Rest the hands at the right knee with palms facing up.

2. **Left Hand:** Fold the index finger at the base of the thumb. Press the index finger's second phalange with the thumb tip. Keep the middle, ring and little finger extended. Rest the hand on the left knee with palms facing up.

BENEFITS

1. Helps in removing fatigue from the spinal muscles.
2. Improves blood circulation around the spine.
3. Encourages the energy or *Prāṇic* flow in the *Cakras*
4. Calms down the nervous tension.
5. It is a great *Mudrā* to practice before meditation for maintaining the meditative pose.

Daṇḍa Svāsthya Mudrā

GAṆEŚA MUDRĀ

Mudrā for healthy digestion

The elephant-headed *Gaṇeśa* is the deity who overcomes all obstacles. It is a *Saṁyukta* (both hands) *Mudrā*.

FORMATION

Hold your right hand in front of your chest, with the palm facing outward. Keep the hand parallel to the floor. Bend the fingers towards the center of the palm. Now grip the right hand fingers with the left hand fingers, which has its back facing outward. Move the hands to the level of the heart, right in front of the chest. While exhaling, vigorously pull the hands apart without releasing the grip. This will tense the muscles of the upper arms and chest area. While inhaling, let go of all the tension. Repeat six times and then lovingly place both hands on the sternum in this position. Then, change the hand position: your left palm now faces outward. Repeat the above practice in this position.

BENEFITS

1. This *Mudrā* stimulates heart activity, strengthens heart muscles, opens the bronchial tubes, and releases any type of tension in this area.
2. It opens the fourth *cakra* and gives one courage, confidence, and openness toward other human beings.
3. Since the *Gaṇeśa Mudrā* activates the fire element, which reacts positively to the color red, certain visualizations support activity of the heart and circulation. Visualize the color red–a mosaic, a *maṇḍala*, or a carpet in various tones of red. Now, focus all of your senses on it for a while. Red should strengthen, warm, and widen your heart, giving you the courage to be open and confident.
4. It helps in releasing abdominal discomforts like flatulence, gases, bloating, and cramps, and aids in the digestive process by triggering the *jaṭharāgni* and *tālahṛdya marma*.

Gaṇeśa Mudrā

GARUḌA MUDRĀ

Mudrā for Immunity

Garuḍa is the mystical bird commonly known as eagle. This is the powerful and mighty bird that Lord *Viṣṇu* rides upon. Birds generally have sharp eyes, a distinct sense of orientation, and strong survival instincts. Large birds have such an enormous wingspan and so much strength in their wings that they can let themselves be carried by the wind.

FORMATION

Clasp your thumbs and place your hands, right hand on top of the left hand, on your lower abdomen. Remain in this position for about 10 breaths and then slide your hands up to your navel. Stay there for another 10 breaths. Then place your hands on the pit of your stomach and remain again for about 10 breaths. Finally, place your left hand on your sternum, turn your hands in the direction of your shoulders, and spread your fingers. Do as needed or three times a day for four minutes each. *Garuḍa*, the king of birds and of the air, is the enemy of snakes. It is a *Saṁyukta* (both hands) *Mudrā*.

BENEFITS

1. This *Mudrā* activates blood flow and circulation, invigorates the organs, and balances energy on both sides of the body.
2. It relaxes and relieves pain related to menstrual complaints, stomach upsets, and respiratory difficulties.
3. It also helps people deal with exhaustion and mood fluctuations.
4. It is highly beneficial in case of cancer, especially breast cancer.
5. It helps in increasing the lymphatic drainage.

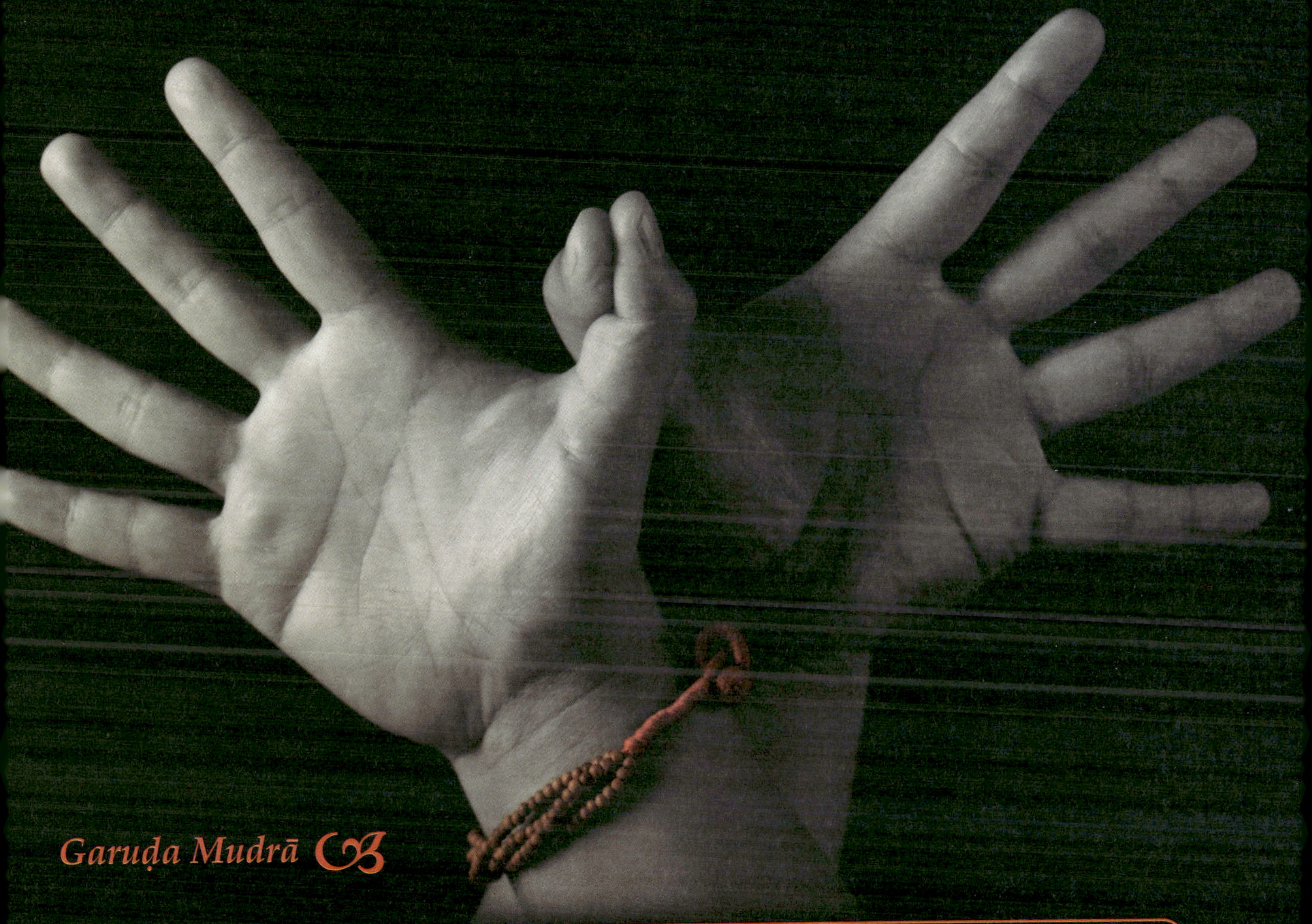

Garuḍa Mudrā

CAUTION
This Mudrā is not advised for those who have high blood pressure

GIRIVARA MUDRĀ

JALA ŚĀMAKA MUDRĀ

Mudrā to release Water Accumulation

Girivara means "mountain" or "lord of mountains." Just like water never stays on the tip of the mountain, but flows down with gravity, *Girivara Mudrā* helps in relieving water accumulation by allowing its smooth uninterrupted flow. It is known as *Jala Śāmaka Mudrā*, which means "one that causes the pacification of water element." It is an *Asaṁyukta* (single hand) *Mudrā* and belongs to *Yoga Tattva Mudrā Vijñāna.*

FORMATION

Bend the index, middle, and ring fingers into the center of the palm. Press them on the top with the thumb. Keep the little finger extended. Rest the hands on the knee.

BENEFITS

1. It helps in relieving urine retention.
2. It allows the easy passing of urine.
3. It also helps in detoxification by relieving the body of accumulated/sedentary toxic fluids.

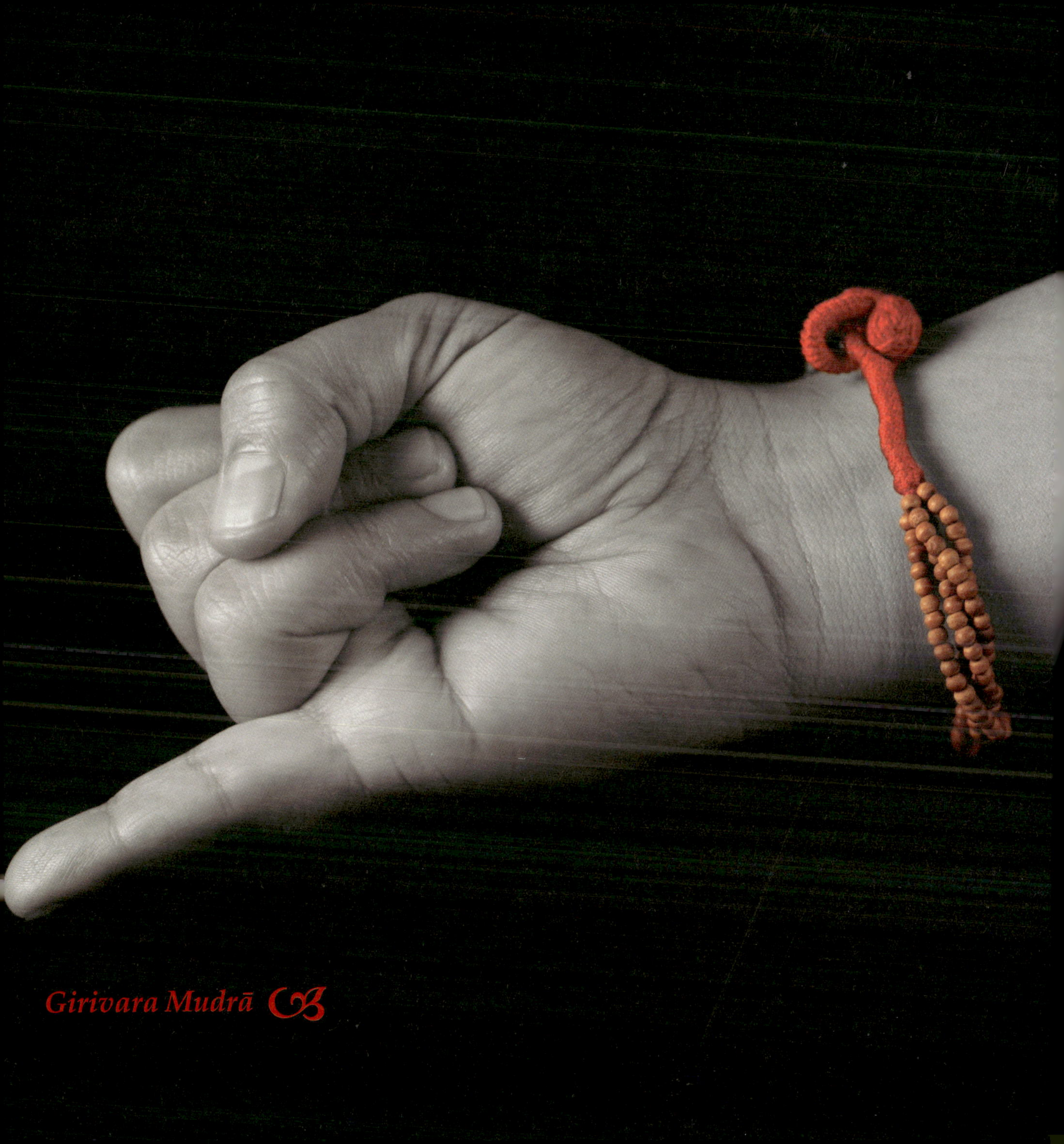

Girivara Mudrā

KĀYĀKALPA MUDRĀ

Mudrā for Detoxification

Kāyā means "skin," and it also means body. *Kalpa* means "transformation, change, revitalization, and rejuvenation." Thus, *Kāyākalpa* means "complete transformation, change, and renewal." It is a *Saṁyukta* (both hands) *Mudrā* and should be practiced on empty stomach, or at least three hours after a heavy meal.

FORMATION

Place each thumb on the inner edge of the third joint of your ring finger. Do this with each hand. Keep all the four fingers spread out and extended, keeping more distance between the ring finger and the middle finger. You may practice this *Mudrā* with both hands, resting them on the knee. It is suggested that the practice of this *Mudrā* be done during fasting and/or during the spring and fall seasons. The practice should be undertaken for a minimum duration of one week, three times a day, with 2 to 5 minutes in each practice session.

BENEFITS

1. As the name suggests, it is a *Mudrā* of cleaning and purification of the *Annamaya Kośa*.
2. It helps in increasing the digestive fire: *Jaṭharāgni*.
3. One may choose to purify any specific element by placing the thumb at the base of the respective finger controlling a specific element.
4. This *Mudrā* is best practiced empty stomach and should not be practiced during fever, menstruation and inflammatory conditions.

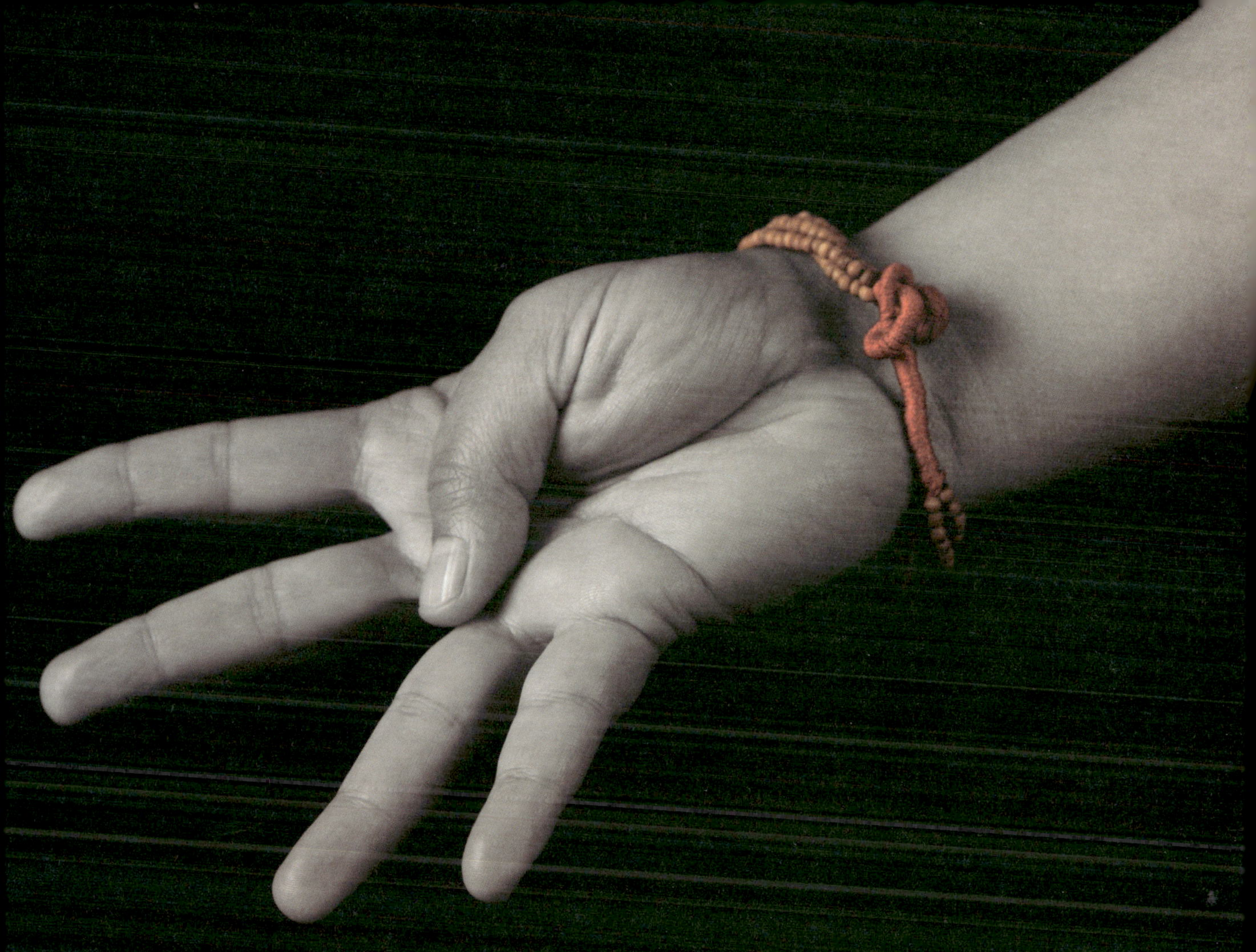

Kāyākalpa Mudrā

CAUTION

This Mudrā should not be practiced in case of sickness, fever, menstruation, or pregnancy. It should not be practiced by children, seniors (above 65 years), and bedridden patients.

KṢEPAṆA MUDRĀ

The Ambrosia of Immortality

Kṣepaṇa means "to let go or release." A *Saṁyukta* (both hands) *Mudrā*, it has its origin in Buddhist (*Mahāyāna*) tradition. *Mahāyāna* also refers to the path of seeking complete enlightenment for the benefit of all sentient beings, and is also called *Bodhisattvayāna*. This *Mudrā* is similar to *Uttarabodhi Mudrā* *(refer to book page 270)* in formation, with the only difference that the direction of this *Mudrā* is pointing downwards.

FORMATION

Interlace the middle, ring, and little fingers of both hands with each other. Extend the index fingers and place them against each other. Cross your thumbs and place each in the hollow of the other thumb. When seated, point the index fingers to the ground. When lying down, point them in the direction of your feet.

BENEFITS

1. The main benefit of this *Mudrā* is that it stimulates elimination through the large intestine, skin (perspiration), and lungs (improves exhalation), as well as removes expended energies.

2. On another level, this *Mudrā* connects one with the nectar or ambrosia of immortality, unveiling the highest truth.

Kṣepaṇa Mudrā

LIṄGA MUDRĀ

Mudrā for Lungs

Liṅga means the "male sexual organ, the phallus." This *Mudrā* is known as *Śiva Liṅga Mudrā*, to symbolize the masculine solar energy. The thumb also represents the spine, the fire element, *Śiva*, and masculine energy. This *Mudrā* is the invocation of all these attributes. It is a *Mudrā* from *Yoga Tattva Mudrā Vijñāna*, and it is also a *Mudrā* in *Hindu* tradition used during prayers and rituals.

FORMATION

Externally interlace the fingers of both hands in such a way that the little finger of the left hand is the downmost and the left-hand thumb extends straight up. Embrace the left-hand thumb with the right-hand index finger and thumb to join the tips at the back of the left hand's palm. Hold the palms together tightly. Hold the hands in front of the chest, with the hands exerting a little pressure against each other. It is a *Saṁyukta* (both hands) *Mudrā*.

BENEFITS

1. It is an excellent *Mudrā* to break the phlegm and relieve a person of frequent coughs and colds.
2. It also works great when the temperature suddenly falls and one shivers in the cold. Practicing this *Mudrā* will generate heat in the body and provide the necessary warmth in cases of hypothermia by retaining body heat.
3. It acts as prevention in case of Raynaud's syndrome, preceding the practice of *Vyāna Mudrā* on a regular basis.
4. It also relieves bronchial spasms and calms down the breath. It is fruitful if practiced by a person suffering from bronchitis, lung cancer, or asthma.
5. It activates the digestive fire by activating the *agni*, which in turn boosts the metabolic rate of the body in case of sluggish digestion.
6. It also helps in cases of low blood pressure, mild paralytic attack, and sinusitis.
7. It is also beneficial in case of hypothyroidism.

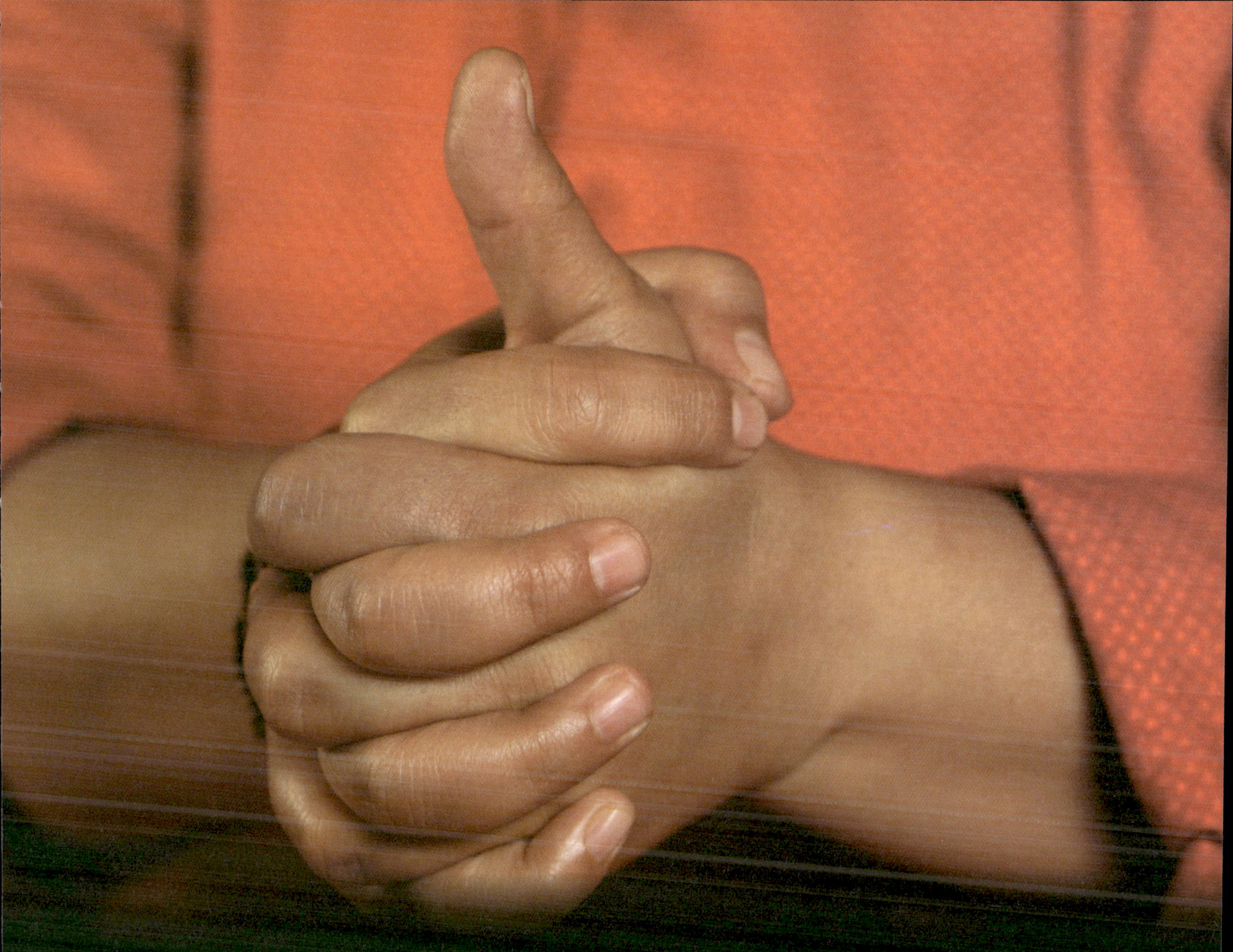

Liṅga Mudrā

CAUTION

One must discontinue the Mudrā in case of dizziness, uneasiness, or nausea. People with acidity/acid reflux/heartburn must observe caution and should discontinue the practice in case of any adverse reaction. One should not practice this Mudrā immediately after meals.

MAHĀJÑĀNA MUDRĀ

Mudrā for Pratyāhāra: Detachment

Mahā means "great," *Jñāna* means "wisdom." The greatest wisdom comes after attachment also known as *Vairāgya*. It is an *Asaṁyukta* (single hand) *Mudrā* that is generally practiced using the right hand.

FORMATION

Bend the little finger and the ring finger (ring finger symbolizes Sun and little finger symbolizes planet Mercury) in the center of the palm; press the back of the second phalange of both these fingers with the thumb pad. The index and the middle fingers are extended; the hands are kept on the knee, or extended sideways like the wings of a bird (in this case, the *Mudrā* is practiced with both hands), or kept at the level of the shoulder, palms facing forward during meditation.

VARIATION

A variation of this *Mudrā* is done by resting the left hand on the left knee in *Jñāna Mudrā*, and the right hand close to the heart in *Jñāna Mudrā*.

BENEFITS

1. It helps in detachment from the past and the future; detachment from the action as well as its fruits; detachment from actions, reactions, and interactions; detachment from childhood traumas, old wounds, fear, and anger; and detachment from all kind of dualities of emotions and experiences.
2. This *Mudrā* helps in the activating and rising of dormant energy from the root center (*Mūlādhāra Cakra)* to the higher centers.

Mahājñāna Mudrā
Variation

MAHĀŚĪRṢA MUDRĀ

Mudrā for Migraines and Tension

Mahā means "great or big," *Śīrṣa* means "head." Here, the meaning of *Mahāśīrṣa* is a person, who thinks a lot, or a person who takes huge responsibilities on himself/herself, or a person in a very high position. This is an *Asaṁyukta* (single hand) *Mudrā*. This *Mudrā* has its origin in *Yoga Tattva Mudrā Vijñāna*.

FORMATION

Bend the ring finger into the center of the palm; join the tips of the thumb, the index finger, and the middle finger. Extend the little finger and rest the hands on the knee, with the hand parallel to the floor or by your side in case of lying down or standing.

BENEFITS

1. It relieves tension, headaches, and migraines.
2. It relieves tension from the sensory and facial organs like eyes, nose, and jaw.
3. It distributes the concentrated energy that tends to get blocked, into the rest of the body.
4. It also helps in eliminating mucus congestion in the frontal sinuses.

Mahāśīrṣa Mudrā

MṚGA MUDRĀ

BIDĀLA MUDRĀ

Mudrā for Irregular Blood Pressure

Mṛga means "deer." *Mṛga Mudrā* is so called because the shadow of this *Mudrā* mimics the head of a deer. In the formation of this *Mudrā*, the middle two fingers put a deep pressure on the first - 1/3rd part of the palm – which is the area of the heart and lungs – to help bring about a rhythm in blood circulation and the respiratory system. The index finger and the little finger are extended, allowing for the free and smooth circulation of water and air elements. It is an *Asaṁyukta* (single hand)/*Saṁyukta* (both hands) *Mudrā* of *Yoga Tattva Mudrā Vijñāna*.

FORMATION

Make a fist with both the hands, fingers really digging into the center of the palm. Now, open up the index finger, the little finger, and the thumb, keeping them reasonably extended. Rest the hands on the knee facing up by keeping the elbow straight.

BENEFITS

The basic benefit of this *Mudrā* is to bring a balance of high as well as low blood pressure – that is, to maintain an optimum blood pressure.

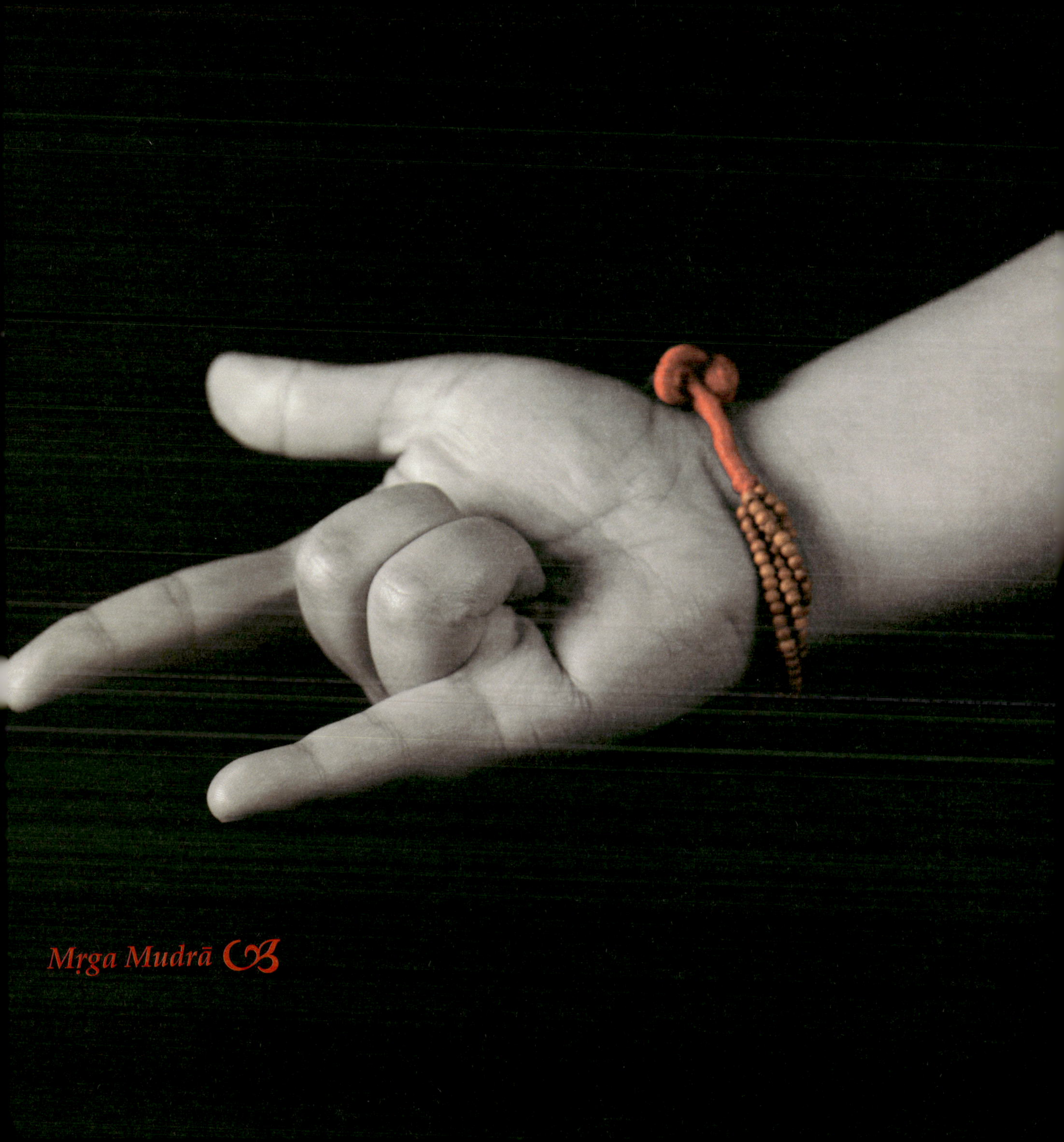

Mṛga Mudrā

MUṢṬI MUDRĀ

Mudrā for Strength and Willpower

*M**uṣṭi* means "fist." It is an *Asaṁyukta* (single hand) *Mudrā* of *Hindu* tradition.

FORMATION

Bend your fingers inward and place your thumbs over the fingers.

BENEFITS

1. *Muṣṭi Mudrā* activates the liver and stomach energy, promotes digestion, and helps cure constipation.
2. It also helps in strengthening the willpower and brings confidence.

VARIATIONS

It has many variations like *muṣṭika* (fist with both hands), *muṣṭi-mṛga* (with middle three fingers forming a fist and little finger and thumb extended out), *muṣṭi-svastikā* (hands in fist, crossed over at wrist level on abdomen), and *vajra muṣṭi* (with thumb inside fist). *Muṣṭikā-mṛga* and *Muṣṭi-svastikā* are practices in Indian classical dances. *Vajra muṣṭi* is a *Tantric Mudrā* common in Japanese Buddhist tradition.

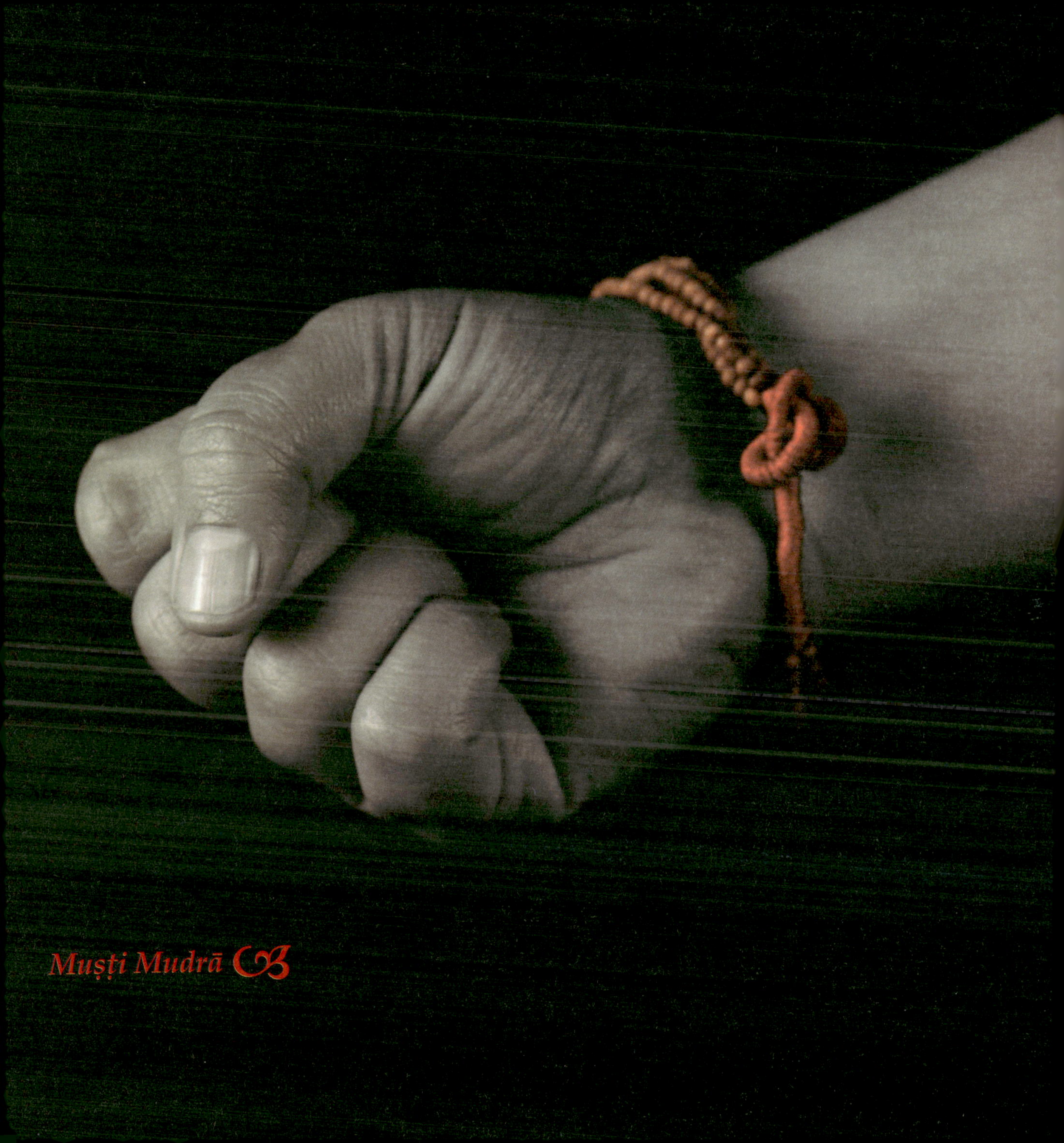

Muṣṭi Mudrā

PŪṢAN MUDRĀ

Mudrā for Nausea/Sickness/Solar Plexus

Pūṣan is another name for Sun. *Pūṣan Mudrā* is a *Saṁyukta* (both hands) *Mudrā*.

FORMATION

Part I: **Left Hand:** Join the tips of the thumb, the ring finger, and the little finger, and keep the index and middle fingers extended. This *Mudrā* symbolizes giving with the left hand and receiving with the right hand.

Part II: **Right Hand:** Join the tips of the thumb, the middle finger, and the ring finger, and keep the index and little fingers extended as in *Apāna Mudrā*. This *Mudrā* symbolizes giving and letting go.

BENEFITS

1. The regular practice of this *Mudrā* helps in digestion process, especially in cases of people suffering from heaviness, bloating, and indigestion post-meals.
2. It influences the energy currents that are responsible for absorbing and utilizing food, as well as helping with elimination by activating the *samāna* and *apāna vāyus*.
3. It intensifies breathing and, therefore, the absorption of oxygen and the release of carbon dioxide in the lungs.
4. It has a relaxing effect on the solar plexus (the area of the stomach, the liver, the spleen, and the gall bladder), regulates energies in the autonomic nervous system, mobilizes energies of elimination, and detoxifies.
5. It has an excellent effect on general or acute nausea, sea sickness, flatulence, and that sensation of fullness one feels after meals.

Prāna Mudrā
Apāna Mudrā

SANDHI MUDRĀ

Mudrā for Healthy Joints

Sandhi means "joint." It is a *Saṁyukta* (both hands) *Mudrā* of *Yoga Tattva Mudrā Vijñāna*.

FORMATION

In the right hand, join the ring fingertip with the tip of the thumb in *Pṛthivī Mudrā* (earth element gesture), keeping the middle, little, and index fingers extended. Rest the hand on the right knee. With the left hand, join the middle fingertip with the tip of the thumb in *Ākāśa Mudrā* (space element gesture), keeping the little, ring, and index fingers extended. Rest the hand on the left knee.

BENEFITS

1. The main benefit of this *Mudrā* is to mobilize the energy blockage around the main joints like knee, hip, neck, and shoulder activating the *vyāna vāta*.
2. It helps in easing out the joint pain.
3. Meditation practice in this *Mudrā* acts as a catalyst in releasing stiffness from the joints.

Ākāśa Mudrā
Pṛthivī Mudrā

ŚAṄKHA MUDRĀ

Mudrā for Speech Disorders

Śaṅkha means "conch." It is a *Saṁyukta* (both hands) *Mudrā*. It is used in *Yoga Tattva Mudrā Vijñāna* as well as in Indian classical dances.

FORMATION

To perform this *Mudrā*, fist the thumb of the left hand by keeping it at the centre of the palm of the right hand with the fingers, and then join the thumb of the right hand with the remaining fingers of the left hand at the tips. It forms the shape of a conch or *Śaṅkha*. This *Mudrā* is practiced any time of the day except after meals. One can perform this *Mudrā* in *Sukhāsana* or *Vajrāsana*, and should perform it for at least 10 minutes at a stretch to benefit out of it. Slowly increase the time limit to 45 minutes. One can also perform it in 3 sittings of 15 minutes each. It is a *Saṁyukta* (both hands) *Mudrā*.

BENEFITS

1. It removes speech disorders like stammering and stuttering. It gives sweetness to voice and renders it an attractive quality.
2. It removes disorders related to tonsils and throat. It also balances the thyroid gland, thereby bringing hormonal balance.
3. It keeps the navel center in order, making the person healthy and helping to keep the nervous system healthy and active.
4. It alleviates abdominal disorders and improves the digestive system.
5. It also helps an advanced *sādhaka* to meditate upon *anāhata nāda*.

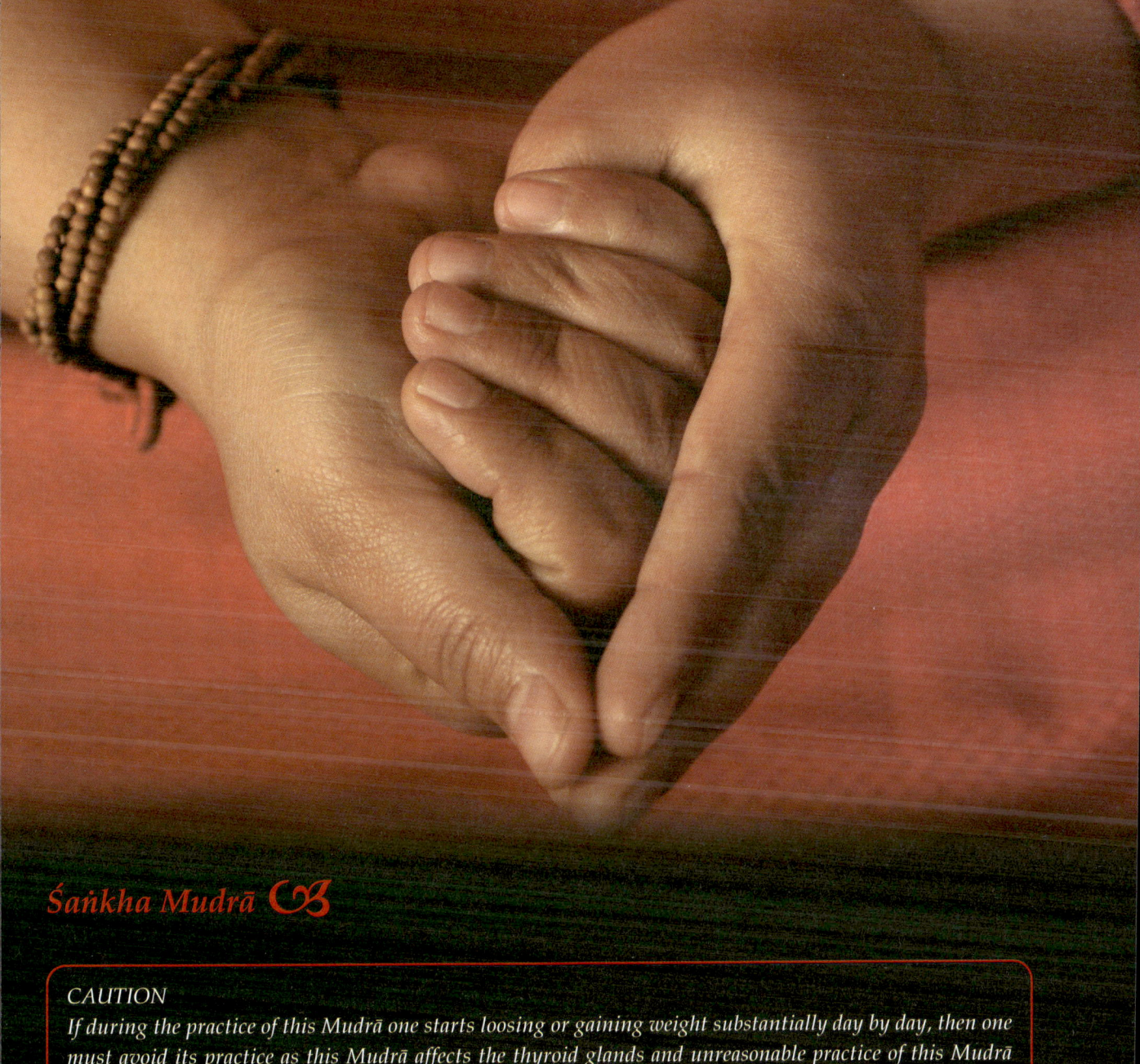

Śaṅkha Mudrā

CAUTION

If during the practice of this Mudrā one starts loosing or gaining weight substantially day by day, then one must avoid its practice as this Mudrā affects the thyroid glands and unreasonable practice of this Mudrā may hypo/hyper-activate the thyroid glands.

Śūnya Mudrā

Ākāśa Śāmaka Mudrā

Mudrā for Hearing Impairment

Śūnya means "void, ether, or space." It can be explained by many names. This is an *Asaṁyukta* (single hand) *Mudrā* and it has its origins in *Yoga Tattva Mudrā Vijñāna*. Ether is the subtlest of the five elements and the first element in creation of the (five organs of senses) *jñānedriya*, the (five organs of action) *karmendriya*, *manas*, and *buddhi*. It is the gateway to higher consciousness or a bridge to the other dimension. An imbalance in this element affects the hearing, perception, and cognition of sound, making it difficult to hear, recognize, and interpret sounds within the range of human perception. It is the *Ākāśā Śāmaka Mudrā*. *Ākāśā* means "ether" and *Śāmaka* means "to decrease;" hence, it is the *Mudrā* that decreases the excess ether element.

FORMATION

Bend the middle finger at the mount/base of the thumb and then press the second phalange (joint) of this finger with the thumb. Keep the rest of the three fingers (index, ring, and little) extended. Rest the hand on the knee with the palms facing up. Practice it using one hand or both hands.

BENEFITS

1. *Śūnya Mudrā* is a first aid in relieving earache.
2. It helps in neutralizing the air pressure that builds up during the take-off and landing in a flight. One may safely memorize it as Take-off and landing *Mudrā*.
3. It also relieves the uneasiness, pain, and dizziness related to airsickness.
4. It is highly beneficial in cases of mild to severe hearing impairment.

Śūnya Mudrā

Śvāsa-Nalikā Mudrā

Mudrā for healthy Bronchioles

Śvāsa means "breath/air" and *Nalikā* means "tube or channel." A channel through which the breath/air flows. *Śvāsa-nalikā* is "bronchiole" in english and is a main part of the lungs as a respiratory organ. This *Mudrā* helps building inner strength as well as strengthening the bronchioles to fight infections and inflammations. It is an *Asaṁyukta* (single hand) *Mudrā* of *Yoga Tattva Mudrā Vijñāna*.

FORMATION

Extend the right hand at the level of the chest; keep the elbow bent by the side of the chest. Open the right palm; bring the right little finger at the mount of the thumb. Rest the ring fingertip on the first phalange (joint) of the thumb from the inner side. Join the middle fingertip to the tip of the thumb, and extend the index finger.

BENEFIT

The main benefit of the *Mudrā* is in strengthening and stretching the bronchioles to prevent bronchitis, recurrent asthma attacks, and shallow breathing, and in opening up the heart to release negative emotions and experiences.

Śvāsa-Nalikā Mudrā

Śvāsī Cikitsā Mudrā

Mudrā for Asthma

Śvāsī means "one who breathes heavily" and *Cikitsā* means "therapy." This *Mudrā* helps in healing the lungs by clearing up the inflammation and deepening the breath. It is a *Saṁyukta* (both hands) *Mudrā* of *Yoga Tattva Mudrā Vijñāna*.

FORMATION

Bring the palms of both hands at the chest level. Face the palms to each other, keeping them a few inches apart. Bend the middle finger of hands inwards, keeping the index, ring, and little fingers extended and spread upwards. Join the middle finger's bent part from second phalange to the nail tip, back to back, as you point them downwards. Try not to bend the first phalange of the middle finger. The thumbs do not touch each other. Spread and extend the thumbs like the rest of the fingers.

BENEFITS

1. This *Mudrā* is a first aid in case of an acute asthma attack.
2. One may practice this *Mudrā* before meditation as it also helps in deepening the breathing and releasing bronchial spasms.
3. It is a wonderful combination with the *Śvāsī Nalikā Mudrā*. The practice of *Śvāsī Nalikā Mudrā* precedes the practice of *Śvāsī Cikitsā Mudrā*.
4. It pacifies the *kapha doṣa* from the channels of *prāṇa*.

Śvāsī Cikitsā Mudrā

SURABHĪ MUDRĀ

DHENU MUDRĀ

Wish-Fulfilling Mudrā

Surabhī is a synonym for cows; it also means, the fragrant one. According to the Monier Williams *Sanskrit*-English Dictionary (1899), *Surabhī* means fragrant, charming, and pleasing, as well as cow and earth. *Kāma* means "desire or passion," and *Dhenu* means "cow." *Kāmadhenu* is a divine Bovine-Goddess described in *Hindu* mythology as the mother of all cows. She is a miraculous "cow of plenty" who provides her owner whatever he desires. *Hindu* scriptures portray her as the mother of all other cattle. The scriptures provide an account of the birth of *Kāmadhenu* in which she emerged from the churning of the cosmic ocean.

FORMATION

Let the two palms face each other and keep them parallel to each other. All the fingers extend pointing upwards. Rest the hands at the level of the chest.

Part I: Move the ring finger of the left hand to join its tip to the tip of the little finger of the right hand. Similarly, the ring finger of the right hand joins the tip of the little finger of the left hand.

Part II: Move the middle finger of the left hand to join its tip to the tip of the index finger of the right hand. Similarly, the middle finger of the right hand joins the tip of the index finger of the left hand.

Part III: Keep the thumbs spread out, not touching any part of the hand and pointed towards the heart.

Surabhī Mudrā

Variations: *This Mudrā has four variations:*

1. ***Vāyu-Surabhī Mudrā:*** A variation of the basic *Surabhī Mudrā*, it helps to eliminate all ailments resulting from the increase of wind in the system. To form this, attain the basic *Surabhī Mudrā* and touch the tip of the left-hand thumb at the base of the index finger of the right hand, and touch the tip of the right-hand thumb at the base of the index finger of the left hand. This completes the *Vāyu-Surabhī Mudrā.*
2. ***Śūnya-Surabhī Mudrā:*** By increasing the ethereal vacuity, it helps the *Sādhaka* to increase the hearing power manifold. To form this, attain the basic *Surabhī Mudrā* and touch the tip of the left-hand thumb at the base of the middle finger of the right hand, and touch the tip of the right-hand thumb at the base of the middle finger of the left hand. This completes the *Śūnya Surabhī Mudrā.*
3. ***Pṛthivī -Surabhī Mudrā:*** It helps to cure all ailments of the stomach generated due to defects in the digestive system, and is especially effective for people with chronic digestive ailments. To form this, attain the basic *Surabhī Mudrā* and touch the tip of the left-hand thumb at the base of the ring finger of the right hand, and touch the tip of the right-hand thumb at the base of the ring finger of the left hand. This completes the *Pṛthivī -Surabhī Mudrā.*
4. ***Jala-Surabhī Mudrā:*** This *Mudrā* helps to cure and eliminate diseases related to bile. It helps in curing diseases related to urine and assists in easy passage of urine. To form this, attain the basic *Surabhī Mudrā* and touch the tip of the left-hand thumb at the base of the little finger of the right hand, and touch the tip of the right-hand thumb at the base of the little finger of the left hand. This completes the *Pṛthivī Jala-Surabhī Mudrā.*

(Note: These four variations are just for your reference and the pictures of these are not included in this book. These are advanced Mudrā and you may practice them after mastery over the basic Surabhī Mudrā.)

BENEFITS

1. *Surabhī Mudrā* is a very effective and powerful *Mudrā*. By itself, this *Mudrā* helps a *Sādhaka* (an aspirant practitioner) to break any barriers that he/she may face when on the threshold of *samādhi* (the ultimate meditation).
2. In this *Mudrā*, the ethereal elements combine such as to magnify and multiply their powers and

produce powerful results on the body. *Vāyu* (air element) meets *Ākāśa* (ether element) to stabilize the *Cakra* (circle) of the universe. *Pṛthivī* (earth element) meets *Jala* (water element) to produce the generative power of the universe.

3. With constant practice, this *Mudrā* helps to stabilize and strengthen the *Maṇipūra Cakra* (solar plexus). During the awakening of the *Kuṇḍalinī Śakti* (the life force seated dormant at the *Mūlādhāra Cakra*), it generally gets stuck at *Maṇipra Cakra*. The regular practice of this *Mudrā* makes the *cakra* strong enough to withstand the rising force as well as helps it to move upwards to a higher center.

4. One may do a *Saṅkalpa* (internal resolution) of the desire one wishes to be fulfilled before the practice, and then practice the *Mudrā* to make it a *Sakāma* practice (Sa means "with"; *Kāma* means "passion" or "desire"; thus, it is a practice that is done with a particular desire in the heart).

Surabhī Mudrā

TSE MUDRĀ

Mudrā for Depression

A *Mudrā* of Chinese and Tao tradition, it is an *Asaṁyukta* (single hand) *Mudrā*. *Tse* means "strong and powerful like a rock." It has masculine energy.

FORMATION

The formation of this *Mudrā* is like making a fist with the thumb tip resting at the root of the little finger. To trigger the strength hidden in this *Mudrā*, inhale as you form the fist, rest the fist on the thighs with knuckles facing up, hold the breath, and internally chant your personal *mantra*; when you feel the need to exhale, relax your abdomen and release the fist. Do this four to five times, or as long as you enjoy the process.

BENEFITS

1. It helps in cases of depression, inertia, and dullness removing *tamas* and invoking *sāttvika rajas.*
2. It helps in awakening the masculine solar energy of the body activating the *piṅgalā nāḍī.*
3. It helps in relieving constipation, and strengthens the digestive system.
4. It helps in relieving gases and flatulence.
5. It helps in releasing repressed emotions and in channelizing anger and aggression.

Kim Tawm, an authority on Chinese medicine, writes that according to the Taoist monks, *"Tradition says that this Mudrā chases away sadness, reduces fearfulness, turns away misfortune and bad luck, and overcomes depression."*

Tse Mudrā

ŪRU MUDRĀ

MUDRĀ FOR EASY BREATH

Sukhada Prāṇāyāma

Ūru means "thighs." This *Mudrā* is a *Saṁyukta* (both hands) *Mudrā*.

FORMATION

Sit in *Vajrāsana* and rest your palms on your thighs facing midline. Keep all the fingers together and extended. The thumbs are facing the inner thighs joint. Try to keep the elbows straight.

BENEFITS

1. One of the main benefits of this *Mudrā* is that it is a preparation for meditation as well as relaxation. It naturally invokes the rhythm of comfortable breath and establishes *Sukhada Prāṇāyāma*: easy, without sound, continuous, smooth and deep breath.
2. It helps in the practice of *Śītalī-karaṇa*: the relaxation and calming down of the body, the mind, and the nervous system before the practice of *Yoga Nidrā*.
3. This *Mudrā* may be practiced by anyone just to calm down the nervous system and *vāta doṣa*.
4. It helps in cases of fatigue, stress, and exertion.
5. It also helps in dealing with hypertension.

Ūru Mudrā

VARUṆA MUDRĀ

Mudrā to Relieve Congestion

Varuṇa is the God of water element. This *Mudrā* is from *Yoga Tattva Mudrā Vijñāna* and is a *Asaṁyukta* (single hand) *Mudrā*.

FORMATION

Bend the little finger of right hand into palm and hold in place with right thumb. Wrap the left-hand fingers around the back of the right hand and press left thumb over right thumb. Keep the palms facing up and rest the *Mudrā* on the lap.

BENEFITS

1. It balances water element in the body by redistribution of fluids.
2. It helps in relieving mucus congestion from the sinuses, bronchioles, digestive tract, and lungs.
3. It may also help in cases of flatulence and bloating.

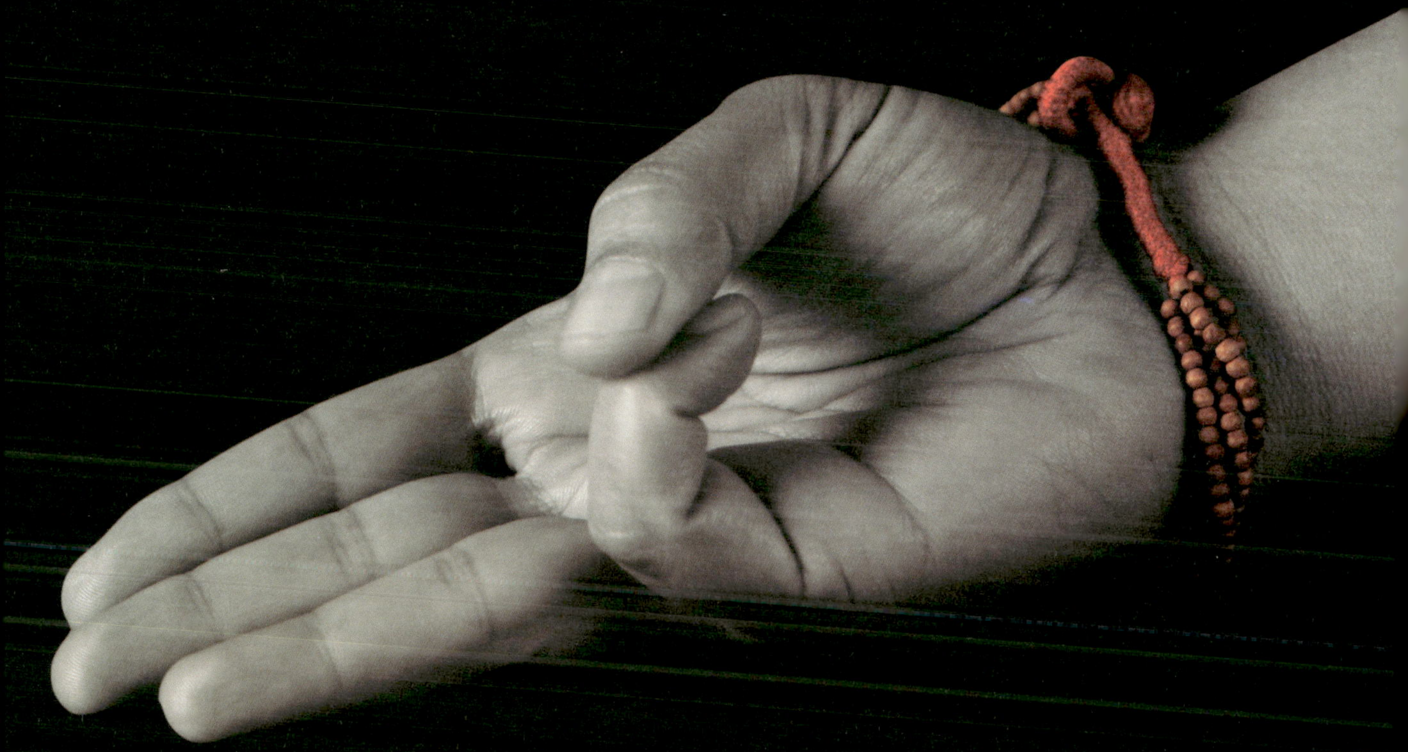

Varuṇa Mudrā ଓ

CAUTION

Do not practice this Mudrā in case of dry cough

Viparīta Namaskāra Mudrā

Madhumeha Mudrā for Diabetes

Viparīta means "reverse," this *Mudrā* is similar to *Namaskāra Mudrā* in formation but is a reverse formation. It is a *Mudrā* of *Yoga Tattva Mudrā Vijñāna* and is a *Saṁyukta* (both hands) *Mudrā. Madhu* means "honey" and *Madhumeha* means "one who is overflowing with sweetness"–known as diabetes in modern language. It is based on the science of *mardana* (acupressure) and *marma cikitsā*, and activates the pancreas by putting pressure in the center of the palms as you join them back to back for the formation of this *Mudrā*.

FORMATION

Join the back of the hands from nails to the base of wrist, thumbs facing outwards and the little finger towards the heart. Extend and point all the fingers upwards. Spread the thumb out 90 degrees from the rest of the hand, and point away from the body, putting a pressure in the center of the palm, which is the acupressure region for pancreas. Rest the hands close to the chest in the center of the chest bone.

BENEFITS

1. Activates the pancreas.
2. Improves circulation of *prāṇa, tejas* and *ojas* around the pancreas.
3. Stimulates the digestive fire and *samāna vāyu*.
4. Activates the *tālahṛdya marma* and *maṇibandha marma*.

Viparīta Mudrā

CAUTION

Keep an eye on your blood sugar levels during the sādhanā of this Mudrā. Go for a laboratory test/ primary physician after a practice of 2 weeks (3 times a day for 5 minutes in each session)

Summary

"Nothing has the greatest power to heal, but self", has been my vision, my mission, my realization and an essential part of the message that I have been sharing since I began my journey in *Yoga*. It sounds like a very empowering and catchy phrase, but to understand it might take life time of experiences... multiple contrations and extensions... reaching out and reaching within!
What better tool can nature bless us with than we ourselves, who else do you think has the ability to delve into the deepest core and secret of your being and dig out the reason for the conflict with your own body and mind?

The Self is the most powerful entity, the key lies in becoming aware of this secret so that it does not remains a secret! Just taking a deep breath, brings your attention from the outside to the inside, this itself allows for the realization that it is all about me and no one else...
Yes, it is easy to look outside but have you ever found your real answers/ solutions there... anyone?

The blessing of *Mudrā* has been bestowed upon us, but its practice is what shall bridge the gap between the state of health and us. Don't loose any chance to connect to self…explore these *Mudrās*, one at a time and practice it for few days to see its effect. Do not loose hope if you do not see any tangible result, be assured that each cell of your body is moving every time you are in practice and there is a subtle ripple effect building up…each cell is pregnant with dynamic energy, all we have to do is to connect. Do not loose any moment…

Nothing to loose

Nothing to gain

Neither the happiness...

Nor the pain!

Be on the tides

or on the plains...

Neither too mad...

Nor too sane

At times "nothing"

At times just a "name"

In the moment, it is all a "game"

It is still this moment

That should not go in "vain"

Yoga Tattva Mudrā

Five Element Mudrās

Mudrā of Five Great Elements:
Yoga Pañca Tattva Mudrā / Pañca Mahābhūta Mudrā

Pañca means "five," *Mahā* means "great," and *Bhūtas* mean "elements." The five *Mudrās* in this category are all *Asaṁyukta* (single hand) *Mudrās* and are a classic example of *Yoga Tattva Mudrā Vijñāna*. Each *Mudrā* helps in restoring one of the five elements (earth, water, fire, air, ether) to their perfect balance. These *Mudrās* are very specific and practiced after a thorough understanding of the disturbance in the body.

PṚTHIVĪ MUDRĀ

EARTH GESTURE

The Mudrā of Strength and Solidity

Pṛthivī means "earth," *Vardhaka* means "to increase," and so, this is a *Mudrā* that increases the earth element in the body. It is commonly known as *Pṛthivī Mudrā* or *Pṛthivī Vardhaka Mudrā.* It is an *Asaṁyukta* (single hand) *Mudrā.* It belongs to the *Yoga Tattva Mudrā Vijñāna* and *Yogic* tradition.

FORMATION

Touch the tip of the thumb to the tip of the ring finger, keeping the rest of the three fingers (index, middle, and little) extended. Rest the hands on the knee as you sit in any meditative pose.

BENEFITS

1. It compensates for the excess of *rajasic guṇa*.
2. It helps boost the blood circulation in the body.
3. It increases tolerance and patience.
4. It helps in grounding during meditation.
5. Since this *Mudrā* is an association of the earth element with the powerful sun, it brings strength and solidity to the body.
6. It helps increase the earth element, which expresses itself as flesh and bones. This can be extremely fruitful in cases of emaciation, debilitating diseases, and muscle wasting, as also for people for whom it is difficult to add muscle mass to the body and in cases of inexplicable weight loss.
7. It wards off weakness, fatigue, and dullness, and invokes *prāṇic* energy in the body.
8. It adds to the aura of a person by working on the *sūkṣma śarīra* and activating *prāṇic* circulation by forming a strong and powerful electromagnetic field.

Pṛthivī Mudrā

Jala Mudrā

Water Gesture

The Mudrā of Hydration and Luster

Jala means "water" and *Vardhaka* means "to increase." It is also known as *Jala Vardhaka Mudrā*. This *Mudrā* increases the circulation of fluids in the body and is an *Asaṁyukta* (single hand) *Mudrā*. It belongs to the *Yoga Tattva Mudrā Vijñāna* and *Yogic* tradition.

FORMATION

To form this *Mudrā*, join the little fingertip with the tip of the thumb, keeping the rest of the three fingers (index, middle, and ring) straight/ extended.

BENEFITS

1. As the name suggests, this *Mudrā* is an association of water element with the fire. *Varuṇa* is the God of water element.
2. It is also a thirst-quenching *Mudrā* that activates the salivary glands.
3. It helps in the purification, distribution, and circulation of bodily fluids, relieving dehydration.
4. It activates the kidney functioning by relieving it of urine retention.
5. It is excellent for curing skin disorders like skin infections, dryness, and dark patches.
6. It purifies the blood and takes care of many blood disorders.
7. It brings luster and glow to the body and prevents pre mature aging of the skin.
8. It helps ease constipation.
9. You may practice this *Mudrā* instead of sipping water when practicing *Yoga*, as it helps in activating the water element while exercising or while practicing *Yoga*.
10. It also helps in absorption of the nourishment from the skin (topically applied, like oils, lotions, and cremes) into the deeper layers of skin.

Jala Mudrā

CAUTION
Make sure you do not press the tip of the little finger near the nail as it causes dehydration rather than hydrating the system.

AGNI MUDRĀ

FIRE GESTURE

The Mudrā of Metabolism

Agni means "fire," this *Mudrā* helps in balancing as well as activating the fire element. It is also called *Pṛthivī Śāmaka Mudrā*. *Pṛthivī* means "earth" and *Śāmaka* means "to reduce." Hence, this *Mudrā* reduces excess earth element. It is an *Asaṁyukta* (single hand) *Mudrā*. It belongs to the *Yoga Tattva Mudrā Vijñāna* and *Yogic* tradition.

FORMATION

Bend the ring finger from the second phalange at the base of thumb and press it with the thumb at the second phalange of the ring finger itself. Keep the rest of the three fingers straight and perform it in sitting position only.

BENEFITS

1. It helps mobilize and burn extra fat of the body by balancing the metabolic rate.
2. It burns the excess phlegm.
3. It boosts sluggish digestion.
4. It improves appetite.
5. It is very effective in reducing increased cholesterol (bad cholesterol) levels.
6. It provides heat and energy to the body in case of cold climates.
7. It decreases earth element in the body and improves concentration and retention.
8. It decreases the *tamasic guṇa* like inertia, laziness, inertness, and lack of motivation and passion.

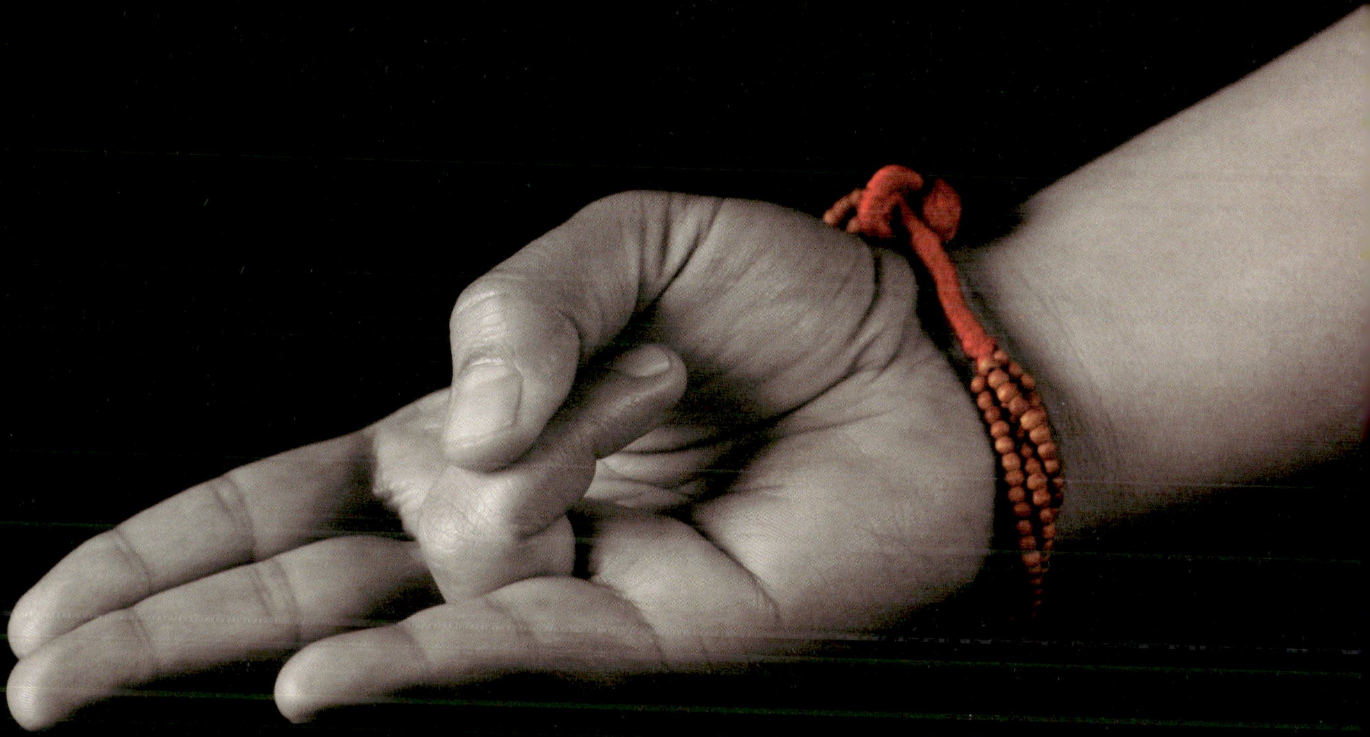

Agni Mudrā

CAUTION

One must perform it on empty stomach. Keep it for at least 15 minutes at a stretch and two to three times daily, to achieve the results. One must discontinue performing this Mudrā in case of acidity, heartburn, or indigestion.

VĀYU MUDRĀ

AIR GESTURE

The Mudrā of Pain Relief

Vāyu means "air" and *Śāmaka* means "to neutralize" or "to nullify." *Vāyu Mudrā* is also known as *Vāyu Śāmaka Mudrā* in *Ayurveda*. It is an *Asaṁyukta* (single hand) *Mudrā*. It belongs to the *Yoga Tattva Mudrā Vijñāna* and *Yogic* tradition.

FORMATION

Bend the index finger from the second joint to the root of the thumb, and press the back of the second phalange with the thumb. Keep the other three fingers (middle, ring, and little) as straight as possible. This can be practiced before or after meals.

BENEFITS

1. It releases extra wind from the stomach (flatulence) and the body, thereby taking care of pains and aches as a first aid.
2. It helps in rheumatic pains, gout, paralysis, Parkinson's disease, chest pains, etc., and in any pain that is caused due to imbalance of air element.

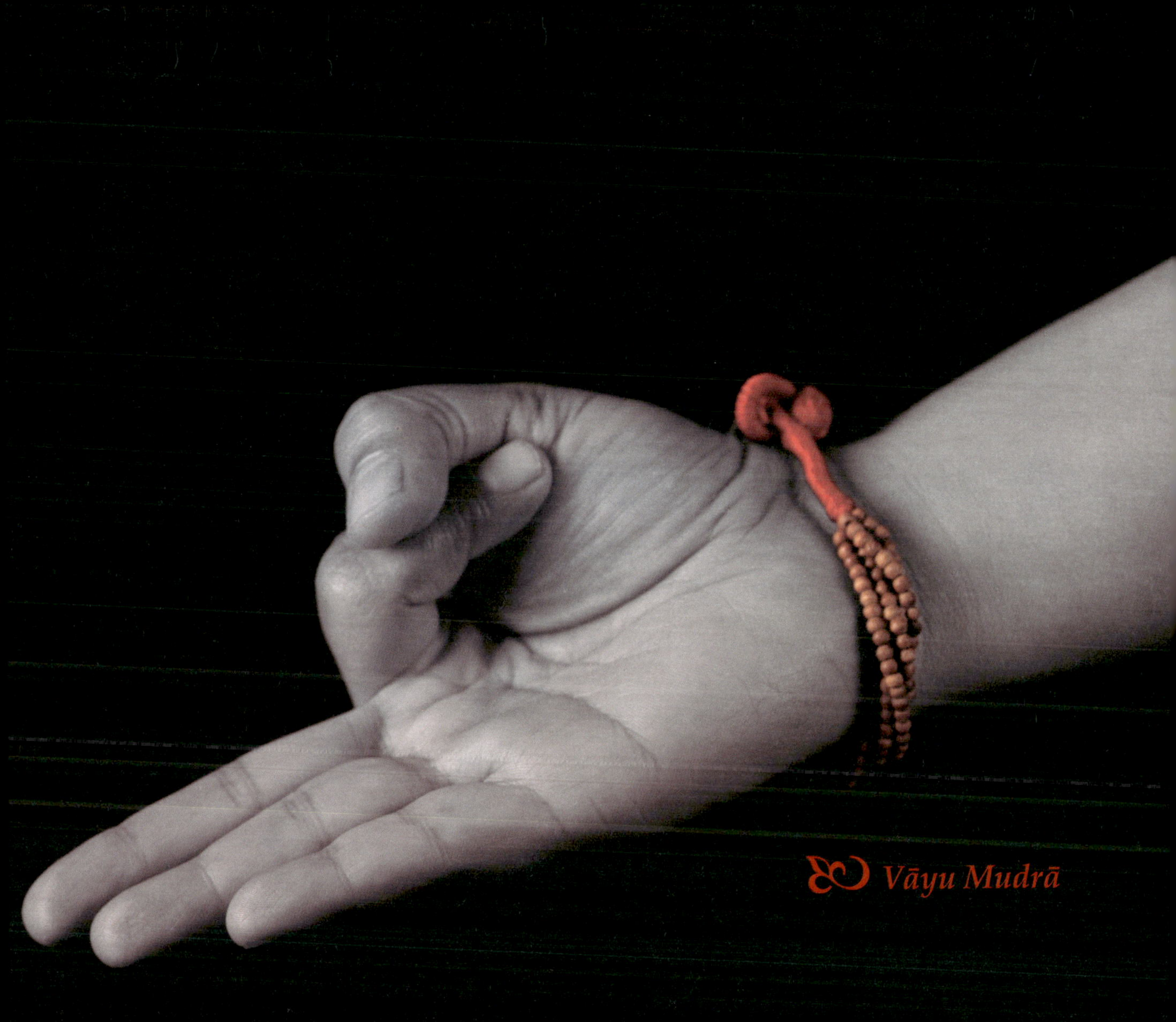

Vāyu Mudrā

CAUTION
This Mudrā works through alternating the air current by decreasing and then increasing it; so, care should be taken to practice it only for therapy purposes and it should be released as soon as relief is attained.

Ākāśa Mudrā

Ether Gesture

The Mudrā of Creation and Annihilation of Space

Ākāśa is the "space element" and *Vardhaka* means "to increase." This *Mudrā is* commonly known as *Ākāśa Mudrā*, it is also called *Ākāśa Vardhaka Mudrā* in *Ayurveda*. It is an *Asaṁyukta* (single hand) *Mudrā*. It belongs to the *Yoga Tattva Mudrā Vijñāna* and *Yogic* tradition.

FORMATION

Join the tip of the middle finger with the tip of the thumb, keeping the rest of the three fingers (little, ring, and index) straight. The best time for practicing this *Mudrā* is in the morning, by sitting in either *Sukhāsana* or *Padmāsana*.

BENEFITS

1. As the name suggests, this *Mudrā* is a combination of ether element (middle finger) with the sun (thumb) and thus come the powers to heal any ailment pertaining to sound. It is excellent to increase the sensitivity to hear sounds. It is a boon in combination with *Śūnya Mudrā* for those hard of hearing
2. This *Mudrā* activates the calcium and phosphorus absorption into the bones, so it is helpful in cases of weakness of bone, like osteoporosis and osteopenia.
3. Due to its inherent quality of releasing tensions and keeping the mind calm and serene, this *Mudrā* is practiced during meditation. It is also a great *Mudrā* for an anxious and ever-processing mind.
4. It is a first aid in case of dizziness.
5. This *Mudrā* is successful in taking care of the "lockjaw" experienced at times during yawning, or during mental tension or over-exertion.

ॐ Ākāśa Mudrā

Summary

A balance and harmony of the five elements is the basic foundation of physical, mental and emotional well being and co-ordination. 10-minute meditation on these *Mudrās* is a very simple way to keep the elements in balance and in harmony.

Pañca Tattva Mudrā Meditation:

1. Take a comfortable seated posture with straight spine.
2. Allow your breath to become diaphragmatic.
3. Allow the breath to attain the four qualities (silent, deep, without breaks and prolonged).
4. Begin the practice of *Pañca Tattva Mudrās* with the *Ākāśa Mudrā*, sequentially going through all the other four, ending with the *Pṛthivī Mudrā*.
5. Hold each *Mudrā* for at least 2 minutes in each hand.
6. Although it is not necessary to be in contemplative mode, but generally the practice itself will trigger a meditative state of mind and breath.

A daily practice of this would ensure a healthy metabolism, glowing skin, mobile joints, focused mind and sharp senses.

I promise my being to be an instrument in the hands of Nature so that …

I may

Spread like fragrance in Air

Ignite the spirit of enlightenment like Fire

Bind the humans together like Water

Support and ground like the Earth

Dissolve the Space within and outside to become One

Yoga is Union and Sublimation

I have the Same Intention…

Pañca Prāṇa Upāsanā Mudrā

The Mudrā of Five Vital Currents

The word *Pañca* means "five," *Prāṇa* means "vital energy current," and *Upāsanā* means "worship." The series of five *Mudrās* refers to the five main vital *prāṇic* currents in the *prāṇamaya kośa* (the second energetic sheath). The five main vital currents are *prāṇa, samāna, vyāna, udāna,* and *apāna*. We shall discuss these five vital airs as we discuss their *Mudrās*. Here, it is important to note that the proper distribution and functioning of these five airs are important to accomplish the smallest of tasks and to perform the minutest of movements. The use of this series is to be before the intake of food to allow for the proper absorption and assimilation of energy from the food. Now, let us discuss them one by one in the series to be practiced, although they can also be practiced individually as a therapy.

PRĀṆA MUDRĀ

The Glorious Mudrā

Prāṇa is the forward and inward moving energy impulse that helps in drawing energy in the form of food, sunlight, water, and air into the body. This is the most vital current - as long as this current is in the body, the body is considered living, and as soon as it leaves the body, the body is said to be inert and dead. The region of *prāṇa* current is the head and chest region. This *Mudrā* is also known as *Kapha Kāraka-Pitta Nāśaka Mudrā*, one that increases the earth element and reduces too much fire, and activates and triggers the nourishment principle in the body. In the ritual of food intake, this is the first *Mudrā* that is practiced by holding a little bit of food in-between the little finger, the ring finger, and the thumb. The *mantra*, *OM Prāṇāya Svāhā*, is recited and then the morsel is taken in with the intention that the food becomes *prāṇic* energy and distributed in the body for assimilation and further processes.

FORMATION

This *Mudrā* is formed by joining the tip of the little finger and the ring finger with the tip of the thumb, and the other two fingers (middle and index) are kept straight. It can be done by both the hands at the same time as a *Saṁyukta Mudrā*. Rest the hands on the knees by keeping the elbow straight. It should preferably be done on empty stomach.

BENEFITS

1. It acts like a storehouse of *prāṇa* or energy, and is also called the "glorious *Mudrā*."
2. It is highly recommended in case of poor, blurred vision and locked pupils.
3. It enhances the absorption of vital nutrients and vitamins from the diet, boosting the energy levels of the body.
4. It is also a wonderful *Mudrā* for bedridden people, providing them energy and strength.

Prāṇa Mudrā

A variation of this *Mudrā*, known as *Pitta Kāraka-Kapha Nāśaka Mudrā*, can be practiced by bending the little and ring fingers at the base of the thumb and pressuring the second phalange of these two fingers together with the thumb. *Pitta Kāraka* means one that increases *(Kāraka)* the fire *(Pitta)*, and *Kapha Nāśaka* means one that melts/ destroys *(Nāśaka)* and mobilizes the fat *(Kapha)*, mucus, and excess earth element from the body. This is an excellent Mudrā for people having a *kapha* excess or a pitta deficiency in their bodies, especially in case of sluggish digestion, poor basal metabolic rate and inertia.

SAMĀNA MUDRĀ

The Gesture of Assimilation

Samāna means "similar," and here, it refers to converting food into a form that is utilized by the body as nourishment. The movement of *samāna* is clockwise-centripital and its region is the abdominal region. It is also known as *Tridoṣa Nāśaka Mudrā*. *Tri* means "three," *Doṣa* means "bodily humors," and *Nāśaka* means to "annihilate" or "neutralize." This *Mudrā* pacifies all the three bodily humors, namely *vāta* (air imbalance), *pitta* (fire imbalance), and *kapha* (earth and water imbalance). This is the main vital current in digestion of food. Before intake, the food is held in the *Mudrā* and the *mantra*, *OM Samānāya Svāhā*, is recited before ingesting the food. It can be practiced as *Saṁyukta Mudrā* (both hands) or *Asaṁyukta Mudrā* (single hand).

FORMATION

Join the index, middle, ring, and little fingertips with the thumb tip to balance the *samāna vāyu* in the body. In Indian tradition, food is ingested using hands; thus, all the food fingers and thumb naturally make the *Samāna Mudrā* and help in the process of digestion.

BENEFITS

1. It helps in digesting the food properly.
2. It reduces the formation of gases and acids in the body.
3. It balances the *pañca vāyus* (five vital airs) and the *pañca tattvas* (five elements).
4. It helps in strengthening and detoxification of the liver.

Samāna Mudrā

VYĀNA MUDRĀ

VĀTA KĀRAKA MUDRĀ

The Mudrā of Circulation

Vi means "to spread," it also means "diffusion." *Vyāna* is one of the five vital airs; its main function is the distribution of the digested food material as nourishment into the entire body. Its main seat is the arms and the legs. This vital air helps in any and every kind of possible movement in the body. It is also known as *Vāta Kāraka Mudrā*. *Vāta* means "air current," and *Kāraka* means "to cause movement or circulation." This *Mudrā* helps in creation of movement impulse in the entire body as and when required, at both physical and *prāṇic* levels. Before intake, the food is held in the *Mudrā* and the *Mantra*, *OM Vyānāya Svāhā*, is recited before ingesting the food.

FORMATION

Join the tip of the index and the middle finger with the tip of the thumb, keeping the other two fingers (ring and little) reasonably straight. It can be practiced as *Saṁyukta Mudrā* (both hands) or *Asaṁyukta Mudrā* (single hand).

BENEFITS

1. It normalizes high blood pressure or hypertension.
2. It relaxes and calms the mind.
3. It strengthens the whole nervous system and veins.
4. It helps in vision problems, especially when it is practiced after *Prāṇa Mudrā*.
5. It helps in regaining lost vital energy as well as distribution of heat in the body, maintaining the same temperature throughout the body.
6. It is especially beneficial to improve the range of motion.
7. It is extremely beneficial in the case of Reynaud's syndrome.

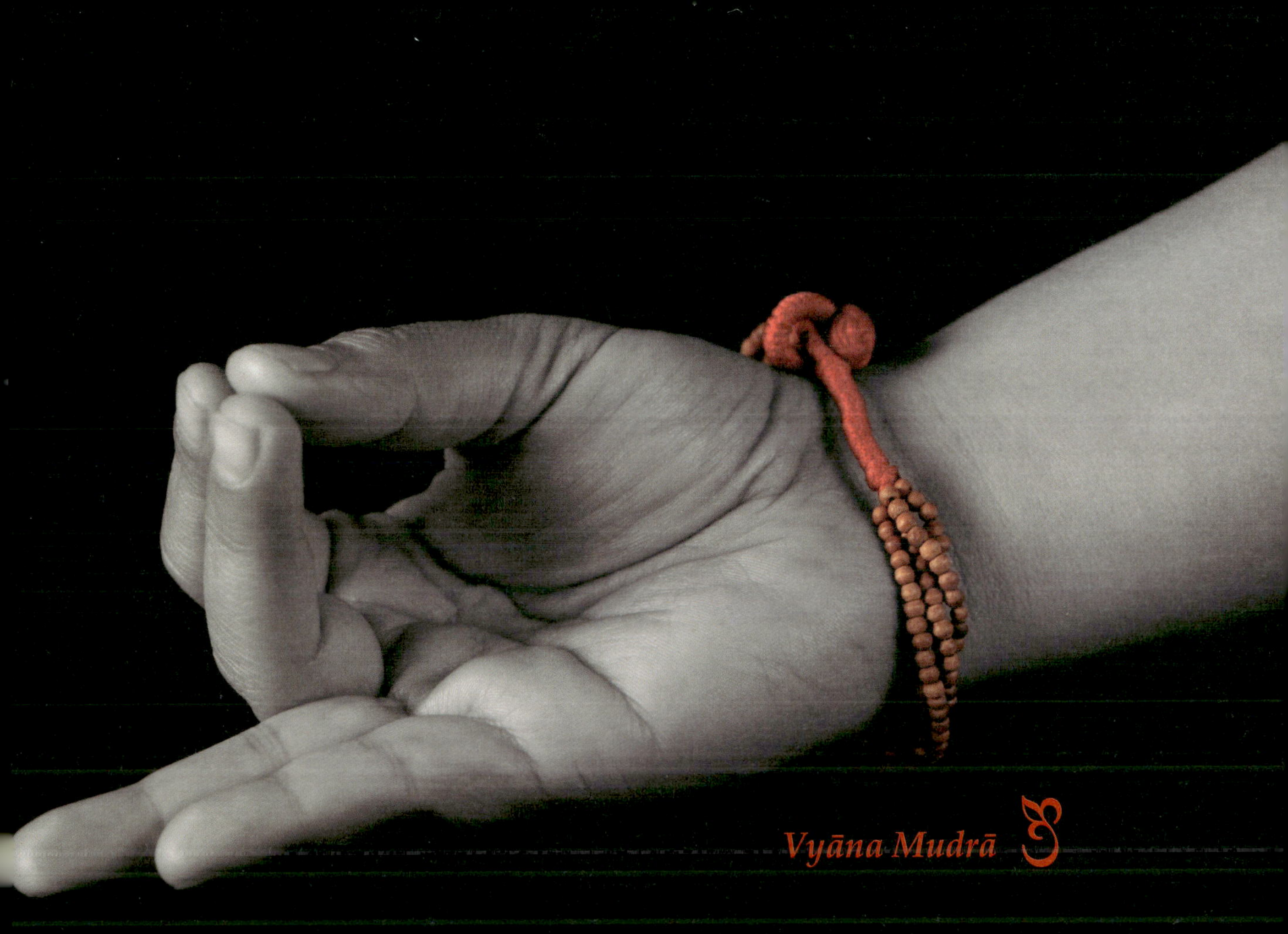

Vyāna Mudrā

A variation of this *Mudrā* is when the index and middle fingers are pressed at the base of the thumb, in which case it becomes the *Vāta Nāśaka Mudrā*. *Vāta* means air imbalance and *nāśaka* means to annihilate or destroy. Practice of *Vāta Nāśaka Mudrā* pacifies the aggravated *vāta* humor. It is, therefore, an excellent *Mudrā* for people with a pronounced *vāta* constitution (*vāta doṣa*).

UDĀNA MUDRĀ

The Mudrā for Directing Energy Upwards

Ud means "to rise above" or "to become so light that you may fly." *Udāna* is vital air, which is the final product of the churning of food into nourishment, to form the essence of food, which then nourishes the higher *cakras*, the brain, and the throat. Its seat is the chest and the throat region, and the direction of movement is upwards. Before intake, the food is held in the *Mudrā* and the *Mantra*, *OM Udānaya Svāhā*, is recited before ingesting the food.

FORMATION

Join the tips of index, middle, and ring fingers with the tip of thumb, while the little finger is separate and extended. This forms the *Udāna Mudrā*. It can be practiced as *Saṁyukta Mudrā* (both hands) or *Asaṁyukta Mudrā* (single hand).

BENEFITS

1. The practice of this *Mudrā* develops the flow of energy and *chetanā* (alertness) in all parts of the body, especially the head and chest region. This is one of the main functions of this *Mudrā*.
2. It helps in the balance of thyroid gland.
3. It helps in making the voice sweet and melodious.
4. It strengthens the ability to express through voice and creativity.

Udāna Mudrā

APĀNA MUDRĀ

The Mudrā of Detoxification/ Letting Go

Apa means "downward movement". Here, it signifies the release of the waste products formed in the process of digestion. It is one of the most vital airs in the body, as it is equally important to get rid of toxins as it is to provide nourishment to the body. The seat of this vital air is the lower abdomen, the pelvis, and the legs. Before intake, the food is held in the *Mudrā* and the *Mantra*, *OM Apānāya Svāhā*, is recited before ingesting the food.

FORMATION

Apāna Mudrā is formed by joining the tips of the thumb, the middle finger, and the ring finger, keeping the little finger and the index finger extended. It can be practiced as *Saṁyukta Mudrā* (both hands) or *Asaṁyukta Mudrā* (single hand).

BENEFITS

1. *Apāna Mudrā* is a combination of the *Ākāśa- Vardhaka* (*Ākāśa:* ether element) and the *Pṛthivī Vardhaka* (*Pṛthivī:* earth element) *Mudrā*. Apart from an increase of the elements' space and earth, *Apāna Mudrā* brings about an increase of *vāta* and *kapha* humors and, therefore, a decrease of *pitta* humor.
2. The *Apāna Mudrā* can be used to overcome disorders like anuria (absence/obstruction of urine), constipation, flatulence (gas), piles, and absence of sweat.
3. It is also beneficial to practice this *Mudrā* in the last week of third trimester of pregnancy for easy delivery (the labor pains and the delivery process are a movement controlled and regulated by *apāna vāyu*. By the practice of this *Mudrā*, we naturally awaken this air current [downward and outward movement known as *apāna vāyu*]).
4. It helps in case of scanty flow during menstruation.
5. It can also be beneficial in dissolving and pushing out stones from the kidney, liver, and pancreas.

Apāna Mudrā ॐ

CAUTION

This Mudrā should not be practiced during pregnancy and excess flow during menstrual cycle. (Can be practice to reduce the excess flow by joining the tip of middle two fingers with thumb).

A variation of this *Mudrā* is when the middle and ring fingers are bent from the second phalange and pressed on the top with the thumb, keeping the little and index fingers extended. This version of *Mudrā* is helpful in cases of diarrhea, excess flow during menstrual cycle, excess sweating, and irritable bowel syndrome (IBS).

Summary

Pañca Prāṇa Upāsanā Mudrās can easily be practiced by one and all before meals. They invoke a feeling of gratitude and connection with the process of eating *(Anna Grahaṇ)*. In addition, they help in balancing the main vital current known as *Mukhya Prāṇas*.

Practice this short exercise for revising these set of *Mudrās* before your lunch/ dinner. This ritual is known as *parishincāmi* (encircling with water), and the eating of small helpings of rice is known as *prāṇahoothi* (offering to the vital breaths). It is performed twice a day when rice is eaten. All other meals are considered "extra" or secondary *(upabhojanam)*. There is actually philosophical significance to the *parisecana* and *prāṇahoothi*. *Parisecana mantra* is sort of a "protection" for the food we are about to eat.

1. *Parisecana*

Take a comfortable seated posture, preferably cross-legged position *(sukhāsana)* on the floor. Chant the mantra: *Satyam tvartena parishincāmi* (O Food! You are true. I encircle you with divine righteousness.) And circumambulate the food with a sprinkling of water. This sprinkling of water is known as "*parisecana*." At night, this mantra is: *Rtam tvā satyena parishincāmi.*

2. *Prāṇahoothi*

Perform the following *Prāṇahoothi*. Use only the thumb, index finger and middle finger of the right hand and take a very little amount food and swallow it without touching the teeth. The idea is that by first making an offering to the *Prāṇas* we pay homage to their life-giving power by virtue of their performing the bodily activities that are crucial to our survival. In this way, this ritual recognizes that not only is food important to survival, but the very bodily functions that we take for granted are essential, and we owe all of this to the Supreme, who sits as the superintending power behind all bodily activity, no matter how mundane.

- *Om Prāṇaye Svāhā* (Hold *Prāṇa Mudrā* in left hand) and meditate upon the mouth region
- *Om Apānāya Svāhā* (Hold *Apānā Mudrā* in left hand) and meditate upon the lower body below the navel
- *Om Vyānāya Svāhā* (Hold *Vyānā Mudrā* in left hand) and meditate upon the limbs (arms, hands, legs and feet) and heart
- *Om Udānaya Svāhā* (Hold *Udāna Mudrā* in left hand) and meditate upon the throat and chest region
- *Om Samānāya Svāhā* (Hold *Samāna Mudrā* in left hand) and meditate upon the navel region
- *Om brahmaṇi ma ātmā -amrtatv āya.* This means, "May my self be united in the Supreme, so that I may attain immortality"

Realized people, while eating, do as follows:

before and after their meal, they "dress up" the Prāṇa with water.

The Prāṇa receives clothing in this manner, and it does not remain naked.

-- Chhandogya 5.2.2 & Brhadaranyaka 6.1.15

Cikitsaka Sparśa Mudrā

Therapeutic Mudrās of Touch

Sparśa means "Touch." We are an embodiment of the divine, yet seeking happiness in the outside world because we have lost contact with our own self. *Sparśa Mudrā* as a meditation and therapy technique enables an individual to connect with one's body in a friendly way, leading towards an inner source of bliss. Being respectful to one's body with awareness is the key to derive maximum benefit from this technique. It restores the mental peace and provides a wonderful experience of relaxation and opening of the lungs. In *Tantra Yoga*, the body is seen as a powerful and useful instrument in a seeker's quest for truth. The body is used as a medium of being mindfully aware and present in this very moment.

Sparśa Mudrās lock and redirect the *prāṇic* and psychic energies into different part of the lungs through *Vibhāga Prāṇāyāma* (*Vibhāga* means "sections," and here, it denotes sectional breathing into different lobes of the lungs). Sit in *Vajrāsana* (thunderbolt pose) for adequate expansion of lungs three-dimensionally, any time of the day for 10 minutes to 30 minutes, to practice all the three or one of these.

ADHAMA PRĀṆĀYĀMA with ADHAMA SPARŚA MUDRĀ

Adhama Prāṇāyāma is diaphragmatic breathing for the lower lobes of lungs. It is practiced as *Saṁyukta* (both hands) *Mudrā*.

VARIATION I

a) **Front:** Rest the palms on the front lower lobes of the lungs. Each palm rests on the edge of the floating ribs and the beginning of the diaphragm (fingers facing each other). Count until 6 as you inhale, and count 1, 2, 3…6 as you exhale. Do the practice three times.

b) **Sides:** Then, move your palms at the same level on the sides of the ribs, and repeat a similar breathing pattern three times.

c) **Back:** Finally, move your hands to the back with fingers pointing towards each other, and thumbs pointing down. Repeat the same breathing pattern for three times.

d) **Three-Dimensional Breathing:** Combine front, side, and back breathing as you keep moving hands from front to side to back sequentially, marking time until 2 counts in each section as you inhale, and then as you exhale from back to side to front, mark 2 counts each. Repeat this round three times.

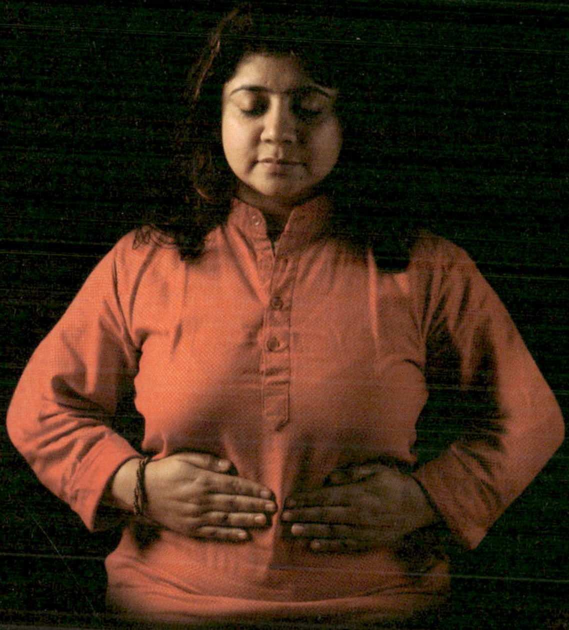

Front

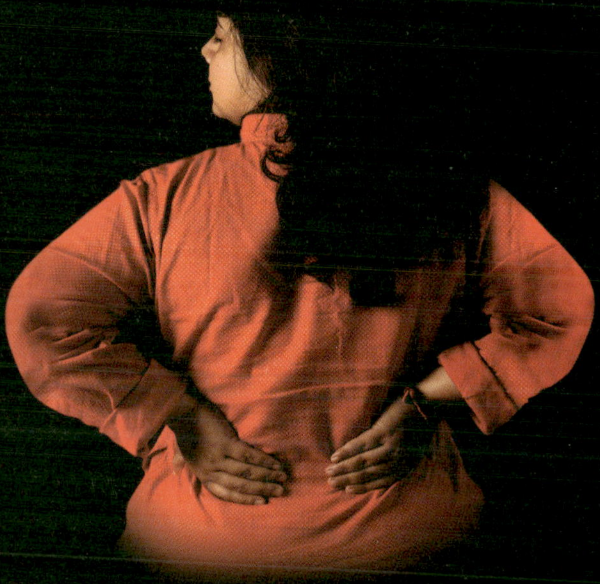

Back

Sides

VARIATION II

Alternate Hand *Mudrā: Cin Mudrā* (join the tip of the index finger at the first phalange [joint] of the thumb, keeping the rest of the three fingers reasonably straight). Practice of this *Mudrā* naturally directs the breath towards the lower lobe of the lungs. It is practiced as *Saṁyukta Mudrā* (both hands).

Post-Practice: After completing practice of variation I or variation II, rest your hands on the lap in *Yoga Mudrā* (interlace the fingers and thumb and rest them on your lap). Allow for natural breathing as the lower lobes of the lungs are energized with fresh supply of oxygen.

BENEFITS

1. It opens up the lower lobes of the lungs.
2. It releases the bronchial spasms from this region of the lungs.
3. It increases lung capacity.
4. It massages the reproductive and the excretory systems by increasing oxygen flow and absorption into these organ systems.
5. It improves blood circulation to the lower limbs.

Cin Mudrā

Yoga Mudrā

MADHYAMA PRĀṆĀYĀMA with MADHYAMA SPARŚA MUDRĀ

Madhyama Prāṇāyāma is thoracic or intercostals breathing for the middle lobe of lungs. It is practiced as *Saṁyukta* (both hands) *Mudrā*.

VARIATION I

a) **Front:** Palms rest on the front middle lobe of the lungs. Each palm rests on either side of the chest cavity (fingers facing each other). Count until 6 as you inhale, and count 1, 2, 3…6 as you exhale. Do the practice three times.

b) **Sides:** Then, move your palms at the same level on the sides of ribs, and repeat a similar breathing pattern three times.

c) **Back:** Finally, move your hands to the back with fingers pointing towards each other at the level of the chest, and thumbs pointing down. Repeat the same breathing pattern for three times.

d) **Three-Dimensional Breathing:** Combine front, side, and back breathing as you keep moving hands from front to side to back sequentially, counting until 2 in each section as you inhale and then, as you exhale from back to side to front, 2 counts each. Repeat this round three times.

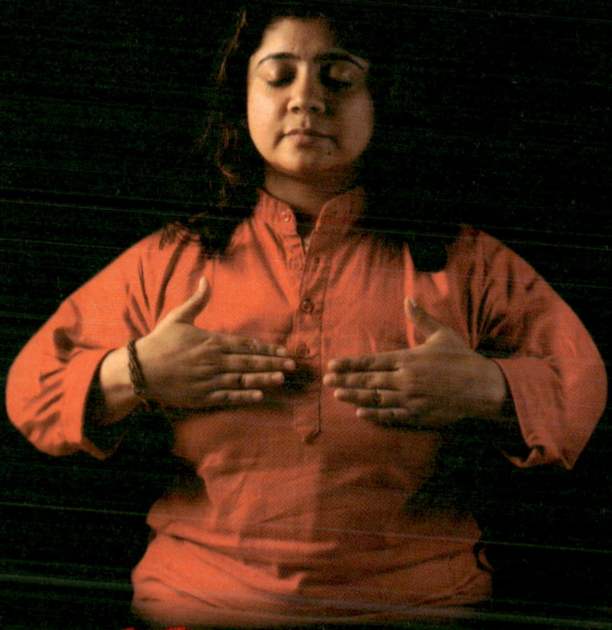

Front

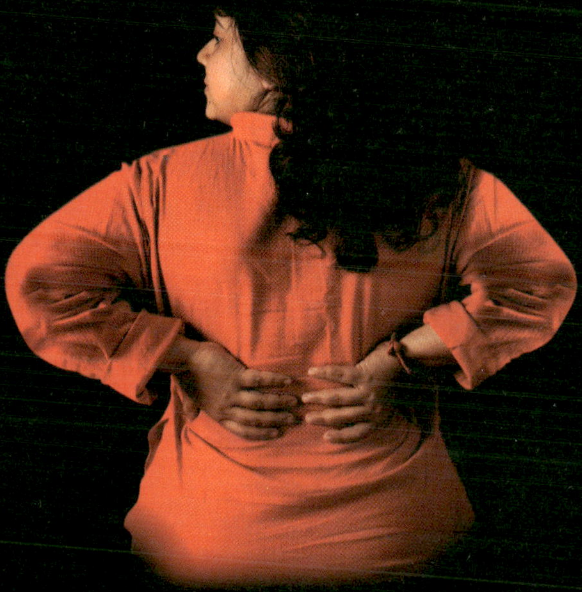

Back

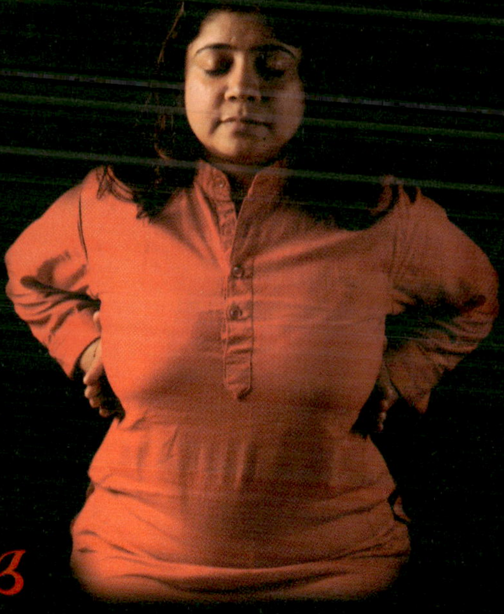

Sides

VARIATION II

Alternate Hand *Mudrā: Cinmaya Mudrā:* Fold the index finger and join its tip with the tip of the thumb, folding the rest of the three fingers like a fist in the center of the palm. Rest the hands in *Cinmaya Mudrā* on the lap, with the palms facing down and the knuckles facing each other. Practice of this *Mudrā* naturally directs the breath towards the middle lobe of the lungs. It is practiced as *Saṁyukta* (both hands) *Mudrā.*

Post-Practice: After completing practice of Variation I or Variation II, rest your hands on the lap in *Yoga Mudrā* (interlace the fingers and thumb and rest them on your lap). Allow for natural breathing as the lower lobes of the lungs get energized with the fresh supply of oxygen.

BENEFITS

1. It helps in opening up the middle lobes of the lungs, which are generally congested and need oxygenation.

2. It releases the bronchial spasms from this region of the lungs.

3. It increases lung capacity.

4. It improves blood circulation to the abdominal organs and boosts the digestive system.

5. It boosts gastric/digestive fire (putting pressure in the center of the palm, as you fold the middle, ring, and little fingers to form a fist, gives acupressure to the points related to the abdominal organs, especially the stomach, small intestine, and gall bladder, thereby awakening the digestive juices and the catabolic reaction taking place in the stomach and small intestine after the ingestion of the food).

Cinmaya Mudrā

Yoga Mudrā

Ādyama Prāṇāyāma with Ādyama Sparśa Mudrā

Ādyama Prāṇāyāma is clavicle breathing for the upper lobes of lungs. It is practiced as *Saṁyukta* (both hands) *Mudrā*.

VARIATION I

a) **Front:** Rest the palms on the front upper lobe of the lungs. Each palm rests on either side of the thorax (above the chest cavity, near the collar bones/clavicle), with fingers facing each other. Count until 6 as you inhale, and count 1, 2, 3…6 as you exhale. Do the practice three times.

b) **Sides:** Then, move your palms on the sides of the hipbones instead of under the armpits, and repeat the breathing pattern for three times.

c) **Back:** Finally, lift your arms up with palms facing back; stretch your arms to feel the stretch in the armpits; and bend your elbows to rest your palms on either side of the shoulder blade, keeping the elbows and forearms as close to each other as possible. Repeat the breathing pattern three times.

d) **Three-Dimensional Breathing:** Combine front, side, and back breathing as you keep moving hands from front to side of hip, to upper back sequentially, counting until 2 in each section as you inhale, and then, as you exhale from upper back to hip side to front, 2 counts each. Repeat this round three times.

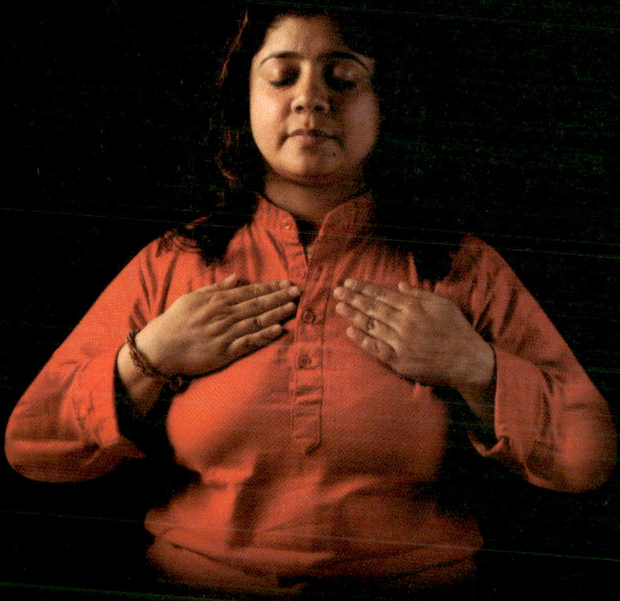

Front

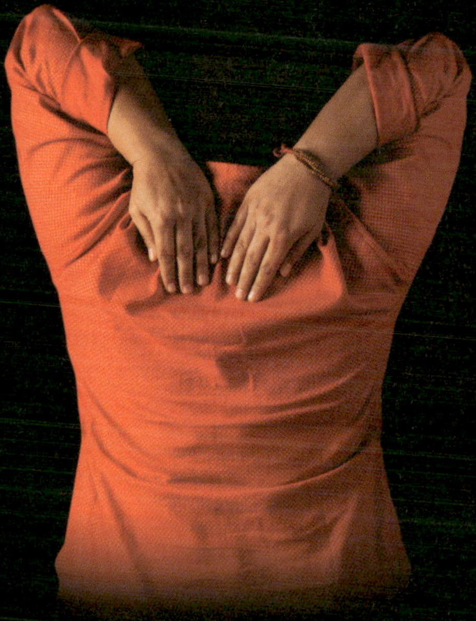

Back

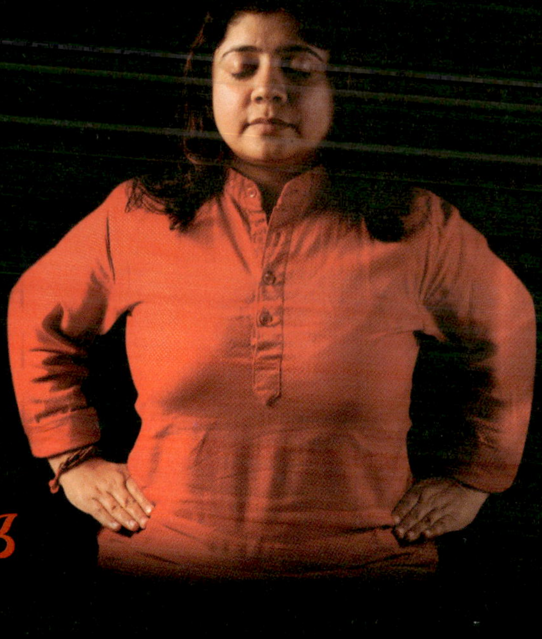

Sides

VARIATION II

Alternate Hand *Mudrā*: *Ādi Mudrā:* Make a soft fist with the thumb tucked inside, and rest the fist on the lap with palms down and knuckles facing each other. Practice of this *Mudrā* naturally directs the breath towards the upper lobe of the lungs. It is practiced as *Saṁyukta* (both hands) *Mudrā.*

Post-Practice: After completing practice of Variation I or Variation II, rest your hands on the lap in *Yoga Mudrā* (interlace the fingers and thumb and rest them on your lap). Allow for natural breathing as the lower lobes of the lungs get energized with the fresh supply of oxygen.

BENEFITS

1. It releases the bronchial spasms from this region of the lungs.

2. It increases lung capacity.

3. It boosts the lymphatic drainage.

4. It improves blood circulation to the head, neck, and arms.

Yoga Mudrā

MAHAD YOGA PRĀṆĀYĀMA with MAHAD SPARŚA MUDRĀ

Mahad Yoga Prāṇāyāma is the full *Yogic* breathing. This is the combination of the first three *Prāṇāyāma: Adhama, Madhyama,* and *Adyama Prāṇāyāma*, with *Adhama, Madhyama,* and *Adyama Sparśa Mudrā*. The practice of *Mahad Yoga Prāṇāyāma* opens up all the three lobes of the lungs three-dimensionally, allowing for complete expansion and contraction with minimum pressure on the lungs. It is practiced as *Saṁyukta* (both hands) *Mudrā*.

VARIATION I

To practice this *Sparśa Mudrā,* rest the left palm on the left side of the chest in the center.

a) **Inhalation:** As a first step, rest the right-hand palm on the right front lower lobe of the lung for 2 counts, and then move the right palm to the right front middle lobe of the lung for next 2 counts, and finally, move the right palm to the right front upper lobe of the lung for next 2 counts.

b) **Exhalation:** As you exhale, rest the left palm on the left middle part of the chest. For the first 2 counts, keep the palms on right front upper lobe of the lung, then move the right palm to the right front middle lobe of the lung for next 2 counts, and finally, move to the right front lower lobe of the lungs for 2 counts. This is one round; practice 2 more rounds of the *Prāṇāyāma*.

Yoga Mudrā

VARIATION II

Alternate Hand *Mudrā:* *Mahad Mudrā:* Make a fist with both hands with the thumb tucked inside, and place them by the side of the navel. Let the palm face the abdomen– Let the fist face up and the little finger side of the fisted palm be close to the abdomen. It is practiced as *Saṁyukta* (both hands) *Mudrā.*

Post-Practice: After completing practice of Variation I or Variation II, rest your hands on the lap in *Yoga Mudrā* (interlace the fingers and thumb and rest them on your lap). Allow for natural breathing as the lower lobes of the lungs get energized with the fresh supply of oxygen.

BENEFITS

1. It helps in diffusion of life force: *(Prāṇa)* in the whole body.

2. It activates and balances all the *Pañca Prāṇas.*

3. It naturally brings awareness to the *Prāṇamaya Kośa.*

4. It is a wonderful *Mudrā* to practice before the *Prāṇayāma.*

5. It pacifies the *Vāta Vikṛti.*

Mahad Mudrā

Summary

Touch speaks to us more than any other sense faculty. When we touch a part of the body, we directly communicate to that region or part of the body. These set of *Mudrās* can be practiced any time of the day - before or after meals. A general suggestion is to avoid them after meals, since the breath is heavy as the body goes in active metabolic mode to digest the food and the blood flows towards the abdominal organs. In case you do not have enough time or are in a situation that you are not able to practice the entire series, you may practice only the *Mahad Yoga Prāṇāyāma* with *Mahad Sparśa Mudrā* or the *Yoga Hasta Mudrā* for 3-5 minutes as per the availability. Get in touch with yourself, as that is the most important thing we are missing in our present day lifestyle. It may seem superficial and superfluous that how just by holding the hand in a specific way or touching a region of the chest cavity may help in connecting to self – "Just do it a couple of times and see/ feel for yourself!"

Still as I am

Energy moves through me

Waves and thrill

Thrills and Chills...

Within

I move

Outside...Still

May it invoke the stillness in you

As I still myself...

May I still YOU!

Prāṇāyāma Sparśa Mudrā

Mudrā to direct the prāṇa

In the practice of breath discipline, *Mudrās* play a key role in the redirection of *prānic* energy in specific channels and activating the various *mukhya vāyus* (five *prāṇas*). Let us try to understand the most common *Prāṇāyāma Mudrā* known as *Viṣṇu Mudrā* (hand gesture of Lord *Viṣṇu*) or *Nāḍī Śodhana Mudrā*.

Viṣṇu Mudrā

Hand Gesture of Lord Viṣṇu

Nāḍī Śodhana Mudrā

This is one of the hand gestures used to alternate the breath through the nostrils during *Nāḍī Śodhana Kriyā* and *Anuloma Viloma Prāṇāyāma*. In this *Mudrā*, the right hand is used, as it is associated with giving, while the left is associated with receiving. It is an *Asaṁyukta* (single hand) *Mudrā*.

FORMATION

Bend the middle and index fingers into the center of the palm, and keep the little finger and the ring finger extended, thumb extended at right angle to the middle and index fingers. The *Mudrā* is done with the right hand and turned towards the face during the practice of *Nāḍī Śodhana Kriyā* (a detoxification technique for the subtle channels in the subtle body) and *Anuloma Viloma Prāṇāyāma* (a traditional *Prāṇāyāma* for balancing the activity of *Iḍā Nāḍī* [moon, cooling, feminine energy channel represented through left nostril] and *Piṅgalā Nāḍī* [sun, heating, masculine energy channel represented through right nostril], so that the *prāṇic* energy can move into the central channel known as *Suṣumnā Nāḍī*.

The *Viṣṇu Mudrā* helps in balancing and filtering of the *Māruta* (air element) to form *Prāna,* as it triggers the *Phanā marma* points on either sides of the nostrils, due to the position of the thumb and fingers on the nostril during the inhalation and exhalation. The energies of fire (thumb), earth (ring finger), and water (little finger) elements are allowed to flow freely, whereas the energies of air (index finger) and ether (middle finger) current are harnessed in the formation of this *Mudrā*.

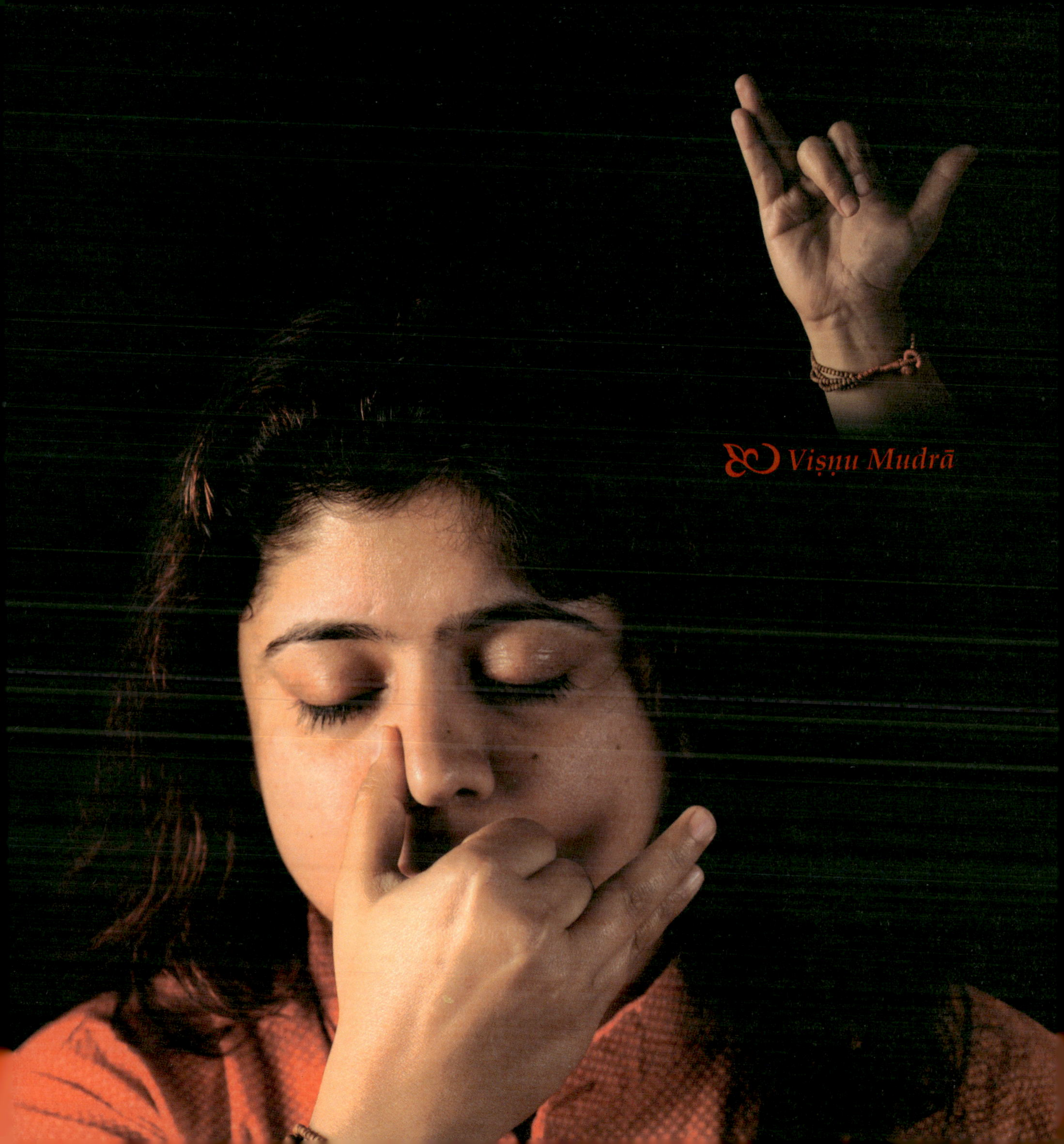

Viṣṇu Mudrā

Summary

Every *Yogic* text has written extensively and laid the maximum importance on redirecting of the energy in the proper energetic pathway. For avoiding the leakage of *Prāṇā* and intensifying its force with *Sattva*, to drive the subtle energy into the *Suṣumṇā Nāḍī*, various *Mudrās* are employed. The finest way of doing this is the practice of *Prāṇāyāma*. Very few traditions lay emphasis on the importance of *Mudrās* in the practice of *Prāṇāyāma*. Right practice of *Mudrās* can help trigger the *prānic* switches (*Marma* points) connecting the physical, energetic, mental, emotional and subtle bodies. I would suggest you to practice *Nāḍī Śodhana Kriyā* with and without the use of *Mudrā* to see the effect.

You sit here for days saying, "This is strange business". You're the strange business. You have the energy of the sun in you, but you keep knotting it up at the base of your spine. You're some weird kind of gold that wants to stay melted in the furnace, so you won't have to become coins.

–Rumi.

My breath is my thread

On breath do I tread…

A path of union awaits me

A dream of happiness chases

The moment is now for all the goodness

The moment is here for all the oneness

I wonder how breath leads to freedom

Tell me Oh Teacher! The secret of my breath

Show me Oh Teacher! The path to death (not physical here - Liberation from the vicious cycle of life and death)

For I am naive and see both as same

You say my breath, body and my mind are all the same

My excuse to be them is absolutely lame

Oh Student "The path to breath is simple and short

Just focus on breath and welcome aboard!!"

Chapter - III

Ādhyātmika Hasta Mudrā

Sprituality has been hyped these days, and people often try to buy and own it in the name of gold, silver and diamond studded idols, temples, fancy pilgrimages, wearing gems, accessories, incense etc. The easiest and simplest way to leading a spiritual life is by understanding the true meaning of it. Being spiritual is being connected, not to the world outside but the one within. Developing the mental faculties to make them sharp and deep enough to reach the inner realms of subtlety is the road to freedom, which is often termed as "Spirituality." *Vedas* and *Yogic* texts have always provided clear and simple solutions to a real and meaningful life that can lead us back to the truth. One such offering is *Mudrās* where the texts on *Laya Yoga* speak highly of meditation on *Cakras*. The practice of *Sapta Cakra Mudrās* is very deep and intense, to trigger the communication between the five sheaths, seven energy vortices and three bodies.

Abhaya Mudrā

The Gesture of Fearlessness and Reassurance

MEANING AND SIGNIFICANCE

This *Asaṁyukta Mudrā* (single hand) is common to *Hindu*, Buddhist, Japanese, and Chinese Buddhist traditions. In *Hindu* and Buddhist traditions, this *Mudrā* is generally held by a deity (Gods and Goddesses), whereas in Japanese and Chinese Buddhist traditions, it is practiced by priests and devotees. The *Mudrā* symbolizes protection, boon, blessing, fearlessness, courage, and reassurance. When held at the level of the chest, as in Thai Theravada Buddhist tradition, it symbolizes "warning" and conveys "halting/stop." In the *Yoga Tattva Mudrā Vijñāna* as per the *Yogic* tradition, it is performed with both hands and symbolizes courageousness, transcending fear and emotional weakness.

FORMATION

The *Mudrā* is formed by keeping the right hand at the shoulder level with palm facing outward, all the fingers and the thumb extended and relaxed. The left hand can be kept with the palm cupping the knee or facing upward.

Abhaya Mudrā

AGNI- ŚĀLĀ MUDRĀ

THE SYMBOL OF FIRE PIT

MEANING AND SIGNIFICANCE

This is a *Tantric Mudrā*, prevalent in *Vajrayāna* and *Mantrayāna* Buddhist Japanese tradition. It is a *Saṁyukta Mudrā* (both hands) generally practiced with *mantra* chanting. The priest or devotee generally practices this *Mudrā* at the time of meditation, performing a ritual or offering prayers. This *Mudrā* is symbolic of a fire pit, which in this case is the burning of all the *saṁskāras* (deep-seated impressions, subconscious patterning) in the inner fire through meditation. It is very similar to the *Yoga Dhyāna Mudrā.*

FORMATION

This *Mudrā* is practiced by placing the right hand on top of the left hand, palms facing upwards, and thumbs and fingers extended towards the midline. The fingers and thumbs are separated and not touching each other, and are kept parallel to each other. The thumbs touch each other at the tips and are kept relaxed, making the electromagnetic circuit. It helps in taking one into deep states of meditation. The hands thus formed in this *Mudrā* are kept at the level of the navel or on the lap during meditation.

Agni-Śālā Mudrā

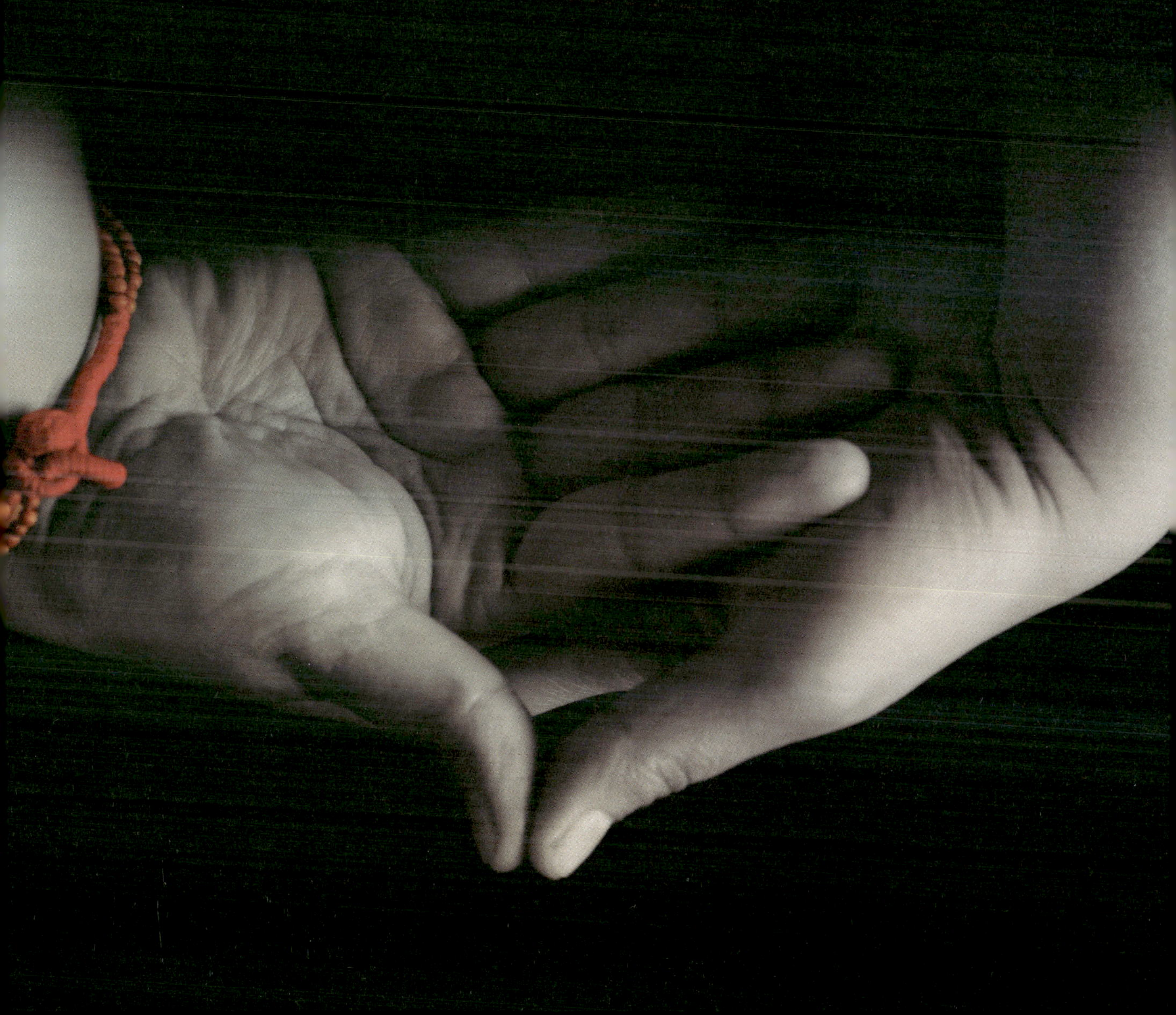

AGNI-CAKRA MUDRĀ

THE WOMB OF COMPASSION

MEANING AND SIGNIFICANCE

This *Tantric Mudrā* is prevalent in *Vajrayāna* and *Mantrayāna* Japanese Buddhist tradition. It is a *Saṁyukta Mudrā* (both hands). The priest or devotee generally practices this *Mudrā* at the time of performing the rites of *Garbhadhātu Maṇḍala* prayers. It may or may not be accompanied by *mantra* chanting. *Garbhadhātu Maṇḍala* is a *Vajrayāna* Buddhist tradition known as "womb realm." The name of the *maṇḍala* derives from Chapter 2 of the *Sūtras*, where it is said that *Mahāvairocana Buddha* revealed the *maṇḍala's* secret teachings to his disciple *Vajrasattva* from his "womb of compassion." The seed syllable of the *Mahāvairocana* in the *Garbhadhātu Maṇḍala* is a simple and short "a," which is experienced by simply opening the mouth and exhaling. The sound thus produced is "a," which is a hidden sound in every consonant. It is thus called - the mother of all *Mantras*.

FORMATION

Bend the little, middle, and ring fingers of both hands into the center of the palm; rest the thumbs on the inner sides of the middle finger. Keep the index finger extended and join the tips of the index fingers of both hands to each other. Also making sure that the tips of the second pahalange of the little and ring fingers of both hands are also touching each other.

Agni-Cakra Mudrā ☙

AGNI-CAKRA ŚAMANA MUDRĀ

MEANING AND SIGNIFICANCE

This is a *Tantric Mudrā*, prevalent in *Vajrayāna* and *Mantrayāna* Buddhist Japanese tradition. It is a *Saṁyukta Mudrā* (both hands) generally practiced with *mantra* chanting. The priest or devotee generally practices this *Mudrā* at the time of performing a ritual or offering prayers. There are two variations of this *Mudrā*.

VARIATION I

Fingers are folded in the center of the palm to make a loose fist, and the thumb is softly pressed in-between the index and the middle fingers, pointing upwards. Both the fists are touching each other along the outside edges of the palm. The palm side of the hands faces you.

VARIATION II

Fingers are folded in the center of the palm to make a loose fist, and the thumb is softly inserted between the index and the middle fingers inside the fist. Both the fists are touching each other along the outside edges of the palm. The palm side of the hands faces you.

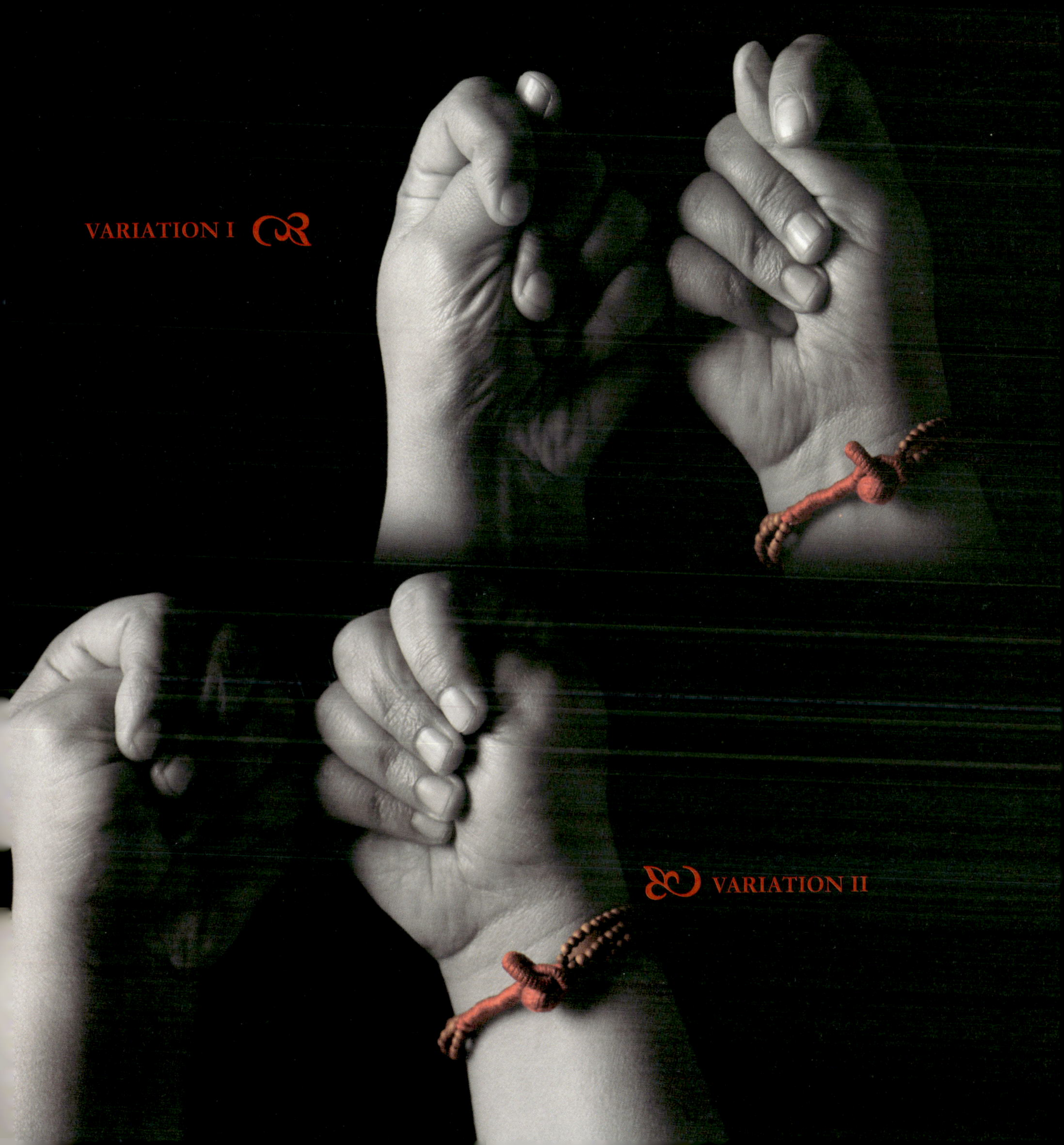
VARIATION I
VARIATION II

BHŪMI-SPARŚA MUDRĀ

THE GESTURE OF SURRENDER AND EARTH AS WITNESS

MEANING AND SIGNIFICANCE

Bhūmi means "earth" and *Sparśa* means "touch." This is the *Mudrā* of taking Mother Earth as witness. The *Mudrā* has its own variations in *Theravada* Buddhist tradition and *Yogic* tradition.

In the *Theravada* Buddhist tradition of Thailand, the *Mudrā* symbolizes *Buddha's* enlightenment under the *Bodhi* tree. There, he summoned the earth Goddess *Sthavara* as a witness. Alternatively, it is believed that *Śākya-muni* formed *Bhūmi-sparśa Mudrā* while meditating on truth. He overcame the obstructions of the demon *Māra* and formed this *Mudrā* by touching the earth as a witness to this event.

In *Yogic* tradition, this *Mudrā* is practiced at the end of a session. It facilitates letting go of all negativity, toxins, and emotional blockages by draining/surrendering them down to Mother Earth. The *Mudrā* is formed by joining the index finger with the thumb, like in *Jñāna Mudrā.* While seated in a meditative pose, the hands extend all the way so that the ring, middle, and little fingers touch the ground. This *Mudrā* is performed with both hands, with both arms extending on their respective sides.

FORMATION

The *Buddha* forms this *Mudrā* in a meditative pose. Rest both your hands on the knees, with palms facing away from the body, fingers tips (middle, ring, and little) touching the floor, keep the thumb and the index finger in *Jñāna Mudrā*.

Bhūmi-Sparśa Mudrā

CIN MUDRĀ

MUDRĀ OF ULTIMATE REVELATION

MEANING AND SIGNIFICANCE

This *Mudrā* of *Hindu* tradition symbolizes spiritual unfolding, supreme consciousness, and revelation of the absolute one. It is an *Asaṁyukta* (single hand) *Mudrā*, practiced during meditation. *Cin Mudrā* has similar affects on the subtle body as *Jñāna Mudrā*.

Cin Mudrā symbolizes the growth of a *Yogic* mind from *Tamas* (darkness, inertia) to *Sattva* (lightness, purity). It is a *Mudrā* of unified consciousness. It activates the "*Gupta Nādī*: secret channel" of consciousness that goes to the *hrid- guhā* (the cave of the heart) as one the hands on the knees in the *Mudrā*. It creates a *prānic* circuit which allows the *prāṇa* to circulate in the body releasing and dissolving any energetic blockages as well as forming the new energetic pathways. In this *Mudrā* each finger has a specific representation:

- Thumb - Supreme Soul
- Pointer(Index) - Individual Soul
- Middle - Ego
- Ring - Illusion
- Little - Karma

Cin Mudrā

Ego, illusion and *karma* are the three impurities that the *yogi* is tries to remove from his/ her life in order to unite their Individual Soul with the Supreme Soul and experience that divine, blissful state of union they strive for. It also helps in balancing the basic bio-rhythms of sleep and hunger. It helps one to stay in the state of *dhāraṇā* by slowly generating the alpha brain wave modulation. It calms down the *rajasic* tendencies and brings forth a sense of clarity and *sattva*. It has a special effect on the *Mūlādhāra cakra*, awakening the sleeping life force. The regular practice of this *Mudrā* brings a balance of the sympathetic and para-sympathetic nervous system. Doing *Cin Mudrā* is a physical representation and reminder of this goal and serves to refocus and re-energize the practitioner.

FORMATION

Place palm face down. Index finger and thumb join at the tip. The ring, middle, and little fingers are kept relaxed. The subtle pressure between the index finger and the thumb is almost as if you are holding the essence of truth in a pinch.

Dharma-Cakra Mudrā

Gesture of Righteousness/ Dharma

MEANING AND SIGNIFICANCE

A *Mudrā* in the Buddhist tradition, symbolizes the setting of the wheel of right action *(dharma)* into motion. It is a *Saṁyukta* (both hands) *Mudrā*. It captures and seals one of the most important moments in the life of *Buddha* – the occasion of his first sermon after attaining Enlightenment in the Deer Park at *Sarnath*. There is a deep symbolism in this *Mudrā*: The *Mudrā* itself means setting the wheel of right action into movement; it is a *Mudrā* of transition as well as transformation. The circle formed by the index finger and the thumb symbolizes the union of method and wisdom, or the union of individual consciousness with cosmic consciousness.

The three extended fingers of the right hand represent the three vehicles of *Buddha's* teachings:

- the middle finger represents the "hearers" of the teachings
- the ring finger represents the "solitary realizers"
- the little finger represents the *Mahāyāna* or "Great Vehicle"

The three extended fingers of the left hand symbolize the "Three Jewels" of Buddhism, namely the *Buddha* (the enlightened being), the *Dharma* (right action or righteousness), and the *Sangha* (spiritual community).

FORMATION

The thumbs and index fingers of both hands touch and form a circle like in *Jñāna Mudrā*. The other three fingers of each hand are extended. Often, the left palm is turned toward the body and the right palm is away from the body. One variation of this *Mudrā* is made when the tips of the index finger

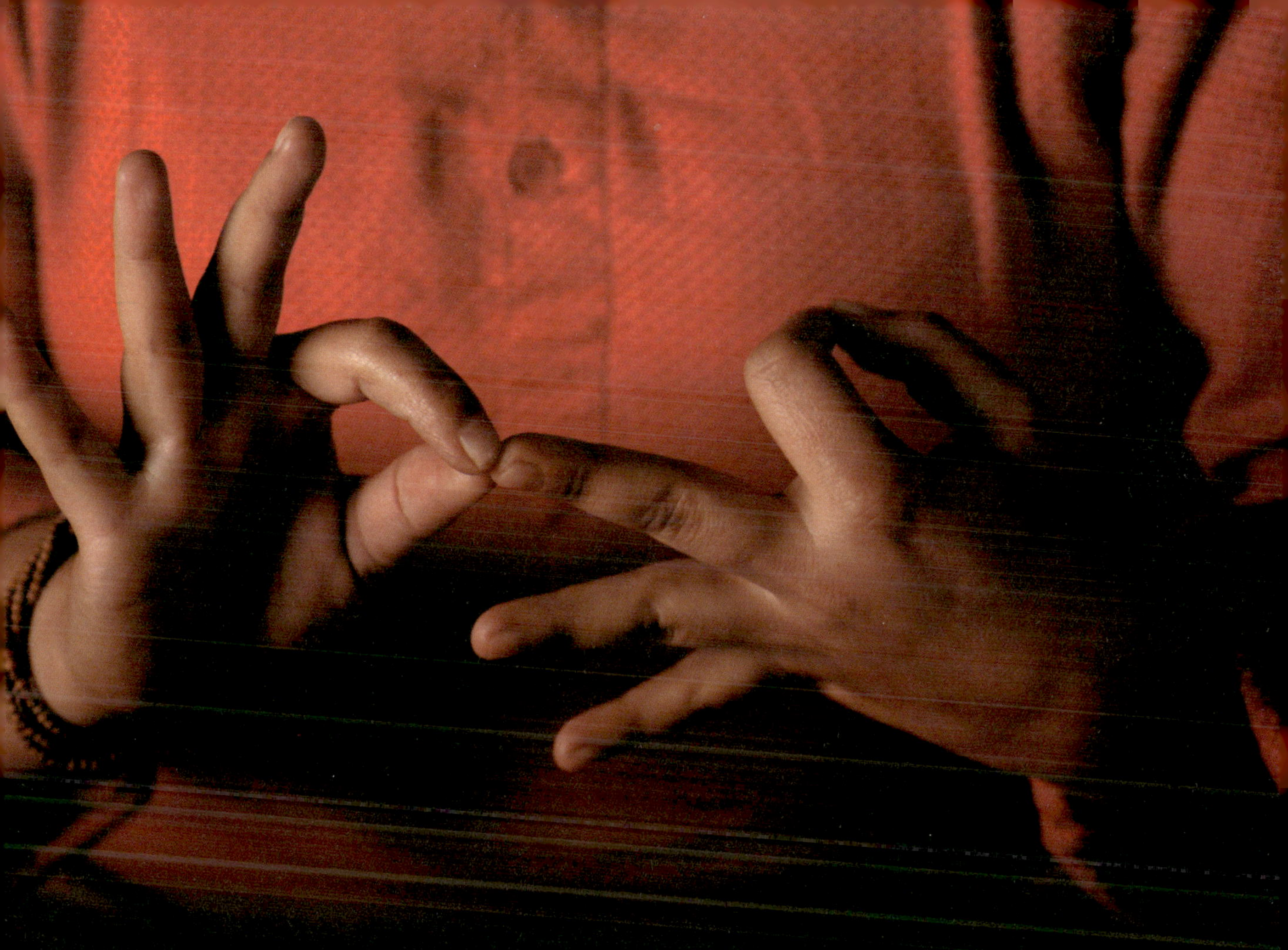

Dharma Chakra Mudrā

and the thumb of each hand are touching each other after forming circle. The second variation of this *Mudrā* is when the left-hand middle fingertip touches the tip of the circle formed by the thumb and index finger of the right hand. Significantly, in this *Mudrā*, the hands are held in front of the heart,

Dhyānī Mudrā

Gesture of Meditation & Peace

One who is absorbed in the state of meditation, becomes meditation.

MEANING AND SIGNIFICANCE

The *Mudrā* has a variation in the Buddhist and *Yogic* traditions. In the Buddhist tradition, *Dhyānī Mudrā* is a *Saṁyukta Mudrā* (both hands) of concentration held by a variety of *bodhisattvas*. In the *Yogic* tradition, *Dhyānī Mudrā* is a *Mudrā* of peace and represents transcendence of dualities. As per the *Yoga Tattva Mudrā Vijñāna*, it is practiced during meditation. The subtle body forms an electromagnetic circuit enhancing communication between the two brain hemispheres, calms the nervous system, and makes the breath *sūkṣma* (subtle).

FORMATION

This *Mudrā* is practiced by resting both hands on lap with the right hand on top of the left hand. Left hand is used as a base and right hand rests over it. Keep palms facing upwards, with thumb tips almost touching each other. Fingers are extended towards the base of the wrist of opposite hands, touch each other. Keep a very relaxed gesture.

Dhyānī Mudrā

VARIATION

Join the tip of the thumb with the tip of the index finger. The hands are kept over each other on the lap, right hand up and left hand as a base. Palms face upwards, with the middle, ring, and little fingers extending towards the opposite hand's wrist. Focus on the breath and the pulsation of contact between the index finger and the thumb.

Jñāna Mudrā

The Wisdom Seal

MEANING AND SIGNIFICANCE

A *Mudrā* from *Yoga Tattva Mudrā Vijñāna*, it symbolizes attainment of wisdom and is a part of *Hindu* tradition. It is one of the most common and most praised *Mudra*. It is also called *Vāyu Vardhaka Mudrā* in *Ayurvedic* terms – *Vardhaka* means "to increase" and *Vāyu* means "air." It is done at the time of meditation by adopting any of the meditation poses.

The practice of the *Mudrā* redirects the *prāṇic* energy back to the body, creating an electromagnetic circuit. It helps increase the neural transmission for better retention, recalling, and cognition. It is a *Mudrā* for building concentration and focus. The regular practice of this *Mudrā* helps in increasing the activity in the gray matter of the brain. It is excellent for a nervous, anxious, and forgetful mind.

FORMATION

This *Mudrā* is formed by palm facing upwards, resting on respective knees, with index finger and thumb joined at the tip, or index finger slightly folded with the thumb resting on the index finger nail, keeping the ring, middle, and little fingers relaxed and extended. It is an *Asaṁyukta* (single hand) *Mudrā*.

It also symbolizes that, "I (the consciousness in the practitioner) am beyond the three states of mind (*suṣupti*: deep sleep, *jāgrat:* awake, and *svapna:* dreaming); the three kinds of bodily humors *(vāta:* air, *pitta:* bile, *kapha:* mucus); the three planes of existence (physical, astral, and cosmic); the three levels of time (past, present, and future), and the three attributes *(sattvic, rajasic,* and *tamasic).* I am the union of individual consciousness:*prakṛti* (index finger) with supreme consciousness: *puruṣa* (thumb)." The intention when one practices this *Mudrā* is, "I am beyond the union of masculine and feminine energy, and I transcend this union for the absolute one."

Jñāna Mudrā

Hākinī Mudrā

Gesture of Smṛti (Memory) and Dhāraṇa (Concentration)

MEANING AND SIGNIFICANCE

Hākinī (form of *Śakti*) is a *Hindu* Goddess who presides at the *ājñā cakra* (third eye center). Goddess *Hākinī* is described as having six moon-like faces. She holds a skull, a small drum, a rosary, and a book; two other arms are lifted up in a gesture of dispelling fear and granting blessings. It is a *Saṁyukta Mudrā* (both hands) that connects the left and right hemispheres of the brain. It is a *Mudrā* of memory, concentration, and one pointed focus. This *Mudrā* can be extremely useful for children or students during their learning, memorizing, and recalling stages.

FORMATION

To form this *Mudrā*, place all the fingertips together without touching any other part of the palm. Point the fingers up towards the sky and keep the hands at the level of the chest or abdomen. When this *Mudrā* is used with harmonization of the breath *(Sama-Vṛtti Prāṇāyāma:* same ratio of inhalation and exhalation – that is, 1:1), it brings amazing results (especially when recalling content).

Hākinī Mudrā

Kubera Mudrā

The Mudrā of Immense Wealth and Treasure

MEANING AND SIGNIFICANCE

Kubera is the chief treasurer of all wealth and riches in *Hindu* tradition. In Buddhism, he is known as *Vaiśravaṇa*, the patronymic form of *Hindu Kubera* (also equated with *Pañcika*). In Jainism, he is known as *Sarvānubhūti*. In the *Viṣṇudharmottara Purāṇa, Kubera* is described as the embodiment of *artha* (wealth, prosperity, glory) as well as *Arthaśāstras* and the treatises related to it.

This *Mudrā* is used in Indian classical dances to depict the glory of *Kubera* through stories enacted in dance forms. It can be used as a spiritual *Mudrā* to invite and invoke knowledge and wisdom in abundance. It is also regarded as a *Mudrā* that bestows the practitioner with the blessing of wealth and abundance. It may be combined with *Kubera mantra (Oṁ Śaṁ Kuberāya Namaḥ)* by holding the intention in the cave of the heart for the fulfillment of desires related to wealth, abundance, and prosperity. It is also said that the practice of this *Mudrā* helps find hidden treasures. It is an *Asaṁyukta* (single hand) *Mudrā*.

FORMATION

Touch the tip of the thumb, the index finger, and the middle finger together. Bend the other two fingers in toward the center of the palm. Practice any time of the day.

Kubera Mudrā

MĀTAṄGĪ MUDRĀ

THE GESTURE OF ROYAL SPEECH AND CREATIVITY

MEANING AND SIGNFICANCE

Mātaṅgī Mudrā is a *Tantric Mudrā* of *Hindu* tradition. *Mātaṅgī* is a *Hindu* Goddess who is a form of *Sarasvatī* (Goddess of wisdom and speech) incarnated as the daughter of *Mātaṅga Ṛṣi*. She is one of the ten *Mahāvidyās (mahā* means "great" and *vidyā* means "knowledge" or "wisdom"); the other nine are *Kālī, Tārā, Ṣoḍaśī, Bhuvaneśvarī, Bhairavī, Cinnamastā, Kāmalā, Dhūmavatī, and Bagalā-Mukhī.* The *Mahāvidyās* represent some form of incarnation or manifestation of the Divine Mother. They are, in this sense, also to be regarded as *Vidyās* or different approaches to *(tantric)* knowledge. *Mātaṅgī* resides in the throat *cakra* and is radiant like the moon. *Mātaṅgī* is invoked to achieve command over speech, creativity, and knowledge. It is a *Saṁyukta Mudrā* (both hands). The practice of this *Mudrā* can be done with or without *mantra* at any time of the day but especially during certain *tantric* rituals or meditation practices. The therapeutic aspect of this *Mudrā* strengthens the wood and the earth elements, and the energies and circulation in and around the heart, the stomach, the liver, the pancreas, and the kidneys. The spiritual aspect of the *Mudrā* helps in strengthening the life force in *Maṇipūra Cakra and Viśuddhi Cakra.*

FORMATION

To form this *Mudrā*, interlace all the fingers and then raise the middle finger of both hands, pointing them upwards, touching each other for the entire length of the finger. One can choose to focus the awareness on the throat or the solar plexus.

Mātaṅgī Mudrā

SĀÑJALI MUDRĀ

THE MUDRĀ OF LOVING OFFERING

MEANING AND SIGNIFICANCE

This *Mudrā* is similar to *Namaskāra Mudrā* and *Añjali Mudrā*. This *Mudrā* is practiced at the beginning or end of a prayer ceremony, meditation, or personal *mantra japa*. It is also a gesture of loving offering of flowers or any other gift to the deity, Guru, teacher, etc. It may also be practiced at the end of meditation or *Yoga āsanas* to offer the practice to the holy feet of the master, teacher, guide, or instructor. It is a *Saṁyukta Mudrā* (both hands).

FORMATION

Join the palms together, keeping a slight hollow in the center of the palm. A gift such as *japa mālā* or flowers is kept in the hollow of the hands.

Sāñjali Mudrā

VARIATION

Join the palms together, keeping a slight hollow in the center of the palm. A gift such as *japa mālā* or flowers is kept in the hollow of the hands.

SIGNIFICANCE

This *Mudrā* symbolizes loving offering. It invokes the *Śṛṅgāra Rasa*, the emotion of selfless love and beauty. It can be practiced during *Āvāhane* (at the time of invocation), *Pūjanānte* (at the commencement of a ritual) and *Visarjane* (at the time of immersion of the energy invoked). It is one of the most common *Hasta Mudrā* used in the *Yajna* (sacred fire ceremony) and *Vedic* rituals. It brings a sense of surrender and abundance. It enables the *Sādhaka* to share his/her emotions of love and thankfulness to the deity/ master/ teacher/ elders. It allows the *Sādhakas* to connect with the *Anāhata Cakra* thus the offering becomes the extension of his/ her heart field. It is a non verbal communication of love, abundance, beauty, thankfulness and surrender between the receiver and the giver.

SAṄKALPA MUDRĀ

THE MUDRĀ OF POWERFUL RESOLVE/ SEALING INTENTION

MEANING AND SIGNIFICANCE

This is a *Mudrā* of *Hindu* tradition. This *Mudrā* marks the beginning of any auspicious activity and is called the *Mudrā* of resolve. Prior to undertaking any task or project, whether spiritual or social, one needs to see the goal clearly as well as have a clear and powerful intention to reach the goal. It helps the practitioner to be in the moment, "the eternal now," as well as acknowledge the connection of the past, the present, and the future with the eternal space, which holds everything together. The resolve or the goal is visualized, mentally recited, and at times spoken aloud while holding the hands in this *Mudrā,* as he/she states the date, time, and place, the performer, the proposed activity, and the purpose, prior to the commencement of worship. Practicing of this *Mudrā* helps invoke clarity, purity, self-confidence, and courage, which are required to reach the goal. This is a *Saṁyukta Mudrā* (both hands) and is practiced by resting together both palms.

FORMATION

There is a slight hollow at the center of the palm symbolic of holding the vision and the intention. The tips of the finger and the thumb are touching each other and the fingers are kept close to each other. The *Mudrā* thus formed is kept at the level of the heart, slightly away from the body, by keeping the elbows bent comfortably. Alternately, this *Mudrā* can be practiced by keeping one palm over the other, pointing the fingers of the top hand towards the thumb of the lower hand and fingers of the lower hand pointing towards the outer edge of the little finger of the top hand. There is hardly any pressure in-between the fingers and the palms. It is a relaxed *Mudrā*.

Saṅkalpa Mudrā

As per the traditional Indian medicine system: *Ayurveda*, the center of the palm is one of the strongest and most powerful therapeutic *marma* points (subtle energy meeting points) called *Tālahradīya*; by connecting one *marma* point to another, we trigger the communication at the subtlest layer of our being.

ŚIVA MUDRĀ/ ĪŚVARA MUDRĀ

THE GESTURE OF DIVINE INVOCATION

MEANING AND SIGNIFICANCE

This is a *Mudrā* used in *Hindu* tradition during the invocation of the energy of the *īśvara* (manifested form of divine energy). It is a *Saṁyukta* (both hands) *Mudrā*. It is also used as a *tantric* gesture common to Japanese Buddhist tradition and practiced by a priest or a devotee. This *Mudrā* is generally used during the rites and rituals of invocation of *īśvarī* (Godly or Divine) energy, during meditation practices, or to trigger the energy in the body in case of extreme fatigue or during recovery from a chronic disease. The hands are kept on the lap parallel to the floor, while sitting in any meditation posture.

FORMATION

To practice this *Mudrā*, join the palms together and keep them facing each other. Now, interlace the middle finger and the ring finger with each other, keeping the index finger and the little finger stretched out and touching each other from base to tip. Keep the thumbs alongside each other, allowing them to touch each other from the inner edge from base to tip.

Śiva Mudrā

Śiva Liṅga/ Naṭarāja Mudrā

The Gesture of Masculine Energy

MEANING AND SIGNIFICANCE

Śiva is considered to be one of the Trinity (*Brahmā*: creator, *Viṣṇu*: sustainer, *Śiva*: one who annihilates or one who presides over dissolution) in *Hindu* tradition. Lord *Śiva* is usually worshipped in the abstract form of *Śiva Liṅga* (masculine energy). The meaning of *Śiva* is "the auspicious one." The *Śiva Liṅga* is regarded as a "symbol of the great power of the universe that is all-auspiciousness."

Śiva Liṅga is a hand gesture in *Hindu* tradition; it is a *Saṁyukta* (both hands) *Mudrā*. This *Mudrā* has spiritual as well as therapeutic importance. It is highly beneficial in case of dullness, fatigue, and lack of confidence and willpower. It helps in the invocation of the masculine principle and energy in the subtle layers of the being. It stimulates the physical, mental, and emotional strength in a person. This hand gesture is extremely beneficial in case of poor posture during meditation or otherwise. The acupressure points triggered alongside the thumb with the formation of the *Mudrā* sends a subtle nerve impulse to the spine to realign the vertebrae. It also helps in strengthening the middle and the lower back. It is a *Mudrā* for bringing in the principles of logic, focus, concentration, posture, and strength. Follow the rules of therapeutic *Mudrā* to gain its therapeutic benefits. For its use as a spiritual *Mudrā*, use it during meditation. It is also used by priests and devotees during certain rites, rituals, and prayers.

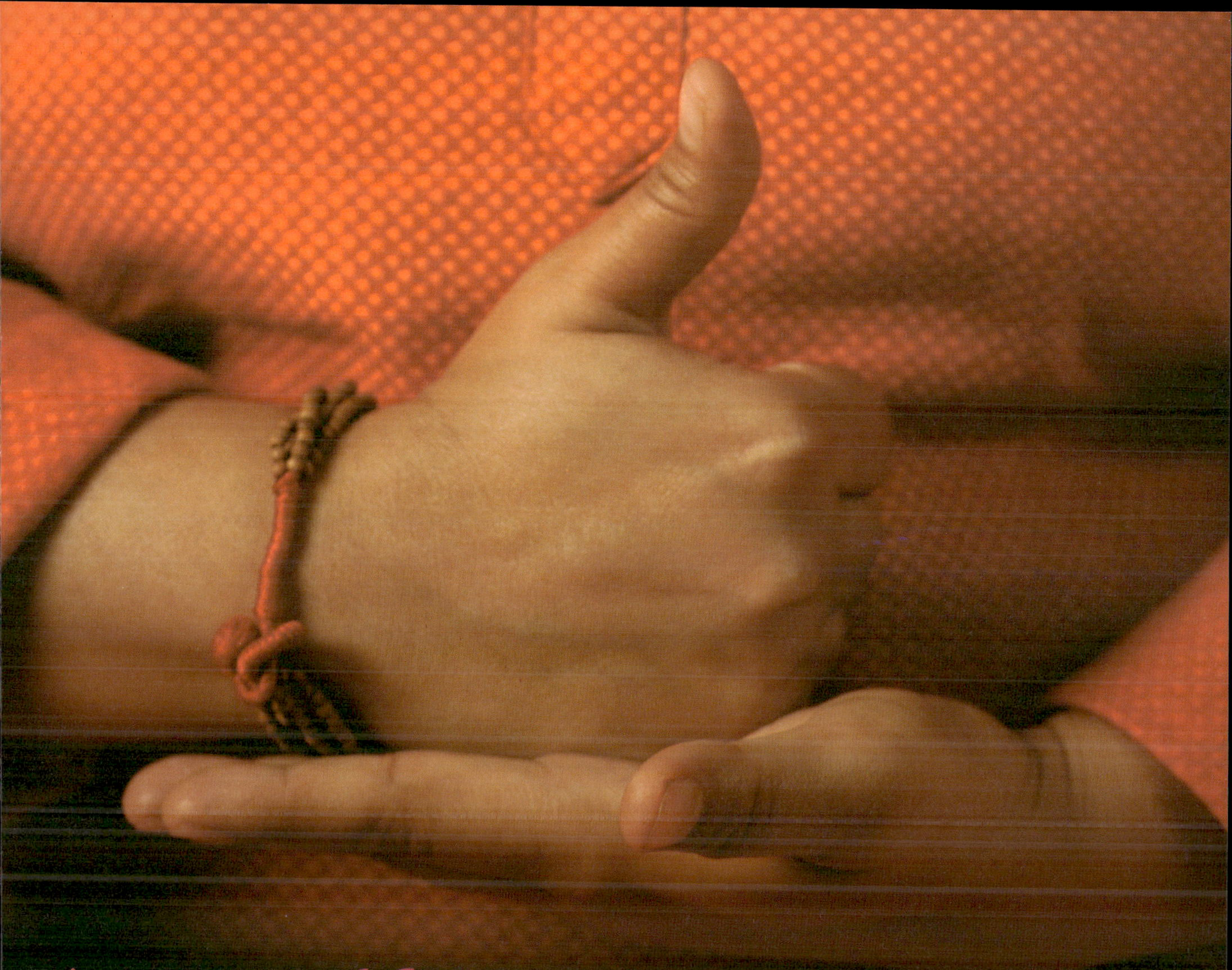

Śiva Liṅga Mudrā

FORMATION

To form this *Mudrā*, make a fist with the right hand, with the thumb stretched upwards. Keep the left hand with the palm facing up, at the level of lower abdomen or navel, with the fingers and the thumb touching each other. Place the fist formed with the right hand on top of the left hand.

UTTARABODHI MUDRĀ

THE GESTURE OF SUPREME ENLIGHTENMENT

MEANING AND SIGNIFICANCE

It is one of the ten most important Buddhist *Mudrās*. *Uttara* means "realization" and *Bodhi* means "to be an enlightened one." This is a *Saṁyukta Mudrā* (both hands), a gesture of perfection, supreme enlightenment, union, balance, and inner connection. It is practiced during meditation with or without the use of a *mantra*. It is also seen in Japanese Buddhist tradition as a *Tantric Mudrā* held by the priest or devotee. This *Mudrā* is frequently seen in images of *Vairocana*. To practice this *Mudrā*, bring the two palms together and interlace all the fingers except for the index finger. Let the index fingers touch each other and point upwards. The *Uttarabodhi Mudrā* strengthens the metal element, which is associated with the energy of the lungs and the large intestine. The metal element has a direct relationship with the nervous system and anything that conducts electrical and/or energetic impulses.

FORMATION

Interlace the little, middle, and ring fingers, extend the index fingers, and join them at the tips to each other; extend the thumbs in opposite directions and join them at the tip. There are two variations of this *Mudrā*. The first variation is when the thumbs are interlaced and hands are kept at the level of the solar plexus, parallel to the floor. In the second variation, thumbs are joined at the tip and pointed down towards the earth, and the index fingers are pointing up to the sky (symbolic of the union and transcendence of the dualities). It is a highly energizing *Mudrā* and can be practiced any time of the day.

Uttarabodhi Mudrā

VARADA MUDRĀ

THE GESTURE OF BLESSINGS AND MERCY

MEANING AND SIGNIFICANCE

This *Mudrā* of *Hindu* and Buddhist traditions is adopted by Gods, Goddess, priests, Gurus, and masters to bless the devotee, the student, or the disciple. A blessing gesture of mercy conveys an intention to fulfill desires or grant a boon. It is an *Asaṁyukta Mudrā* (single hand), done generally by left hand.

FORMATION

To form the *Mudrā*, there are many different positions of the hand. In one variation, the left hand is held at left-knee level while sitting cross-legged during meditation. In a second variation, the left hand is held at the level of left thigh with the arm extending downwards. To form the *Mudrā*, place the palm outwards, with fingers and thumb extended and pointing downwards, as if pouring or giving something away. The palm is kept completely relaxed. At times, it is done in combination with *Abhaya Mudrā*.

Varada Mudrā

YONI MUDRĀ

THE GESTURE OF FEMININE ENERGY

MEANING AND SIGNIFICANCE

This is a *Tantric Mudrā* that belongs to Buddhist, *Hindu* Buddhist, and *Yogic (Yoga Tattva Mudrā Vijñāna)* traditions. In each tradition, it has a different purpose, hand formation, and meaning. Common in all of them, however, is the underlying principle of feminine energy. It is a *Saṁyukta* (both hands) *mudrā*.

This *mudrā* is among the eight *mudrās* that are practiced after the chanting of *Gāyatrī Mantra (*the most important and the oldest *Vedic mantra)* and among the other 32 *mudrās* that are used in the invocation of energy. It is a highly spiritual *mudrās* and can be used as a therapeutic *mudrā* in case of infertility or debilitating diseases like cancer, multiple sclerosis (MS), and acquired immune deficiency syndrome (AIDS). In some case studies, this *mudrā* has been useful to combat palsy and nervous disorders by bringing about communication, connection, and harmony between the two brain hemispheres and the sympathetic and para-sympathetic nervous system.

FORMATION

Join the thumb, the middle finger, and the little finger at the tip. Keep the index finger and the ring finger stretched out. Bring the inner edges of both palms together towards the midline so that the ring fingers cross each other making the "X" or cross sign. Grip the tip of the left-hand ring finger with the right-hand index finger and the tip of the right-hand ring finger with the left-hand index finger. Now, slide the thumb at the base of the ring finger, and stretch the middle finger and the little finger straight. Keep the hands at chest level.

Yoni Mudrā

VAJRAPRADAMA MUDRĀ

THE GESTURE OF UNSHAKABLE TRUST

MEANING AND SIGNIFICANCE

Vajra has several meanings that include "thunderbolt" or "lightning bolt" and "diamond," all of which bring to mind the image of something luminous, powerful, and indestructible. *Vajra* also means "the true self, which contains these qualities." *Pradama* means "trust" or "confidence." *Vajrapradama mudrā* evokes unshakable self-confidence and inner strength. It is a *Tantric Mudrā*, prevalent in *Vajrayāna* and *Mantrayāna* Japanese Buddhist tradition.

In Buddhism, the thunderbolt represents the ultimate weapon against doubt. It is a *Saṁyukta Mudrā*. The priest or devotee generally practices this *mudrā* at the time of performing the rites of *Vajradhātu Maṇḍala* prayers. It may or may not be accompanied by *mantra* chanting. *Vajradhātu Maṇḍala* is a *Vajrayāna* Buddhist tradition known as "the diamond realm." This *maṇḍala* is meant to convey *Vairochana's sambhogakāya* (body of perfect rapture), said to be characterized by radiance and emptiness *(Śūnyatā)*. *Yogi/nis* can practice this *mudrā* in *Vajrāsana* (thunderbolt pose) to let go of self-doubt, mistrust of others, or hopelessness in the face of obstacles.

FORMATION

To practice this *mudrā*, interlace the fingers in front of the chest with the palms facing upwards and the thumbs spread out. Open the hands away from each other, creating a gentle stretch to the fingers. The hands in front of the heart form a net or a web and symbolize the interconnectedness of all that exists. By forming the shape of a net or a web in front of the heart, we acknowledge our interconnectedness with all that exists and we awaken compassion for others and ourselves.

Vajrapradama Mudrā

Summary

Through time immemorial, same message of union, oneness, dissolution, love has been passed over in various languages across geographical boundaries, races and eras. The message has not changed, maybe the way it has been communicated has. "Come back home, it's time!" This gift of *Ādhyātmika Hasta Mudrās* is shared with you with the sole intention to bring you back to the cave of your heart. You may practice them for any length of time during your contemplation/ self reflection. Just allow yourself to feel the changes in subtle energy current movements. The most important aspect would be to become a witness.

For you seek me with
Eyes, ears, nose, intellect, hands and feet
Bound are you by senses and actions
And boundless I am…
Reduced to "āṇava"

Re-think Oh Man!
Re-flect Oh Man!
Re-verse Oh Man!
Re-create Oh Man!
…Your thoughts…your visions

For I am the meaning veiled
In the meaning itself
For I am the light in the light itself

Trapped are you by your limitations
Expand and free yourself
From the knowledge and its lack…
You shall be free
For then
You shall see…

SAPTA CAKRA MUDRĀ

MUDRĀ OF CAKRA

Cakras: *Cakra* means "a wheel, a vortex, a focal point of energy, a three-dimensional energy field where more than three energy channels meet." There are seven higher, seven lower, and seven main *cakras*. Here, we shall study the seven main *cakras* in the subtle body in *sūkṣma śarīra*. Each *cakra* relates to a particular rhythm, color, energy pattern, sound vibration, element, organ of action, organ of sense, geometrical pattern, psychical posture, breath pattern, *mantra, marma* point, and *mudrā*. It means that you can tap into that energy field by focusing on any of the elements mentioned above. These are all channels to connect to the massive energy concealed in that particular energy center. The energy in this field is constantly revolving (clockwise and counterclockwise), expanding, shrinking, and pulsing at a particular rhythm and cyclic pattern. The energy in each field is connected to *sthūla śarīra:* physical body, through glands, nerves, and nervous system. In fact, there are some points called *marma* points that are the physical opening of *cakras* on the body. Each *Mudrā* activates a particular movement of energy in our body to enhance the communication between the physical and the subtle body. Let us learn seven such *Mudrā*, and their practice as meditation.

Mūlādhāra Cakra/Root Cakra/Coccygeal Plexus

The physical layer

The *Mudrā* related to this *cakra* is *Vairāgya Mudrā*. *Vairāgya* means "detachment" or "without *rāga*". *Rāga* means "the experience of the duality of emotions." The intention here is to rise beyond the obvious materialistic urges that keep us bound to the animalistic nature, and at the same time to ground ourselves to reality.

FORMATION

Touch the tips of the index finger to the first phalange of the thumb from the inner side of the hand. Rest the hands on respective knees, with the rest of the three fingers extended, palms facing up. It is a *Saṁyukta* (both hands) *Mudrā*.

MŪLĀDHĀRA CAKRA MEDITATION

Bring your attention to the point of contact formed in the *Mudrā*. Allow the *mantra* "*laṁ*" (the seed vibration of this *cakra*) to arise repeatedly in your mind field, silently. The *mantra* may move quickly or slowly. In any case, keep your attention on the space between the genitals and the pulsation that you experience at the point of contact of the *Mudrā*. Allow your mind to naturally be aware of earth, solidity, or form. Allow to rise in your mind field the awareness of the *karmendriya* of elimination, which operates throughout the body, and the *jñānendriya* of smell.

Vairāgya Mudrā

SVĀDHIṢṬHĀNA CAKRA/SACRAL PLEXUS

The emotional layer

The *Mudrā* related to this *cakra* is *Bhairava/ Bhairavī Mudrā*. *Bhairava* or *Bhairavī* is related to the creative energy force in each one of us; it may also be interpreted as the feminine energy or *Śakti*.

FORMATION

To form this *Mudrā*, put your hands on your lap, palms up and on top of each other. Keep the left hand underneath, with its palm touching the back of the fingers of the right hand. The tips of the thumbs touch gently. Concentrate on the sacral *cakra* in the lower abdominal region of the body. It is a *Saṁyukta* (both hands) *Mudrā*.

SVĀDHIṢṬHĀNA CAKRA MEDITATION

When you move your attention upwards towards the second *cakra*, be mindful of the transition and the nature of the shift of energetic, emotional, and mental experience. Allow your attention to naturally find the location of the second *cakra*. Allow the *mantra "vaṁ"* (the seed vibration of this *cakra*) to arise and repeat itself, at its own speed, naturally coming and going. Allow the awarness of water element to arise in the region of the second *cakra* as fluidity in physical, mental or emotional realms. Explore the awareness of the *karmendriya* of procreation and the *jñānendriya* of tasting.

Bhairava /Bhairavi Mudrā

MAṆIPŪRA CAKRA/NAVEL CENTER/SOLAR PLEXUS

The mental or intellectual layer

Maṇipūra means "palace of jewels." The jewels here are the impressions from the subconscious mind, the past-life accomplishments, and the previous birth's good *karmas*. This *cakra* is a focus point of our force of will and our sense of transformation. Concentration and control of our personal energies originate from this point. One's sense of power and authority, and self-control and discipline of the ego, converges here. The *Mudrā* for this cakra is *Agni Namaskāra Mudrā*.

FORMATION

To form this *Mudrā* rest your hands at the level of the abdomen, right in front of the navel, slightly below solar plexus. Let the fingers join at the tips, all pointing forward, with the hands parallel to the floor. Cross the thumbs. Keep the fingers extended forward and do not join the heels of the hands; let there be a hollow triangular space in the center of the palms. This triangular energy represents the fire element. It is a *Saṁyukta* (both hands) *Mudrā*.

MAṆIPŪRA CAKRA MEDITATION

Be aware of the transition as you move to the third *cakra*, at the navel center. Allow the *mantra "raṁ"* (the seed vibration of this *cakra*) to arise and repeat itself, at its natural speed. Be aware of the element of fire, and the many ways in which it operates throughout the gross and subtle body from this center. Be aware of the *karmendriya* of motion, and how motion itself happens in so many physical, energetic, and mental ways. Be aware of the *jñānendriya* of seeing, which you will easily see as related to fire and motion.

Agni Namaskāra Mudrā

ANĀHATA CAKRA/HEART/ CARDIAC PLEXUS

The astral layer

Anāhata means "the unstuck sound, a sound that cannot be created or destroyed, a sound that is innate, and a sound that is subtler than silence." The heart *cakra* is the focus for love and understanding. Feelings that stem from this love – such as forgiveness, compassion, balance, and harmony – radiate from this point. This *cakra* also nurtures the rarified feeling of unconditional or divine love, love that goes beyond the physical. The *Mudrā* for this *cakra* is *Pūrṇa Jñāna Mudrā*, which means complete wisdom: true and pure love.

FORMATION

To form this *Mudrā*, let the tips of your index finger and thumb touch, like in *Jñāna Mudrā* of both hands. Put your left hand on your left knee, cupping the knee, and your right hand in front of the lower part of your breast bone (so a bit above the solar plexus), facing the chest. It is a *Saṁyukta* (both hands) *Mudrā*.

ANĀHATA CAKRA MEDITATION

Observe the transition as you move your attention to the fourth *cakra*, the space between the breasts. Allow attention to become well-seated there, and then remember the vibration of the *mantra* "*yaṁ*" (the seed vibration of this *cakra*), allowing it to repeat at its own speed, while being mindful of the feeling it generates. Be aware of the element of air, and notice how that feels with the *mantra*. Notice how the element of air relates to the *karmendriya* of holding or grasping, whether physically, energetically, mentally, or emotionally. Observe how these relate to the *jñānendriya* of touching, and how that touching is very subtle in addition to being a physical phenomenon.

Pūrṇa Jñāna Mudrā

Viśuddhi Cakra/ Throat or Laryngopharyngeal Plexus

The etheric layer

Viśuddhi means "absolute purity". The throat *cakra* is located in the throat area between chin and the top of the sternum. This *cakra* is linked to power of communication. Through this *cakra*, one can realize truth and knowledge, honesty, kindness, and wisdom, and how these elements can be conveyed through thoughtful speech. The *Mudrā* for this *cakra* is *Viśuddhi Mudrā.*

FORMATION

Interlace your fingers outside, let the thumbs touch at the tips, and pull them slightly up as if you are holding a circular ball of energy in the center of the palm. The hands are kept at the level of the chest or throat. It is a *Saṁyukta* (both hands) *Mudrā*.

VIŚUDDHI CAKRA MEDITATION

Bring your attention to the space at the throat, the fifth *cakra*, which is the point of emergence of space (which allows air, fire, water, and earth to then emerge). In that space, be aware of the nature of space itself, allowing the *mantra "haṁ"* (the seed vibration of this *cakra*) to arise and repeat itself, reverberating many times through the seemingly empty space in the inner world. Awareness of the *karmendriya* of speech (actually, communication of any subtle form) helps in experiencing how that vibrates through space. The *jñānendriya* of hearing aligns with space, speech, and the vibration of *mantra*. Notice the fine, subtle feelings that come with the experience.

Viśuddhi Mudrā

Ājñā Cakra/ Occipital Plexus/ Third Eye Center

The "third eye" is the celestial layer

Ājñā means "permission" – the permission to transcend the five elements, space, time, dualities, the five organs of senses, and the five organs of action. This *cakra* is located in the forehead, right above the eyes. This *cakra* is related to our perception beyond the physical realm. Intuition, insight, imagination, and clairvoyance can all be associated with this *cakra*. One can also focus their realization of their own soul, divine wisdom, and peace of mind on this point. The *Mudrā* for this *cakra* is *Kāleśvara Mudrā*. *Kāleśvara* means "the lord of time and space, one who has transcended and presides over these meters of time and space."

FORMATION

To form the *Mudrā*, bend the index, ring, and little fingers of both hands from the second phalange, pointing them down, and let them touch each other as they bend down. Keep the middle finger extended upwards towards the sky, touching each other at the tip. Keep the thumbs pointed down towards the floor, touching each other at the tip. It is a *Saṁyukta* (both hands) *Mudrā*.

Kāleśvara Mudrā

ĀJÑĀ CAKRA MEDITATION

Gently, with full awareness, transition awareness to the seat of mind at the space between the eyebrows, the *ājñā cakra*. Allow the *mantra* "*OM*" (the seed vibration of this *cakra*) or "*kṣaṁ*" to arise and repeat itself, over and over, as slow waves of *mantra*, or as vibrations repeating so fast that the many *OMs* merge into a continuous vibration. Be aware of how the mind has no elements, but is the source out of which space, air, fire, water, and earth emerge. Be aware of how this space, this mind itself, does no actions, but is the driving force of all of the *karmendriyas* of speech, holding, moving, procreating, and eliminating. Be aware of how this cakra has no sense itself, but is the recipient of all of the information coming from hearing, touching, seeing, tasting, and smelling. Observe keenly how the source of this input is the sensations from the external world, coming through the physical instruments, or coming from the inner world of memories/subtle experiences, presenting on the mental screen through the subtle senses.

SAHASRĀRA CAKRA/CROWN CAKRA

The Ketheric Layer

Sahasrā means "thousand" and here it refers to the "thousand-petaled lotus," where each petal is a vibration of the 50 syllables, with each syllable inscribed 20 times. The crown *cakra* is located at the very top of the head. As one might guess, this *cakra* is associated directly with dealings of the mind and the spirit. This *cakra* is deeply tied to the exploration of one's consciousness and place in space and time. Oneness with the universe, your spirit and will, inspiration, divine wisdom… all the things that deal with the higher self are rooted in this *cakra*. The *Mudrā* for this *cakra* is *Śakti Mudrā.*

FORMATION

To form this *Mudrā*, let the ring fingers point up, touching at their tops. Cross the rest of your fingers, with the left thumb also interlaced. It is a *Saṁyukta* (both hands) *Mudrā*.

SAHASRĀRA CAKRA MEDITATION

Allow attention to move to the crown *cakra*, which has no element *(bhūtas)*, no cognitive sense *(jñānendriyas)*, and no active means of expression *(karmendriyas),* as it is the doorway to pure consciousness itself. Experience how this is the source of mind, which gives birth to five elements, the five cognitive senses, and the five means of expression. The *mantra* (in its subtler, silent form) is that silence (not mere quiet) out of which the rest have emerged. It is experienced as the silence after a single *OM*, merging into objectless, sense-less awareness. Allow attention to rest in that pure stillness, the emptiness that is not empty, which contains, and is, the pure potential for manifestation, which has not manifested yet.

Śakti Mudrā

Summary

Practice the *Sapta Cakra Mudrā* Meditation once a day for one week to feel the energetic pulsation in the subtle layers of your being. It is suggested to not bind with the duration of mediation. The time boundaries naturally fade as one progress in the practice with regularity and discipline.

Disciple asks
: Where should I seek thee my Master?

Master Speaks
: When the two lotuses close
Seek me at the foothills of the cave, Where the currents of fire and water meet
Follow the path of stillness in movement
As you enter the cave, The darkness transforms into light
The sound and silence merge, The movement conjoins stillness
All the boundaries fade, There you seek Me!

Disciple asks:
: When shall I seek Thee?

Master Speaks
: When the Sun becomes the Moon & Moon becomes Sun
Enter the cave
When the seven (7) Wheels pulsate, dance, expand and shrink
Draw within from Nine (9) Gates, The twenty-four (24) Tattvas
Then
You meditate upon the Self, Meditate upon Me

Disciple asks:
: Why shall I seek Thee?

Master Speaks
: Time and again
You have come to Me, In the darkness of silence
You have questioned the Self for its purpose
Within you I reside
Coming back to home is the key!

Gāyatrī Mantra Mudrā

Mudrās in the practice of Gāyatrī

Gāyatrī mantra is also known as *Sāvitrī mantra* and is dedicated to the sun, the source of light and life in the universe. It is derived from *Ṛg-veda* and *Ṛṣi Viśvāmitra* is regarded as the main channel for this *mantra*. *Gāyatrī mantra* is considered to be the *Mahā mantra* and *Veda-mātā* (mother of *Veda* and mother of all *mantras*) owing to the benefits it confers in the form of wisdom, guidance, and prosperity upon the meditator. It is one of the greatest, ancient most, and first *Vedic mantras.*
In the practice of *Gāyatrī mantra*, it is said by the *ṛṣis* (divine seers) in the *Śāstras* that "for one who does not know the *Gāyatrī Mantra Mudrās*, the *mantra* does not yield any results, is fruitless," as stated in the *mantra* here:

Etā Mudrā na jānāti gāyatrī niṣphalā bhavet
Etā Mudrā tu kartavyā gāyatrī supratiṣṭhitā

Gāyatrī mantra recitation is incomplete without the practice of *Mudrā*. Very few people know about it and even less is the number of people who practice it. When practiced with *Mudrā*, this *mantra* is praised to the point where it is described as miraculous and most effective.

There are 32 *Hasta Mudrās* associated with the chanting of this *mantra*. Out of this, 24 are practiced before the chant and 8 after the chant. The 24 *Mudrās* are related to 24 *Tattvas* (elements) as per the *Vedic* theory of evolution of the cosmos. As per *Ayurveda*, the 24 *Tattvas* are 5 organs of action *(karmendriya)*, 5 organs of senses *(jñānendriya)*, 6 *dhātus* (tissues), 5 elements *(pañca mahābhūtas)*, *manas, buddhi, and citta*. The number 24 is also related to 24 reincarnations of *Sanātana Dharma*, 24 *Tīrthankaras* of Jain tradition, and 24 syllables of *Gāyatri mantra.* There is a detailed mention of these *Mudrās* in *Tantra*, Buddhist, and Yogic tradition. These 32 *Mudrās* are also related to the 32 main vertebras.

OM Bhūḥ! OM Bhuvaḥ! OM Svaḥ! OM Mahāh ! OM Janah! OM Tapaḥ! OM Satyam!
OM
Tat savitur vareṇyaṁ (8 syllables)
Bhargo devasya dhīmahi (8 syllables)
Dhiyo yo naḥ pracodayāt (8 syllables)
Om Āpo jyotī raso'mṛtaṁ brahma bhūr bhuvaḥ svar Om

Summarized Meaning of the *Mantra*

The chanting, the rhythm, the words...protect the aspirant

Gāyatrī mantra is dedicated to the Sun, the source of light and life in the universe. This *mantra* is dedicated to Goddess *Gāyatrī*, which means *Śakti*. It means: "We welcome the energies of three planes of existence – The Earth Plane, The Astral Plane, and The Heavenly Plane. We surrender to the light, brilliance, splendor, and golden aura of the Sun that is worthy of our prayers and worship. One who is the dispeller of darkness (*karmas*, ignorance, unawareness, fear and phobias) and the bestower of light (symbol of knowledge – which helps us to go beyond the *tri-guṇas – sattva, rajas*, and *tamas*; rise beyond dualities – likes and dislikes, good and bad, sorrow and happiness, pleasure and pain, life and death), so that it may guide our intellect (mind and attribute) towards the right direction. *(Aham Brahma Asmi* – I AM THAT). The best time for chanting this *mantra* is *Muhūrta* (before sunrise/evening [dusk]), sitting in a meditative pose.

The *24 Mudrās* before chanting *Gāyatrī mantra* are as follows:

sumukhaṁ sampuṭaṁ caiva vitataṁ vistṛtaṁ tathā
dvimukhaṁ trimukhaṁ caiva catuḥ pañcamukhaṁ tathā
ṣaṇmukhādhomukhaṁ caiva vyāpakāñjalikaṁ tathā
Śakaṭaṁ yamapāśaṁ ca granthitaṁ conmukhonmukham
pralambaṁ muṣṭikaṁ caiva matsyaṁ kūrmaṁ varāhakam
siṁhakrānta-mahākrāntaṁ mudgaraṁ pallavaṁ tathā

SUMUKHA MUDRĀ

This is the first *Hasta Mudrā* in the series of 24 *Mudrās* preliminary to *Gāyatrī mantra* chanting. It is a *Saṁyukta* (both hands) *Mudrā* and is a great *Mudrā* for fighting debilitating diseases. The *Sumukha* is another name of *Śiva*. To form this *Mudrā*, face the palms to the midline, so that all the fingers and the thumb are touching each other and curled to form a cavity in the center of the palm. Hold the *Mudrā* at the level of the chest.

SAMPUṬA MUDRĀ

This is the second *Mudrā* in the series of 24 *Mudrās*. *Sampuṭa* means "hidden treasure." Thus, this *Mudrā* helps in releasing the hidden potential within us, which is the real treasure within each one of us. It is a *Saṁyukta* (both hands) *Mudrā*. To practice this *Mudrā*, bring both the palms to midline, and join the fingertips and thumb tips lightly to each other. Now, bring the heels of the palms also close to each other, as if you are holding a garland of fresh flowers in your hand–a very delicate gesture. The hands are held at the level of the chest.

Vitata Mudrā

Vitata means "most acceptable or pleasant." This is an *Asaṁyukta* (single hand) *Mudrā* where both hands are used without touching each other. This is the third *Mudrā* in the series of 24 *Gāyatrī Mantra Mudrās*. To form this *Mudrā*, we keep the hands parallel to each other, palms facing the midline, almost 6-10 inches apart. Hands are kept completely relaxed, to the point that it feels as if they are holding some energy balls in the center of the palms. The *Mudrā* thus formed is kept at the level of the chest.

Vistṛta Mudrā

Vistṛta means "expanded or elaborated." Here, it means the expansion to form five elements. It is an *Asaṁyukta* (single hand) *Mudrā*. This is fifth *Mudrā* in the series. To form this *Mudrā*, simply separate the hands almost shoulder-width apart (double the space between hands, as done in the case of *Vitata Mudrā*). The hands are kept at the level of the abdomen.

Dvimukha Mudrā

Dvimukha means "one who has two faces or is two-faced." Generally, it is used in case of a creature with two faces. Here, it means the multiplication of the *Tattvas*. It is a *Saṁyukta* (both hands) *Mudrā*. To form this *Mudrā*, bring the palms to the midline, so that you touch the tip of the little and the ring fingers to each other; the rest of the two fingers and the thumb are kept apart and spread out. Hands are kept in a relaxed gesture at the level of the chest.

Trimukha Mudrā

Trimukha means "three-faced." At times, it is also used for *Brahman* or to mean holding of the three *Vedas* in the mouth! It is a *Saṁyukta* (both hands) *Mudrā*. To form this *Mudrā*, bring the palms to the midline, so that you touch the tips of the little, ring, and middle fingers of one hand to those of the other hand; the index fingers and the thumbs are kept apart and spread out. Hands are kept in a relaxed gesture at the level of the chest.

Caturmukha Mudrā

Caturmukha means "four-faced." It is a *Saṁyukta* (both hands) *Mudrā*. To form this *Mudrā*, bring the palms to the midline, so that you touch the tip of the little finger, the ring finger, the middle finger, and the index finger to each other, while the thumbs are kept apart and spread out. Hands are kept in a relaxed gesture at the level of the chest.

PAÑCAMUKHA MUDRĀ

Pañcamukha means "five-faced." Here, it also means five elements. It is a *Saṁyukta* (both hands) *Mudrā*. To form this *Mudrā*, bring the palms to the midline, so that you touch the tips of all the fingers and the thumbs to each other. Make sure that you keep a hollow space in the center of the palm – the heels of the palms are not touching each other. Hands are kept in a relaxed gesture at the level of the chest.

ṢAṆMUKHA MUDRĀ

Ṣaṇmukha means "having six faces." It is a *Saṁyukta* (both hands) *Mudrā*. To form this *Mudrā*, bring the palms to the midline, so that you touch the tips of all the fingers and the thumbs to each other, except for the little finger, which is kept spread out. Make sure that you keep a hollow space in the center of the palm – the heels of the palm are not touching each other. Hands are kept in a relaxed gesture at the level of the chest.

ADHOMUKHA MUDRĀ

*A*dhomukha refers to Lord *Viṣṇu*; it also means facing downwards. It is a *Saṁyukta* (both hands) *Mudrā*. To form this *Mudrā*, join the back of the palms from the second phalange to the tips of the fingers, pointing the tips of the fingers towards the chest. The thumbs are raised up, and the cups of the palms are facing you.

Vyāpakāñjalika Mudrā

Vyāpakāñjalika means "all-pervasive surrender." It is a *Saṁyukta* (both hands) *Mudrā*. To form this *Mudrā*, palms face upwards, with the inner edges of the palms (the little finger side) touching each other. Fingers are extended forward, and thumbs are extended outwards and separated a little. The *Mudrā* thus formed is held at the level of the waist.

Śakaṭa Mudrā

Śakaṭa means "carriage." It is a *Saṁyukta* (both hands) *Mudrā*. The hands are facing downwards; the middle, ring, and little fingers are folded into the palm; the index fingers are extended forward, parallel to the floor as well as to each other; and the thumbs are facing each other, touching at the tip and kept 90 degrees to the hand. The *Mudrā* is held at the level of the waist.

YAMAPĀŚA MUDRĀ

Yamapāśa means "snare of the noose of *Yama* (the lord of death)." It is a *Saṁyukta* (both hands) *Mudrā*. To form this *Mudrā*, face the right hand inside with the middle, ring, and little fingers curled into the palm to form a soft fist. The index finger is bent at the second and first joint/ phalange; grip the left-hand index fingertip with it like a hook. In a similar way, fold the middle, ring, and little fingers of the left hand also into the palm keeping the left hand parallel to the floor. The thumbs of both hands are extended. This is *Yamapāśa Mudrā* and it is held at the level of the waist.

GRANTHI MUDRĀ

Granthi means "knot." It symbolizes the interlacing of purity and generosity. This *Mudrā* is a *Saṁyukta* (both hands) *Mudrā*. It also means the summoning/invitation of knowledge. To form this *Mudrā*, interlace all the fingers with each other, towards the midline, palms touching each other and thumbs also interlaced with each other. The *Mudrā* thus formed is at the level of the waist.

Unmukhon-mukha Mudrā

This is a *Saṁyukta* (both hands) *Mudrā* and is done in a two-step process.

Step one: Join the fingers of both hands together; keep the left hand down and the right hand on top. Place the tips of the fingers upon each other.

Step two: In this state, the hands should be rotated so that the right hand comes down and the left up, and then vice versa. This completes the two-step process of this special *Mudrā*.

Pralamba Mudrā

Pralamba means "bending of the upper part of the body forward, leaving it loose to hang down." It is a *Saṁyukta* (both hands) *Mudrā*. To form this *Mudrā*, face both the palms downwards and let them loose; fingers are extended, and the thumb sides of the hands are close to each other. Hands are almost parallel to the floor but not stiff.

Muṣṭika Mudrā

Muṣṭi means "fist," *Muṣṭika* means "handful of." It can also be described as a *Mudrā* for summoning courage, inner strength, as well as physical strength. This is a *Saṁyukta* (both hands) *Mudrā*. To form this *Mudrā*, both hands form a fist, and then, they are brought together so that the second phalanges of the fingers touch each other back to back, and the thumbs touch along their length. The *Mudrā* is held at the waist level.

MATSYA MUDRĀ

Matsya means "fish." Here, it may also mean the water element. It symbolizes the *matsyāvatāra* (incarnation as a fish) of Lord *Viṣṇu* (protector/ sustainer of the universe). This *Mudrā* is common to *Hindu* and Buddhist traditions. It is also a prevalent *Mudrā* in *Yogic* tradition, particularly in *Yoga Tattva Mudrā Vijñāna*. It is a *Saṁyukta* (both hands) *Mudrā*. To form this *Mudrā*, place the right hand over the left hand with the palms of both hands down. Keep the fingers of both hands extended and together. The hands are kept parallel to the floor. Thumbs are extended outwards at a right angle to the palm. Fingers are pointing away from you. This *Mudrā* is held at the waist level.

Kūrma Mudrā

Kūrma means "tortoise." It symbolizes the second incarnation of Lord *Viṣṇu*. It denotes a long peaceful life. It is a prevalent *Mudrā* in *Yoga Tattva Mudrā Vijñāna* of *Yogic* tradition. It is a *Saṁyukta* (both hands) *Mudrā*. To form this *Mudrā*, right palm faces down, middle and ring fingers are curled into the center of the palm, and index and little fingers are extended out parallel to the floor and to each other, too. Left palm is facing up with middle and ring fingers curled into the center of palm; index and little fingers are extended so that the index finger is pointing towards midline. Place the second phalanges of the right hand on top of the second phalanges of the left hand. Touch the tip of right-hand index finger with left-hand thumb, and right-hand little finger to left-hand index finger. The thumb of right hand is at 90 degrees to the palm and extended outwards. The little finger of the left hand can be curled in or kept extended.

Varāhaka Mudrā

Varāha/Varāhaka means "boar", another incarnation of Lord *Viṣṇu*. It is a *Saṁyukta* (both hands) *Mudrā*. To form this *Mudrā*, keep the right palm facing up, curl all the fingers upwards, and keep the fingers together. Now, grip all the four fingers of the right hand with the finger of the left hand, from the index finger side of the right hand. Then, join the tips of the thumbs of both hands together and raise them pointing upwards.

SIṀHA-KRĀNTA MUDRĀ

Siṁha means "lion" and *Krānta* means "revolution." It means transformation and change that come from the courage and ability to face the truth. It is one of the five reincarnations of Lord *Viṣṇu*. It is a *Saṁyukta* (both hands) *Mudrā*. In this *Mudrā*, the hands are kept on either side of the shoulder in line with the shoulder and the chest, raised up and palms facing forward, with fingers and thumbs extended and raised upwards. The hands are in a relaxed gesture.

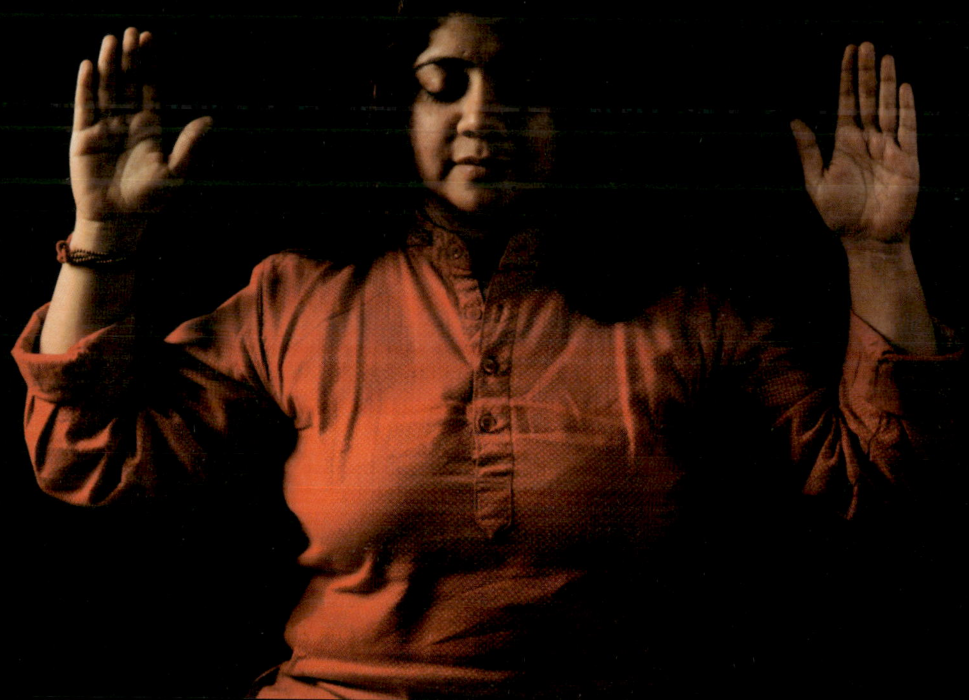

MAHĀKRĀNTA MUDRĀ

Mahākrānta means "great revolution – the great change that follows courage, determination, and clarity." It is a *Saṁyukta* (both hands) *Mudrā*. To form this *Mudrā*, the hands are kept on either side of the shoulder , a little more than shoulder-width apart, raised up, palms facing each other towards the midline, with fingers and thumbs extended and raised upwards. The hands are in a relaxed gesture.

MUDGARA MUDRĀ

Mudgara means "a hammer," a wooden hammer at times. In some places, it also means a bud or a jasmine flower. It is a *Saṁyukta* (both hands) *Mudrā*. To form this *Mudrā*, bend the right arm at the elbow, so that the palm faces outside and the hand is at the level of right shoulder. Make a soft fist with the right hand, with thumb alongside, and bend left hand elbow keeping the left palm in a soft cup like formation. Left-hand fingers are all together and extended.

PALLAVA MUDRĀ

Pallava means "a bud, a sprout, and a tender leaf." Depending upon its context, the meaning keeps changing. It is an *Asaṁyukta* (single hand) *Mudrā*. It is done with right hand. The right palm faces forward, with fingers and thumb extended upwards. The fingers are kept slightly apart and hands are kept shoulder-high and relaxed.

Eight Mudrās are done after the chanting of *Gāyatrī mantra*, as expressed here:

Surabhir jñana-vairāgyaṁ Yoniḥ śaṅkhó tha paṅkajam
Liṅgaṁ nirvāṇakaṁ caiva japānte'ṣṭau pradarśayet

These *Mudrās* are to be done in the sequence suggested below. Each *Mudrā* refers to a state of mind and evolution of consciousness to various planes of existence. One connects with these states and stages while practicing the *Mudrās* as well as connects to the inherent vibrations of these states. With regular practicing of these states of mind, one starts to manifest these states, provided one has purity of intent and intensity of practice.

1. *Surabhī Mudrā*

This *Mudrā* invokes the *Agni Tattva* which rises to unite with the *soma* flowing as a stream from the *Sahasrāra cakra*. It also depicts a state of fulfillment and manifestation of the single most desire of union through liberation.

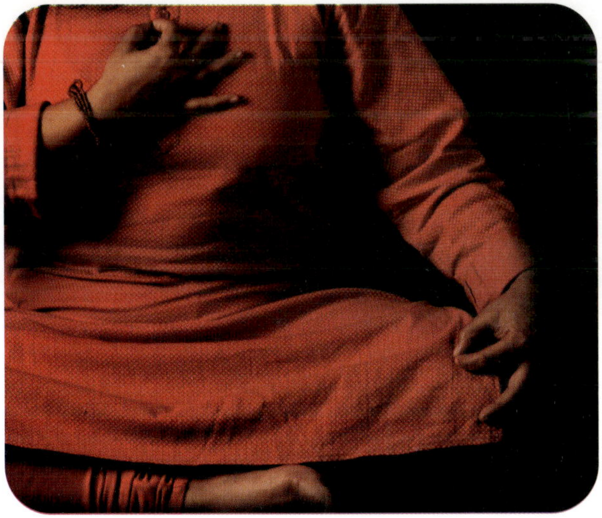

2. *Jñāna Mudrā*

This *Mudrā* is the state of arising and flowing of wisdom which manifests itself as a result of merging of *Agni* in *Soma* and *Soma* in *Agni*. It is a state of awareness of cosmic intelligence known as *Mahad*.

3. *Vairāgya Mudrā*

This *Mudrā* symbolizes and represents the state of detachment from attachment. It is a state of the fullness of "Self" and is achieved by few. It is when we limit to "Self" that we become full ourselves. In this state, there is no *rāgā* or *dwesha*, it is a state of fullness in solitude.

4. *Yoni Mudrā*

Śakti rises from its abode to the *Param Śiva* in *Yoni Mudrā*. The state of mind is that of *Dhyāna* transforming into *Samādhi*.

5. *Śaṅkha Mudrā*

As the *Śakti* rises from the *Mūlādhāra* (known as *Brahamarandhra* or the lower opening of the *Suṣumṇā*), it pierces and passes through the *Anāhata*, then the 10 *Nādas* (The first sound is Chini; the second is Chini-Chini; the third is the sound of bell; the fourth is that of conch; the fifth is that of *Tantri* (lute); the sixth is that of *Tala* (cymbals); the seventh is that of flute; the eighth is that of *Bheri* (drum); the ninth is that of *Mṛdaṅga* (double drum) and the tenth is that of clouds, viz., thunder) are heard and experienced through the practice of the *Mudrā*. It is a state when the '*Bhramara Guhā* (cave of the bumble bee) connects with the '*Hrid Guhā* (cave of the heart).

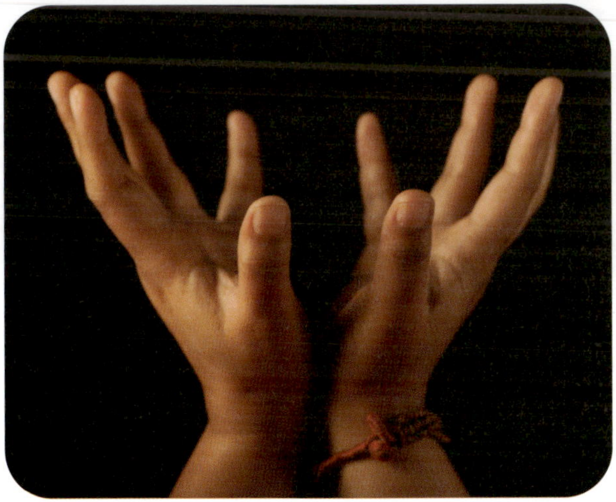

6. *Paṅkaja/Padma Mudrā*

This *Mudrā* symbolizes the opening of the lotuses of the heart, throat and third eye. The *Anāhata Nādas* harmonize the 3 higher *cakras* *(Anāhata, Vishuddhi and Ajna)* with its subtle and unstruck frequencies. This is the state of full blooming of inner potential.

7. ***Liṅga Mudrā***

The state when one becomes *Śiva*. As per the *Śiva Sūtras, "Yatha Tatra Tathan Yatra"* (3.14) which means as here so everywhere. One becomes none and the state of *Śiva* arises from within. This is the state of complete union and merging. This is the state of dissolution.

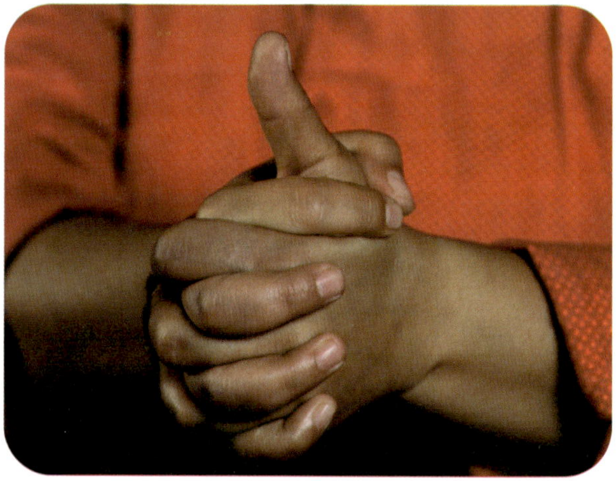

8. ***Nirvāṇa Mudrā***

Nirvāṇa means "ultimate liberation by the union with the supreme." In some contexts, it also means becoming free from grief, suffering, attachment, greed, etc. It is a *Saṁyukta* (both hands) *Mudrā*. Cross the hands at the wrist level, so that the right hand faces right side and the left hand faces left side. Now, cup the hands to each other so that the fingertips are touching each other along with the thumb. Keep the fingers upright and extended softly. The thumbs are facing forward. The hands are kept close to the heart.

Summary

The key feature of *Gāyatrī mantra tapas* is the infusion of the potency of the *Gāyatrī mantra* into every cell of the human body. One of the ways this is achieved is through the use of *Mudrā* (hand gestures) along with with *Gāyatrī* meditation. Start the practice by first becoming familiar with the hand formations and then mastering the sequence. Once the practice of sequencing is achieved, then slowly the 24 *Mudrās* can be practiced with each of the 24 syllables and 8 *Mudrās* by the end of the *Mantra*. Try this practice at dawn, noon and dusk to reap its maximum benefits by tapping into the *sattvik* solar energy. Different texts have been written and complied on *Gāyatrī mantra tapas,* the intention here is to introduce the hidden and mysterious concept of *Mudrās* to the reader.

Śiva Sūtra is a central text for Kashmir Shaivism revealed to a sage Vasugupta in a dream.

Below is the first Sūtra of the first awakening: Shambhavopaya in poetry.

Sūtra 1.1: Chaitanya Atma

Self-Luminous I am
For I am the light
Atman is my nature
Beyond the time and space
I am Spanda
Tuned to fullness
I am the light within the light
Though self luminous I still illuminate
Objects all animate and inanimate
You see the flowers, sky, colors and forms
I see the Self in my own reflection
Pure, still...enlightened in my own nature...

Ṣaḍaṅga-Nyāsa Mudrā

Mudrā: Touch, Protect & Awaken

Ṣaḍ means "six," Aṅga means "body parts." Hence, Ṣaḍaṅga means "six body parts." Nyāsa means "placement." Ṣaḍaṅga Nyāsa means "the placements of the hands in different body parts to sensitize the six main cakras before some tantric rituals." The practitioner touches various parts of the body at the same time pronouncing a mantra and visualising a devata or a bīja (root) mantra. There are many types of Nyāsa, with some being very complex and elaborate. The types of Nyāsa most often encountered in tantric ritual are Ṛṣi Nyāsa, Kara (hand) Nyāsa, Matrika Nyāsa and Ṣaḍaṅga Nyāsa.

Matrika Nyāsa is a form where the 50 letters of the Sanskrit alphabet are placed on the body. As this is done, the practitioner uses various hand gestures (Mudrās). The letters are prefixed with OM and suffixed with namaha.

Ṣaḍaṅga Nyāsa uses bīja connected with long vowels of the Sanskrit alphabet. Aṅga Nyāsa and Kara (hand) Nyāsa are the two forms of Ṣaḍaṅga Nyāsa. When Ṣaḍaṅga Nyāsa is performed on the body, it is called Hṛdayādi-ṣaḍaṅga Nyāsa; and when done with the five fingers and palms of the hands only, Aṅguṣṭhādi Ṣaḍaṅga Nyāsa.

The mantras of Ṣaḍaṅga Nyāsa on the body are used for Kara (hand) Nyāsa, in which they are assigned to the thumbs, the index finger, the middle finger, the fourth, little finger, and the front and back of the palm.

These actions on the body, fingers, and palms also stimulate the nerve centers and nerves. For the attainment of that state in which the sādhaka feels that the bhāva (nature, disposition) of the Devatā has come upon him, Nyāsa is a great auxiliary. It is, as it were, the wearing of jewels on different parts of the body. The bīja of the Devatā are the jewels which the sādhaka places on the different parts of body. By Nyāsa he places his Abhīṣṭa-devatā in such parts, and by vyāpaka-nyāsa, he spreads its presence throughout himself. Nyāsa is also of use in effecting the proper distribution of the Śakti of the human frame in their proper positions so as to avoid the production of discord and distraction in worship. Nyāsa as well as Āsana are necessary for the production of the desired state of mind and of citta-śuddhi (its purification).

Hṛdayāya Mudrā

It is an *Asaṁyukta* (single hand) *Mudrā*. The heart center is touched with the palm in *Hṛdayāya Ṣaḍaṅga Nyāsa Mudrā* for sensitizing the heart *cakra* by chanting this *mantra* along with the *Mudrā*:

Om hṛdayāya namaḥ

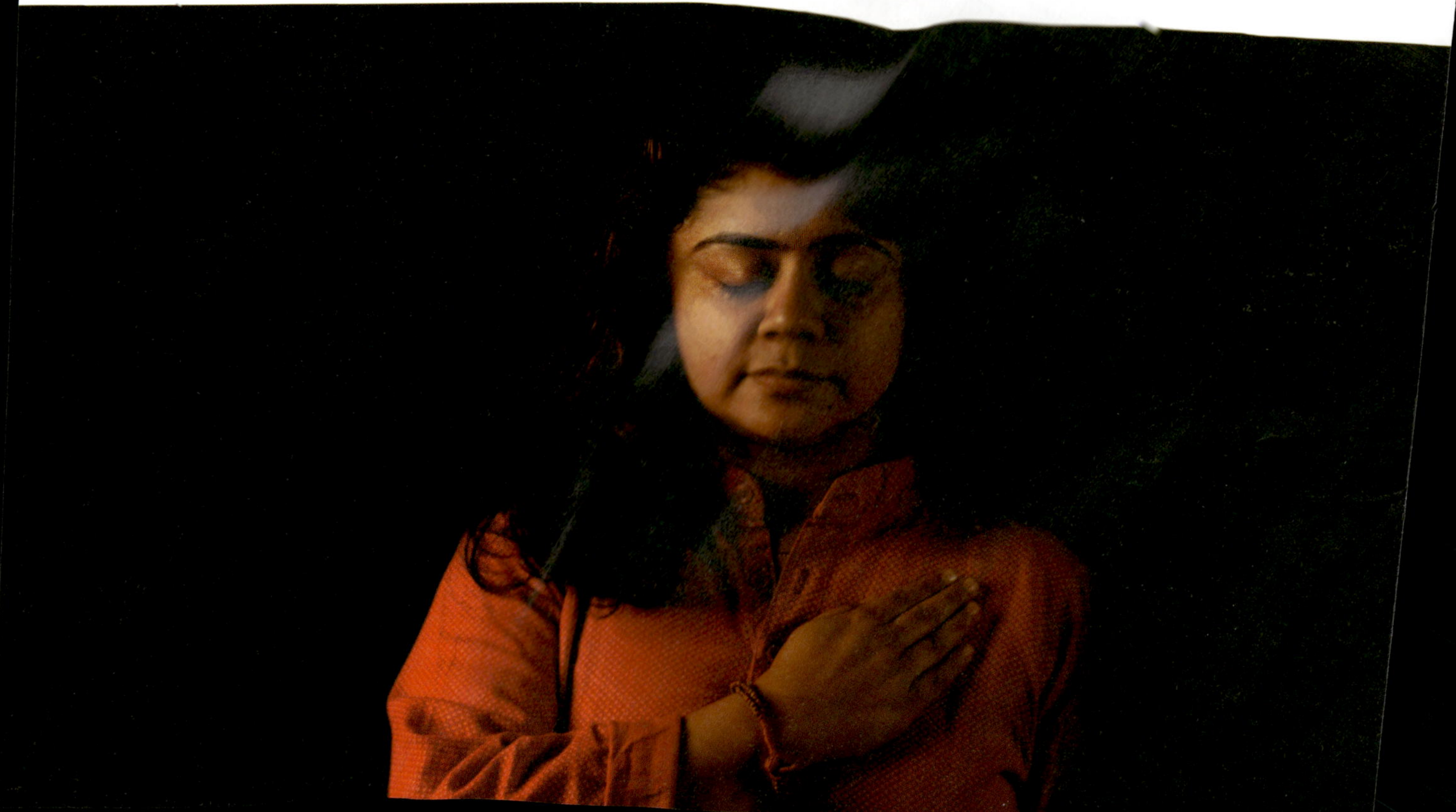

KAVACĀYA MUDRĀ

It is a *Saṁyukta* (both hands) *Mudrā*. Touch the opposite arms by palms, crossing them at the level of the wrist in *Kavacāya Ṣaḍaṅga Nyāsa Mudrā,* for sensitizing the *cakra* by chanting this *mantra* along with the *Mudrā*:

Om svaḥ kavacāya hum

NETRATRAYĀYA MUDRĀ

It is an *Asaṁyukta* (single hand) *Mudrā*. The index finger and the middle finger of the right hand touch the closed eyes one by one, starting with the right eye in *Netratrayāya Ṣaḍaṅga Nyāsa Mudrā,* for sensitizing the third eye *cakra* by chanting this *mantra* along with the *Mudrā*:

Om bhuvaḥ netratrayāya vauṣaṭ

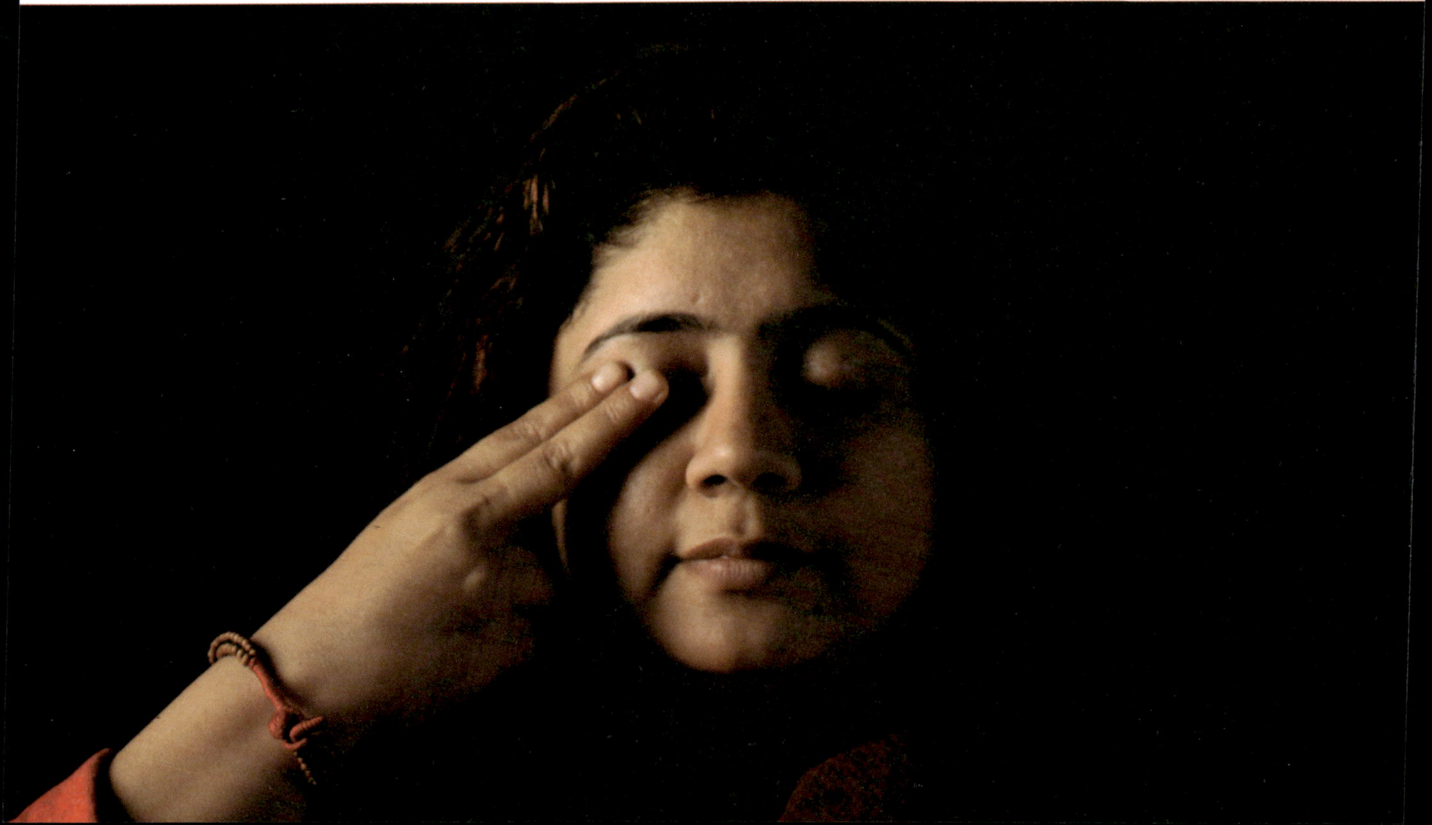

Phaṭ Mudrā

It is a *Saṁyukta* (both hands) *Mudrā*. The index finger and the middle finger of the right hand touch the center of the left-hand palm with a sound in *Phaṭ Ṣaḍaṅga Nyāsa Mudrā*, for sensitizing the *cakra* by chanting this *mantra* along with the *Mudrā:*

Om bhūr bhuvaḥ phaṭ

Śikhāyai Mudrā

It is an *Asaṁyukta* (single hand) *Mudrā*. The right hands form the *Śikhāyai Mudrā* and the thumb of the right hand touches the top of the head (known as *Śikhā*, the tip) in *Śikhāyai Ṣaḍaṅga Nyāsa Mudrā,* for sensitizing the crown *cakra* by chanting this *mantra* along with the *Mudrā*:

Om svaḥ śikhāyai hum

Śirase Mudrā

It is an *Asaṁyukta* (single hand) *Mudrā*. Touch the forehead with the four fingers of the right hand in *Śirase Ṣaḍaṅga Nyāsa Mudrā*, for sensitizing the *cakra* by chanting this *mantra* along with the *Mudrā*:

Om klīṁ śirase svāhā

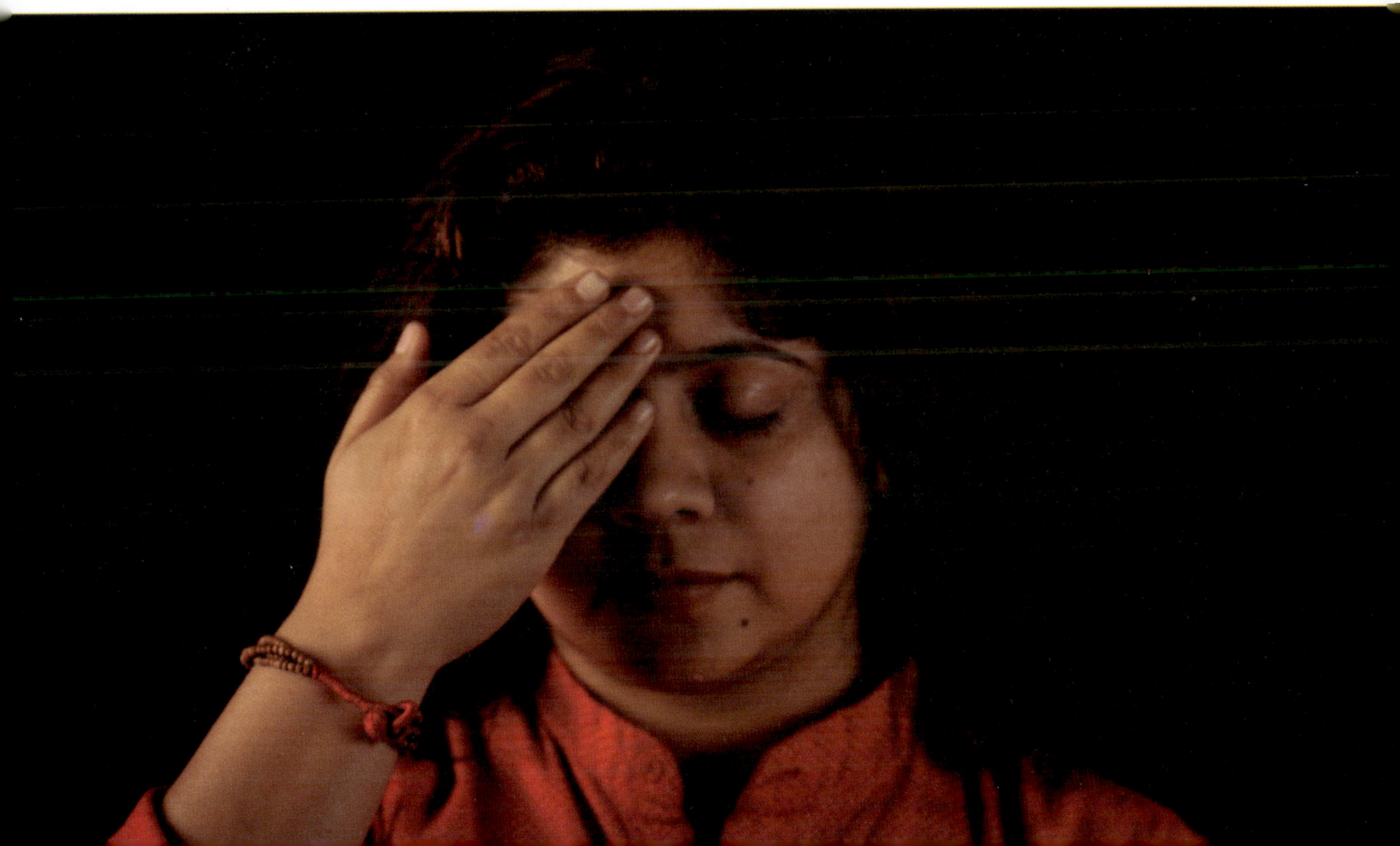

Summary

"Mental worship is superior, and external worship is inferior. By worshipping Devatā, a sādhaka is himself honoured"

- *Niruttara Tantra.*

The practice of *Ṣaḍaṅga Nyāsa* is the practice of bringing life to the body. The application of many and diverse ritual practices such as gestures *(Mudrās)* and touching the various parts of the body *(Nyāsa)* not only have symbolic significance but a psychological basis as well; they deepen concentration and expand the awareness of the aspirants. The *tantrikas* believe that the flesh must be awakened from its dormancy, and this rite symbolically puts the divinities into the various organs of the body. Both *Mudrās* and *Nyāsas* are external expressions of "inner resolve," suggesting that such non-verbal communications are more powerful than the spoken word.

In recent years there has been a growing awareness of the efficacy of such non-verbal communication. A group of scientists studying this form of communication has established that there appears to be an "alphabet" of gestures, postures, body movements which express much more than words can convey. A recent study by the psychologist Albert Mehrabian based on extensive laboratory measurement of the communication between two persons, concluded that only 7% of the message's effect is carried by words, while 93 % of the total impact reaches the 'listener' through non-verbal means. . . Further, feelings are conveyed mainly by non-verbal behaviour.

"||हरी ॐ तत सत||"

From the womb of consciousness
I come on Earth
To bind myself to karmas unlimited
As body: as limitations
Amba gave birth to me
Vama brough me into being
Jyeshtha grew me up
Raudri dissolves me back…
I am one
Yet became Two
To
Give birth to you
I am the womb
I am the fetus
I am the birth
I am its karma
I am its bondage
I am its re-cognition
I am its dissolution
I am ONE yet again…

When it is time...
I fill myself
From the reservoir supreme
A drop in me
A fluid dance I then create
I move, I stop
I stop, I move
When this movement
Fills me to the brim
The churning creates the force within
The energy unimaginable I create in me
But
A push minimal I then need
To rise, dissolve and manifest
To manifest, dissolve and rise
When it is time...

Mudrā Therapy Quick Guide

A

Alzheimer's: *Vāyu Mudrā, Vāta-kāraka Mudrā, Jñāna Mudrā, Prāṇa Mudrā*

Anxiety: *Pṛthivī Mudrā, Jñana Mudrā, Sparśa Mudrā, Cin Mudrā, Vāyu- śāmaka Mudrā, Vāta-nāśaka Mudrā, Mṛta Sañjīvanī Mudrā, Pūṣan Mudrā, Vajra-padma Mudrā, Añjali Mudrā, Ādi Mudrā*

Arthritis: *Sandhi Mudrā, Daṇḍa Svāsthya Mudrā, Vāyu- śāmaka , Vāta-nāśaka, Pṛthivī-vardhaka Mudrā*

Atrophy of muscles: *Pṛthivī Mudrā, Prāṇa Mudrā*

Anus, burning/fissure in: *Pṛthivī Mudrā*

Acidity: *Prāṇa Mudrā, Vāyu Mudrā, Pṛthivī Mudrā, Kapha-Kārak Mudrā, Jal-śāmaka Mudrā*

Appetite (loss): *Samāna Mudrā, Sūrya Mudrā, Gaṇeśa Mudrā, Pṛthivī-śāmaka Mudrā, Prāṇa Mudrā, Liṅga Mudrā*

Anaemia: *Jala Mudrā, Mṛta Sañjīvanī Mudrā*

Abdominal pain: *Vāyu Mudrā, Samāna Mudrā, Muṣṭi Mudrā, Apāna Vāyu Mudrā, Mātaṅgī Mudrā, Agni Namaskāra Mudrā*

Anger: *Pṛthivī Mudrā, Vāyu Mudrā, Cin Mudrā*

Ageing, premature: *Pṛthivī Mudrā, Jala Mudrā*

Acne: *Jala Mudrā, Samāna Mudrā, Kāyākalpa Mudrā*

Anuria: *Apāna Mudrā, Jala Mudrā, Surabhī Mudrā*

Angina pectoris: *Apāna Vāyu Mudrā*

Asthma: *Liṅga Mudrā, Śvāsai Cikitsā Mudrā, Ākāśa Mudrā, Sūrya Mudrā*

Allergy: *Kāyākalpa Mudrā, Liṅga Mudrā, Śaṅkha Mudrā, Sandhi Mudrā, Pṛthivī Mudrā*

Appendicitis: *Apāna Vāyu Mudrā, Pṛthivī Mudrā*

B

Bradycardia: *Vāyu Mudrā*

Brittle nails: *Pṛthivī Mudrā*

Blood pressure (high): *Mṛga Mudrā, Vyāna Mudrā*

Bones, to strengthen: *Pṛthivī Mudrā*

Blood circulation, slow: *Prāṇa Mudrā, Jala Mudrā, Vāyu Mudrā, Vyāna Mudrā*

Backache: *Vāyu Mudrā, Daṇḍa Svāsthya Mudrā, Sandhi Mudrā*

Bloody stools/urine: *Prāṇa Mudrā*

Blood pressure (low): *Mṛga Mudrā, Pṛthivī Mudrā, Śūnya Mudrā*

Bed-wetting: *Jala Śāmaka Mudrā* (the thumb presses the second phalange of the little finger and little finger is bend into the center of the palm, all other fingers extended)

Bronchitis: *Śvāsa Nālikā Mudrā, Śvāsi Cikitsā Mudrā, Liṅga Mudrā, Pṛthivī Mudrā*

Blocked nose: *Śūnya Mudrā, Sūrya Mudrā, Liṅga Mudrā, Hākinī Mudrā*

Brain (to empower): *Jñāna Mudrā, Śakti and Mudrā*

C

Creativity: *Bhairavī Mudrā, Śakti Mudrā, Kāleśvara Mudrā*

Cerebral palsy: *Vyāna Mudrā, Surabhī Mudrā, Yoni Mudrā*

Concentration (lack of): *Jñāna Mudrā, Pṛthivī Mudrā*

Constipation: *Apāna Mudrā, Muṣṭi Mudrā, Surabhī Mudrā, Vāyu Mudrā, Sūrya Mudrā, Jala Mudrā*

Chronic fatigue: *Pṛthivī Mudrā, Prāṇa Mudrā, Pūṣana Mudrā, Muṣṭi Mudrā, Dhyānī Mudrā*

Convalescence: *Pṛthivī Mudrā*

Coldness of body/skin: *Sūrya Mudrā, Liṅga Mudrā*

Cataract: *Vyāna Mudrā, Sūrya Mudrā, Prāṇa Mudrā*

Chest pain: *Liṅga Mudrā, Madhyama Sparśa Mudrā, Apāna Mudrā*

Colds: *Sūrya Mudrā, Liṅga Mudrā*

Cough (wet): *Liṅga Mudrā, Prāṇa Mudrā*

Cough (dry)*: Vāyu Mudrā, Liṅga Mudrā*

D

Dementia: *Vāyu Mudrā, Jñāna Mudrā, Cin Mudrā, Vitarka Mudrā*

Diabetes mellitus: *Viparīta Namaskāra, Apāna Mudrā, Muṣṭi Mudrā, Vāyu Mudrā*

Dizziness: *Pṛthivī Mudrā, Prāṇa Mudrā, Jñāna Mudrā*

Detoxification: *Kāyākalpa Mudrā, Apāna Mudrā*

Deafness: *Śūnya Mudrā*

Dry eyes: *Jala Mudrā, Prāṇa Mudrā*

Dehydration: *Jala Mudrā*

Diarrhea: *Pṛthivī Mudrā, Prāṇa Mudrā, Udāna Mudrā, Samāna Mudrā*

Depression: *Pūṣana Mudrā, Mātaṅgī Mudrā, Pṛthivī Mudrā, Sūrya Mudrā, Jñāna Mudrā, Liṅga Mudrā, Sūrya Mudrā*

Dry mouth throat: *Jala Mudrā*

E

Endocrine disorders: *Surabhī Mudrā, Yoni Mudrā, Śakti Mudrā, Vāyu Mudrā*

Epilepsy: *Vāyu Mudrā, Pṛthivī Mudrā, Surabhī Mudrā*

Ear disorders (pain): *Sūnya Mudrā, Vāyu Mudrā*

Emaciation (weight-loss): *Pṛthivī Mudrā, Prāṇa Mudrā*

Excessive sleep: *Vāyu Mudrā, Sūrya Mudrā, Pūṣan Mudrā*

Eye-ailments (watering): *Sūrya Mudrā, Prāṇa Mudrā*

Eczema (dry): *Jala Mudrā*

F

Flatulence (gas): *Vāyu Mudrā, Muṣṭi Mudrā, Samāna Mudrā*

Frozen shoulder: *Apāna Vāyu Mudrā, Vāyu Mudrā*

Fracture: *Pṛthivī Mudrā*

Feet (cold): *Liṅga Mudrā, Vyāna Mudrā*

Forgetfulness: *Jñāna Mudrā, Pṛthivī Mudrā, Prāṇa Mudrā, Vitarka Mudrā, Dhyānī Mudrā*

G

Gastric ulcer: *Pṛthivī Mudrā*

Giddiness: *Vāyu Mudrā, Pṛthivī Mudrā*

Gas: *Vāyu Mudrā, Apāna Mudrā, Muṣṭi Mudrā, Samāna Mudrā*

Gastritis: *Pṛthivī Mudrā, Apāna Mudrā, Prāṇa Mudrā, Jala Mudrā*

H

Heart weak/ failure: *Jñāna Mudrā, Vyāna Mudrā, Apāna Vāyu Mudrā, Añjali Mudrā, Bhairava Mudrā*

Hypothyroidism: *Sūrya Mudrā, Liṅga Mudrā, Śaṅkha Mudrā*

Hyperthyroidism: *Prāṇa Mudrā, Pṛthivī Mudrā, Vāyu Mudrā*

Hiccups: *Apāna Vāyu Mudrā, Vāyu Mudrā*

Heat (intolerance): *Jñāna Mudrā, Vyāna Mudrā, Pṛthivī Mudrā*

Headache: *Mahā Śīrṣa Mudrā, Apāna Vāyu Mudrā, Vāyu Mudrā*

I

Irregular hear-beats: *Apāna Vāyu Mudrā, Ākāśa Mudrā, Pṛthivī Mudrā, Prāṇa Mudrā, Jñāna Mudrā*

Indigestion: *Samāna Mudrā, Sūrya Mudrā, Prāṇa Mudrā, Muṣṭi Mudrā*

Immunity (weak): *Garuḍa Mudrā, Sūrya Mudrā, Śaṅkha Mudrā, Liṅga Mudrā, Prāṇa Mudrā, Pūṣan Mudrā, Ādi Mudrā, Yoga Mudrā*

Impotence: *Prāṇa Mudrā, Pṛthivī Mudrā, Liṅga Mudrā, Kāmajayī Mudrā*

Infertility: *Yoni Mudrā, Bhairavī Mudrā, Śakti Mudrā*

J

Joint-pains: *Sandhi Mudrā, Vāyu Mudrā, Pṛthivī Mudrā*

Jaundice: *Prāṇa Mudrā, Samāna Mudrā*

K

Kidney ailments: *Apāna Vāyu Mudrā, Apāna Mudrā, Muṣṭi Mudrā*

Kapha (mucous) excessive: *Sūrya Mudrā, Liṅga Mudrā*

L

Loss of memory: *Jñāna Mudrā, Pṛthivī Mudrā*

Lethargy: *Dhyānī Mudrā, Kubera Mudrā, Mātaṅgī Mudrā, Meru Daṇḍa Mudrā, Śiva Liṅga Mudrā, Sūrya Mudrā, Uttarabodhi Mudrā, Vajra-padma Mudrā, Jñāna Mudrā, Vāyu Mudrā*

Loss of taste-sensation: *Bhairavī Mudrā, Jala Mudrā*

Liver ailments: *Samāna Mudrā, Prāṇa Mudrā*

Leucorrhoea: *Apāna Mudrā, Prāṇa Mudrā, Pṛthivī Mudrā*

Lumbago: *Meru Daṇḍa Mudrā, Daṇḍa Svāsthya Mudrā, Sandhi Mudrā, Vāyu Mudrā, Apāna Mudrā*

M

Muscles (to strengthen): *Jñāna Mudrā, Pṛthivī Mudrā*

Multiple sclerosis: *Jñāna Mudrā, Pṛthivī Mudrā*

Mucous (excessive): *Liṅga Mudrā, Sūrya Mudrā, Pūṣana Mudrā, Prāṇa Mudrā, Garuḍa Mudrā, Viparīta Namaskāra Mudrā*

Muscle spasm /cramps/rigidity: *Jala Mudrā, Vāyu Mudrā*

Migraine: *Mahāśīrṣ Mudrā, Vāyu Mudrā, Jñāna Mudrā, Apāna Mudrā*

Mouth ulcers: *Pṛthivī Mudrā, Jala Mudrā*

Menstrual problems:

Scanty: *Pṛthivī Mudrā, Sūrya Mudrā, Vāyu Mudrā, Apāna Mudrā*

Excessive menstruation: *Prāṇa Mudrā, Vāyu Mudrā*

Painful menstruation: *Vāyu Mudrā, Surabhī Mudrā, Apāna Vāyu Mudrā*

Irregular menstruation: *Surabhī Mudrā, Yoni Mudrā, Bhairavī Mudrā*

Mental tension: *Prāṇa Mudrā, Jñāna Mudrā*

Menopause: *Prāṇa Mudrā with Apāna Mudrā, Jala Mudrā*

N

Nausea: *Pūṣana Mudrā*

Nervous (system) disorders: *Jñāna Mudrā, Vyāna Mudrā, Yoni Mudrā*

Numbness in body /hands/feet: *Vāyu Mudrā, Sūnya Mudrā, Pṛthivī Mudrā, Vyāna Mudrā*

Nose/smell disorders: *Pṛthivī Mudrā*

Nervous exhaustion/breakdown: *Jñāna Mudrā, Vyāna Mudrā*

Neck-pain, stiffness: *Vāyu Mudrā, Sandhi Mudrā*

Nausea: *Pṛthivī Mudrā, Apāna Mudrā*

O

Osteoporosis: *Pṛthivī Mudrā, Prāṇa Mudrā*

Obesity: *Sūrya Mudrā, Liṅga Mudrā, Samāna Mudrā*

Odema: *Girivara Mudrā, Sūrya Mudrā, Liṅga Mudrā*

P

Prostatitis: *Pṛthivī Mudrā, Prāṇa Mudrā*

Parkinson's disease: *Vāyu Mudrā, Apāna Mudrā, Apāna Vāyu Mudrā*

Palpitations: *Apāna Vāyu Mudrā*

Psoriasis: *Jala Mudrā, Vāyu Mudrā*

Painful conditions: *Vāyu Mudrā, Apāna Vāyu Mudrā*

Piles: *Pṛthivī Mudrā, Apāna Vāyu Mudrā*

Pneumonia: *Pṛthivī Mudrā, Prāṇa Mudrā, Śaṅkha Mudrā*

S

Stress: *Jñāna Mudrā, Pṛthivī Mudrā, Pūṣana Mudrā, Vāyu Mudrā, Hākinī Mudrā, All 10 Sparśa Mudrā, Añjali Mudrā, Prāṇa Jñāna Mudrā*

Sleepness: *Nidra Mudrā, Vāyu Mudrā, Pṛthivī Mudrā, Prāṇa Mudrā*

Sciatica: *Vāyu Mudrā, Śikhara Mudrā, Śiva Liṅga Mudrā*

Skin (dry-cracked): *Jala Mudrā, Prāṇa Mudrā, Pṛthivī Mudrā*

Skin: Mature, ageing: *Pṛthivī Mudrā*

Sinusitis: *Hākinī Mudrā, Liṅga Mudrā, Mukula Mudrā, Ākāśa Mudrā*

Shivering: *Sūrya Mudrā, Vāyu Mudrā, Jñāna Mudrā, Liṅga Mudrā*

Sweating (absent): *Sūrya Mudrā, Prāṇa Mudrā, Vyāna Mudrā*

Sweating (excessive): *Pṛthivī Mudrā*

Scanty urine: *Girivara Mudrā, Prāṇa Mudrā*

Stammering: *Vāyu Mudrā, Śaṅkha Mudrā, Mātaṅgī Mudrā, Viśuddhi Mudrā*

Sexual debility: *Yoni Mudrā, Kubera Mudrā, Surabhī Mudrā, Kāmajayī Mudrā, Pṛthivī Mudrā, Prāṇa Mudrā*

Swelling: *Sūrya Mudrā, Vyāna Mudrā*

T

Typhoid: *Pṛthivī Mudrā, Jala Mudrā, Jñāna Mudrā, Samāna Mudrā, Śaṅkha Mudrā*

T.B: Pṛthivī Mudrā

Tennis elbow: *Vāyu Mudrā, Vyāna Mudrā, Apāna Vāyu Mudrā, Sandhi Mudrā*

Toothache: *Apāna Vāyu Mudrā, Vāyu Mudrā, Śūnya Mudrā*

Tonsillitis: *Liṅga Mudrā, Viśuddhi Mudrā, Dhyānī Mudrā, Śaṅkha Mudrā, Apāna Mudrā*

Tinnitus (noises in the ear): *Śūnya Mudrā, Pṛthivī Mudrā, Vāyu Mudrā*

U

Urticaria, itching: *Jala Mudrā, Prāṇa Mudrā, Yoni Mudrā, Surabhī Mudrā*

Ulcers in mouth /stomach/intestines: *Pṛthivī Mudrā, Prāṇa Mudrā*

V

Vision: *Prāṇa Mudrā, Vyāna Mudrā*

Voice lost/feeble*: Śaṅkha Mudrā, Pṛthivī Mudrā*

Voice hoarse/strained: *Śaṅkha Mudrā, Mātaṅgī Mudrā, Pṛthivī Mudrā*

Vertigo: *Ākāśa Mudrā, Pṛthivī Mudrā, Vāyu Mudrā*

Vata(air)excessive: *Vāyu Mudrā, Samāna Mudrā, Muṣṭi Mudrā, Gaṇeśa Mudrā*

Varicose veins: *Pṛthivī Mudrā, Vyāna Mudrā, Apāna Vāyu Mudrā, Apāna Mudrā*

W

Weakness: *Jñāna Mudrā, Dhyānī Mudrā, Abhaya Mudrā, Vyāna Mudrā, Prāṇa Mudrā*

Weight-loss (to arrest): *Pṛthivī Mudrā, Vāyu Mudrā, Prāṇa Mudrā*

Water retention: *Girivara Mudrā, Liṅga Mudrā, Sūrya Mudrā*

Watery eyes: *Prāṇa Mudrā*

GLOSSARY (A)*

This is a special glossary where the focus is not merely on translation of the *Sanskrit* word into English, but also on trying to find the meaning as per the root vibration.

- *Abhaya: bhi:* to fear
- *Abhiśeka: sic:* to irrigate, to sprinkle, to pour, to dip
- *Adhama Sparśa:* adhama: lowest, sparsh: to touch
- *Adhomukha:* facing down
- *Ādya:* upper, higher
- *Agni:* fire gesture, *ag:* to go (up)
- *Ahaṁkāra, aham:* I, *kri:* to do
- *Ākāśa:* ether gesture, *kash*: to shine brightly, to see clearly
- *Anja:* One who is decorated with flowers, sandalwood, kumkum, water, honor, respect, etc.
- *Añjali anj:* one who is decorated by flowers, sandalwood, kumkum, water, honor, respect, etc.
- *Apāna: apa:* to flow downwards, *ana:* to breathe, to live
- *Asaṁyukta/Saṁyukta: yoj:* to yoke, to unite
- *Ātmāñjali:* self, omnipresent; *at:* to pervade, to go constantly, *anj:* one who is decorated with flowers, sandalwood, *kumkum*, water, honor, respect, etc.
- *Āvāhana: aa+vah:* to invite, to invoke
- *Bhūmi-Sparśa: bhu:* to exist, *sprish*: to touch
- *Caturmukhī:* having four mouths
- *Cetanā: cit:* to be conscious
- *Cin: cit:* to observe, to perceive, to comprehend, to be aware

---

**: This glossary is provided by Siddhartha Krishna*

- *Cin: cit:* to be conscious
- *Cinmaya: cit:* to know, to be conscious
- *Dharma: dhri:* to bear
- *Dhyānī: dhyai:* to meditate
- *Dvimukhī:* having two mouths
- *Gaṇeśa: gan:* to count, to enumerate, to sum up, *ish:* to rule, to preside over
- *Garuḍa: grii:* to swallow
- *Girivaraa: gri:* to praise, to extol
- *Granthi: grath:* to fasten, to tie together
- *Jñāna: jna:* to know
- *Hākinī:* female demon
- *Haṁsī:* female swan, she who walks gracefully, *han*: to walk
- *Hṛdayāñjali: hri:* to draw, magnetic pull
- *Jala: water gesture, jal:* to be rich, to be wealthy, to be cold
- *Kāleśvara: kal:* to count, to calculate, *ish*: to rule, to own, to reign
- *Kārak: kri:* to do
- *Kailās* (Lord *Śiva's* abode): *K*: Water, *las*: to play, enjoy, sport, to frolic, dance
- *Kāma-jayī: kam:* to desire, *ji:* to conquer
- *Kapitthaka, kapi:* monkey (sits on that tree, as the fruit of that tree is dear to monkey), *stha:* to sit, to reside, to dwell
- *Kashyapa:* name of a *ṛṣi, kashya:* ignorance, *pa:* to drink up (in the sense of "to dry out or to destroy")
- *Kāyākalpa: kaya:* body, *kalpa:* rejuvenation, fitness, competency
- *Kṣepaṇa: kship:* to throw
- *Lakṣ:* to perceive, to observe, to notice
- *Lakṣmi:* the deity of wealth, she who notices a hard-worker

- *Latā:* creeper, creeping plant, *lat:* to wrap, to envelop
- *Laxmi: lakṣ:* to observe, to mark
- *Liṅga: lig:* to go, to know
- *Madhyama: madhya:* in-between, sprish: to touch
- *Mahāt: mah:* to exalt, to magnify, to esteem highly
- *Mātaṅgī: Mātaṅgī* = female elephant
- *Matsya: matsya:* fish, the happy one, *mad:* to be happy, to revel
- *Mṛga:* to chase, to pursue, to seek
- *Mṛta Sañjīvanī: mri:* to die, *jiv:* to live
- *Mudgara: mud:* to rejoice, to be happy, *grii:* to destroy
- *Mudrā: mud*-like *modak:* glad, rejoice, happy, have pleasure, delight
- *Mukula:* half-bloomed flower, *much:* to free, to liberate, one who has detached from one stage to another and not yet taken another form, is in process
- *Muṣṭi: mush:* to steal, *Muṣṭi:* fist, clenched hand (the hand closed to clasp anything stolen)
- *Nāshak: nash:* to destroy
- *Namaskāra: nam:* to bow, *kri:* to do
- *Naṭarāja: nat:* to dance, *raaj:* to reign, to illuminate
- *Nidrā-Hasta: nidra:* sleep, *hasta:* hand, *has:* to laugh
- *Nirvāṇa: nir+vaa:* to blow out
- *Padma-kośa:* lotus bud, *pad:* to go, to acquire, *kush:* to come together, to embrace, to enclose
- *Pañcamukhī:* having five mouths
- *Paṅkaja/Padma:* mud-born, *pach:* to spread, pank: *mud*, mire, muck, *ja:* one who blooms in
- *Pralamba: lamb:* to hang, to depend
- *Prāṇāyāma: a-yam:* to stretch, lengthen out, restrain, extend, hold in
- *Prāṇa: pra:* inward-coming impulse, *ana:* to breathe, to live
- *Pṛthivī: earth gesture, prath:* to spread, to manifest, to extend

- *Pūṣan: push:* to nourish, nurture
- *Puśpa -Añjali, pushp:* to bloom, *anj:* one who is decorated with flowers, sandalwood, kumkum water, honor, respect
- *Puśpa - pūta: pushp:* to bloom, *puu:* to be pure
- *Puśpa -mālā:* that which causes respect, give respect, *pushp:* to bloom, *maa:* to respect
- *Samāna: sam:* similar, *ana:* to breathe, to live
- *Sampuṭa: put:* to clasp, to fold
- *Saṁyukta: yoj:* to yoke, to unite
- *Saṅkalpa: klrip:* to consider
- *Śāmaka: sham:* to appease, to calm
- *Śakaṭa: shak:* to be able
- *Śakti Mudrā: shak:* to be able
- *Śāmaka: sham:* to appease, to calm
- *Śaṅkha: sham:* peace
- *Ṣaṇmukhī:* having six mouths
- *Śikhara Mudrā:* top of a mountain, from *shikha:* the flame of fire, *shii:* to sleep, to rest
- *Śiva Liṅga: Śiva* = in whom all things lie, *shi:* to rest, to lie down, *lig:* to go, to know
- *Śūnya: shvi:* to increase, to grow
- *Siṁha-krānta Mudrā: kram:* to walk, to go
- *Suman: man:* to know, to understand
- *Surabhī: sura:* gods, *rabh:* to desire
- *Sūcī: needle, suuch:* to point, to indicate, to indicate by gesture
- *Tattva Mudrā:* essence of that *(Brahman)*, *tat:* that
- *Tṛmukhī:* having three mouths
- *Udāna: ud:* to raise higher, *ana:* to breathe, to live
- *Ūru: Ūru* = thigh

- *Uttarabodhi: budh:* to know, to realize, to awaken
- *Vāyu: vaa:* to blow, to be defused
- *Vāyu:* air gesture, *vaa:* to blow, to be defused
- *Vairāgya:* detachment *ranj:* to colour, to be affected, to be attached
- *Vajra:* thunderbolt (and also diamond, depending upon the context), *vaj:* to go, to acquire
- *Varada: vri:* to chose, *da:* to give
- *Vardhaka: vridh:* to increase
- *Varuṇa: vri:* to choose, to love
- *Vibhāga:* division, separation, *bhaj:* to distribute, to divide
- *Viśuddhi: shudh:* to become pure
- *Vitarka Mudrā/Manana:* to contemplate, *tark:* light, to infer, try to discover, to speculate about, to reason, to reflect, to shine, to ascertain
- *Vitata: vi+tan:* to spread, to extend
- *Vyāna: vi:* to disperse, spread, diffuse, *ana:* to breathe, to live
- *Vyāpakāñjalika: aap:* to reach, to pervade
- *Yama-pāṣa: yam:* to control, pash: to bind
- *Yoni: yu:* to unite, to worship

GLOSSARY (B)*

This section is merely an effort to find/ share the relative English term for the *Sanskrit* word.

- *Acalāgni:* eternal fire/flame
- *Ādhyātmika*: spiritual, relating to supreme, holy, causes within one's self
- *Agni*: fire
- *Agni- cakra*: the circle of fire
- *Agni-śālā:* the fire pit
- *Agrā:* forward, in front
- *Ākāśa*: ether gesture
- *Apāna:* downward moving, negative force, one of the five vital airs
- *Arcita*: greeting, salutation
- *Aśoka*: devoid of depression, sadness, alternately it is also name of a tree
- *Bhairava*: form of *Śiva*, destroyer of fear, one who has the radiance of fire and is faster than the air
- *Bhairavī*: consort of *Bhairava*
- *Bhramara*: bee, humming sound of a bee
- *Bhūmi-sparśa*: the earth as witness, the act of touching earth with hands
- *Buddhapātra*: *Buddha* here symbolizes upholder of law, *pātra* means a beggling bowl, an empty bowl
- *Cikitsaka:* therapeutic, one who gives therapy: doctor, healer
- *Dharma- Cakra*: the wheel of righteousness
- *Haṁsa:* swan
- *Hṛdayāya*: heart, core, centre
- *Īśvara*: As per *Vedas "ishavasyam idam sarvam,"* which means whatever there is in this world is covered and filled with *Ishvara*. *Ishvara* not only creates the world, but then also enters into everything there is.

**: This glossary is provided by Siddhartha Krishna*

- *Kacchapa/ Kūrma*: turtle
- *Kavacāya:* shield, veil, cover, protection
- *Kubera:* Lord of wealth, the divine treasurer
- *Jala*: water, liquid
- *Latā*: entwinement, string of pearls, creeper, any winding plant
- *Mahā-krānti*: the great revolution
- *Netra-trayāya:* the third eye
- *Nyāsa*: assignment of various parts of the body to tutelary deities, drawing, trust, bringing forward, placing, introducing
- *Mukula*: unbloomed flower bud
- *Muṣṭi:* fist
- *Nāḍī*: pulse, river, vein, tubular organ, artery, tube, flowing water, one that produces sound
- *Namaskāra*: the act of bowing, surrender and acknowledgement
- *Nidrā*: deep sleep
- *Pallava*: tender leaf, part of the paragraph, bud, sprout, particular position of hands in dancing
- *Ṣaḍaṅga*: with the incorporation of body parts, along with body
- *Sāṅjali*: handful of flower, offering with respect
- *Śirase*: head, crown, top
- *Sumukha*: face to face, bright faced, handsome, having a good entrance, favourable, cheerful, learned man or teacher
- *Surabhī*: wish fulfilling cow, lovely, famous, sweet smelling, fragrant, earth, virtuous, gold, perfume, aroma
- *Paṅkaja/Padma*:full-bloomed lotus
- *Padma-kośa*: heart of lotus, lotus bud
- *Prāṇa*: energy, breath of life, life, spirit, one of the five vital airs
- *Pṛthivī*: earth
- *Pūrṇa*: complete, whole, full, contentment, satisfaction
- *Pūṣan*: sun

- *Puśpāñjali*: Handful of/ holding of flowers
- *Puśpa-mālā*: garland of flowers
- *Śakti*: energy flow, feminine strength, female personification of divine energy
- *Śakti-jāgaraṇa*: the uprising of the energy, *Kuṇḍalinī śakti,* the awakening
- *Sandhi*: joint, meeting point, agreement, union, connection
- *Śaṅkha:* conch
- *Samāna*: balanced, similar, one of the five vital airs
- *Śodhana*: cleansing, washing, making clean, purification, act of making pure
- *Śūnya*: void, space, ether, zero, null, void, empty
- *Surabhī Mudrā*: Wish-fulfilling *mudrā*
- *Śvāsa:* breath
- *Udāna*: upward movement, lifting up, one of the five vital airs
- *Ūru*: thighs
- *Vairāgya*: detachment, absesnce of dualities of likes and dislikes
- *Varada*: blessing, giving, boon
- *Varāhaka*: wild boar, ram
- *Vāyu*: Air
- *Viparīta*: reverse, opposite, inverse, unfavourable, inverted, contrary to, turned around, contrary
- *Viṣṭa*: spreading, expansion
- *Viśuddhi*: pure knowledge, complete purification, removal of any doubt or error
- *Vitarka*: a discussion to clear doubts, argument, supposition, instructor in divine knowledge,
- *Vyāna*: diffusion, spreading, moving, one of the five vital airs
- *Vyāvahārika*: general, usual, social, casual

INDEX OF ILLUSTRATIONS

Illustrations **Page**

Illustrations	Page
Fingers, Brain Areas And Tasks	8
The Finger-Brain Lobe Connection	9
Durgā Depicting *Mudrās* In *Vāhanas* And *Astras*	11
Śrī Lalitā Mahā-tripura-sundarī	20
Nṛtya Mudrā	22
Theories Behind the Science of *Mudrā*	39
24 *Tattvas* of *Sāṁkhya*	43
Fingers And *Tattvas*	44
Pañca Prāṇas	47
Acupressure Points In Hands	50
Indian *Thāli*	51
Traditional Way Of Eating Food In *Sukhāsana*	52
Samāna Mudrā	54
Five Main *Marma* Points	59
Minor Nāḍīs In The Palms	66
Cakra In Hands	70
Location Of Planets As Per Astrology	72
Meridian Pathways In Hand	74

Tables

	Page
8 *siddhis* Of *Mudrās*	17
10 *Mudrās* of *Śrī Vidyā*	19
Fingers *Tattvas* & *Bhūtas*	44
Pañca Prāṇas Location And Function	48
Co-Relation Of Five Senses & Eating Food With Hand	52
Relationship between the organs, fingers and emotions	56
Comprehensive Study Of *Cakras*	71
Finger and Corresponding *Mudrā*	73
Rasas, Meaning and Color	97

Om Shantih Shantih Shantih